ARTISTIC LEATHER
OF THE ARTS & CRAFTS ERA

DANIEL LEES

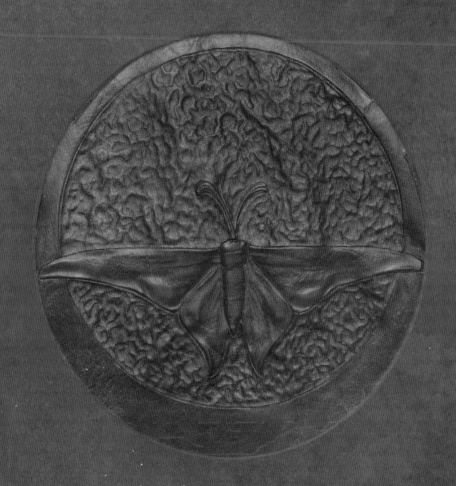

Schiffer Publishing Ltd®

4880 LOWER VALLEY ROAD, ATGLEN, PA 19310

DEDICATION

Without the subtle insistence from "she who must be obeyed" this work
might have languished. "She" is my spouse, the lady Faire, whose collecting
of modeled leather articles became contagious and I caught it!

Designed by John P. Cheek
Cover design by Bruce Waters
Type set in Rennie Mackintosh ITCStd/New Baskerville BT

ISBN: 978-0-7643-3371-2
Printed in China

Schiffer Books are available at special discounts for bulk
purchases for sales promotions or premiums. Special
editions, including personalized covers, corporate
imprints, and excerpts can be created in large quantities for special needs. For more information contact the
publisher:

Published by Schiffer Publishing Ltd.
4880 Lower Valley Road
Atglen, PA 19310
Phone: (610) 593-1777; Fax: (610) 593-2002
E-mail: Info@schifferbooks.com

For the largest selection of fine reference books on this
and related subjects, please visit our web site at:
www.schifferbooks.com
We are always looking for people to write books on new
and related subjects. If you have an idea for a book
please contact us at the above address.

This book may be purchased from the publisher.
Include $5.00 for shipping.
Please try your bookstore first.
You may write for a free catalog.

In Europe, Schiffer books are distributed by
Bushwood Books
6 Marksbury Ave.
Kew Gardens
Surrey TW9 4JF England
Phone: 44 (0) 20 8392 8585; Fax: 44 (0) 20 8392 9876
E-mail: info@bushwoodbooks.co.uk
Website: www.bushwoodbooks.co.uk

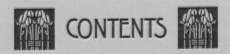# CONTENTS

# AUTHOR'S NOTE

This work is the first to present an insight into the artisans and commercial companies that produced hand-modeled leather in America's early 20th century.

There is an awakening interest in the creative design and its execution on a wide variety of leather articles for the home and personal use. Not so long ago a Roycroft modeled leather twining rose design table mat of 20-inch diameter might have gone unnoticed or at best brought a few hundred dollars. Today it will command spirited auction bidding that will generally hammer down north of two-thousand dollars.

Longtime Arts & Crafts collectors, dealers, and published scholars told the author during his research that this breakthrough book should help both the experienced and the novice A&C collector to understand leather's importance in the period's decorative design. This work covers but a short moment of creative leatherwork in the United States—1900 to 1929—yet its practice extended across the nation. It focuses on personal and household articles rather than the saddle and tack style of leather working.

Although a number of well-known leather artisans were also bookbinders, this too is not the emphasis of this work. The descriptions, shop marks and dozens of full color images should help even new collectors to quickly become proficient in assessing a potential "find" that may be overlooked among antique stores, estate sales, or internet auctions.

Every attempt has been made to discover the most accurate information about the leather artisans and the companies that produced the articles shown. If you have information you believe to be more relevant, please make it known to the author.

FOREWORD
BOICE LYDELL

The leather articles produced during the "Arts and Crafts" movement of the early 1900s undoubtedly rank as the last frontier in recognition and collectability from the period. The pioneering Arts & Crafts movement exhibit at Princeton University in 1972 did present several pieces of Roycroft leather including a wastebasket and a frame. However, in the years after the exhibit, the accessibility, usability, durability, and favored iconic forms of furniture, fine art, pottery, and metalwork, all came to the forefront for recognition and value long before their leatherwork and textile counterparts.

But for me there has always been something irresistible about the antiquity of early 1900s modeled leather objects. Hues of green, gold, black ,or a variety of brown colors subtly worked into the crevasses of artistically sculptured designs leaving a beautifully aged patina to the leather, reminiscent of mellowed carved wood or hand chased and oxidized copper, just cry out to be touched and admired.

While the use of utilitarian leather objects can be traced back to nearly every civilization through all periods of history, it was the intricate and elaborate motifs in relief developed in Medieval Moorish Spain that were generally considered as having the most impact on leatherwork as an art form. Centered around the thriving Spanish city of Cordoba beginning in the eighth century, the area became known for its quality leather production and sophistication of design. It was the work produced at Cordoba over the next few centuries that was the basis of inspiration for the revival by artisans of the Arts and Crafts era.

While many turn of the century Arts & Crafts manufactures, such as Stickley and Forest Craft, generally used leather only as an accessory for functional purposes on furniture or metal objects, others such as the Roycroft or the Cordova Shops of Buffalo, New York, produced a multitude of utilitarian objects of all-leather construction where both artistic expression and usefulness of the leatherwork go hand in hand. Nevertheless, leatherwork can take an artistic prominence even as an accessory to a piece of furniture or art metal object if it is elaborately sculptured or modeled.

I consider myself fortunate when in the 1980s I stumbled across one of the last living modelers of the Roycroft leather department. While "Roycroft Hunting" in the famed Roycroft town of East Aurora, New York, I spotted a Roycroft lantern hanging on a front porch ceiling of a house. After conversing with the owner and eventually purchasing the prized item, they informed me that their next door neighbor used to work in the Roycroft Leather Shop. Visions of new finds were quickly conjured up in my mind as I headed next door to visit Helen Wilson Ess. A shy, but very astute, widower welcomed me to sit and chat in her enclosed front porch where I put forth my best efforts to pursue what Roycroft she might have. But as she produced a cherished one-of-a-kind leather purse that she had modeled for herself in the early 1920s, I quickly become interested in ascertaining a first hand account of the leather modeling process. She kept denying that there would be interest in the old modeled leather art, but I finally coaxed her into telling the story. She lovingly gestured how she crafted the prize purse as I further realized the most important acquisition I could make from her would be her knowledge.

Sometime during the conversation she left and came back with a little wooden box containing her old leather modeling tools. She then proceeded to explain the entire step-by-step process of Roycroft leather modeling. The many hours I spent with her over the next few years would be some of the most cherished of my Roycroft collecting. My visits with her gave me the utmost appreciation for the leather craft and the amount of time and pride the workers put into their trade.

It should be noted that most Arts & Crafts era leather items are fully handcrafted and not merely stamped and assembled by some machine. While many times the same design templates were initially used to score a pattern on modeled leather articles, one should bear in mind that each piece is its own work of art and unique in its detail and coloring to the individual artisan who made it.

About Boice Lydell

Most leading Arts & Crafts scholars and collectors are in accord that there is no one better informed on all things Roycroft than Boice Lydell. He is the keeper of the Roycroft flame and displays his collection in his private Roycroft Arts Museum. An ardent preservationist and revivalist for the Roycroft Campus, Boice has an extensive assemblage of important Roycroft decorative arts including modeled leather. This collection is housed in several buildings on the Roycroft Campus grounds in East Aurora, New York. His museum's archives contain many of the personal effects, photographs and papers of Elbert Hubbard, his family, and the famed workers of the Roycroft. He is regularly called upon to speak on Roycroft and Arts & Crafts topics and is a contributor to scholarly publications and to other researchers who require special knowledge of Roycroft. He is also in the process of developing an encyclopedic reference on handcrafted art-metal objects of the early twentieth century.

ARTISTIC MODELED LEATHER OF THE ARTS & CRAFTS ERA

In 1972 only a few visionaries imagined that an exhibition organized by the Princeton University Art Museum and the Art Institute of Chicago would have created such an intellectual tsunami of reverence for the Arts and Crafts movement. The renewal of interest for a period of U.S. design and production has established a collecting frenzy of the fine art, furniture, ceramics and pottery, metals, and textiles produced in the period 1895 to 1916.

With the new-found interest in the crafts, a few clairvoyant ones recognized the thirst for information about the almost forgotten artisans who made it possible. Scholars and authors, such as David Cathers, Wendy Kaplan, David Rago, Stephen Gray, and others, investigated and reported to us who followed the nuances of success and the demise of the artisan pathfinders. A new group of antique authorities and dealers emerged. A generation of artisans who sought to recapture the spirit of the form and the material began work. It also inspired the architecture and design of "new, but in the manner of" homes and communities. Special interest publications *American Bungalow* and *The Craftsman-Style 1900* emerged with devoted readers who clung to every word about fellow enthusiasts and any new discoveries into the lives of the workers they adore.

This may sound like "preaching to the choir" but there is already evidence of the wave of interest adopted by a new generation of collectors and well-versed pioneers bent on further discovery. In fact, with new internet web sites there have been thousands of sightings of new data with a most notable exception—the artistically decorated and modeled leather of the period.

The expectation of this work is to present new discoveries about artisans who worked in leather and the commercial aspects of U.S. leather goods inspired by the Arts and Crafts movement. With so very little information available (compared to the numerous books and serious essays on Gustav Stickley), there are but a few dealers and collectors nationwide who have an understanding of modeled leather. The most likely reason is that little of the individually produced artistic leather has endured. It is subject to the vagaries of use, abandonment, and falling from grace.

Artisan-Produced Leather

The real treasures (Californian Elizabeth Burton's early work of burned, painted, modeled, and appliquéd or stacked leather comes to mind) are tucked away in private or institutional collections. A century ago, many emerging artists executed their stunning designs on leather. Yet few made the work with leather a continuing career profession. Instead, they became known as silversmiths, jewelers, metal workers, and in Burton's case, an "electrolier" for her novel hammered and pierced metal and shell electrified lamps. She had a good teacher in her Santa Barbara father, Charles Frederick Eaton, who was recognized at the turn of the century as a premier artist, book designer, and leatherworker. Other California champions of the craft during this era include Henry Busse of Los Angeles, The Companeros Colony of Santa Rosa, Charles Frank Ingerson, Bertha and Ellen Kleinschmidt, Lillian O'Hara, Grace Livermore, Lillian Tobey, and Ruth Stensrud Gordon of the San Francisco Bay area.

Early in her formative years, Chicagoan Clara Barck modeled, burned, and stitched leather. Upon receiving a designer's course degree from the Art Institute in 1900 she opened the Kalo (the Greek word for "beautiful") Shop at The Bank of Commerce Building, at 175 Dearborn Street in downtown Chicago. Her colleagues, also Art Institute graduates of the designer's course, were known as the "Kalo girls." In addition to Clara, the original six included Bertha Hall, Rose Dolese, Grace Gerow, Ruth Raymond, and Bessie McNeal. They produced objects in a variety of media including decorated leather, textiles, and copper. Their proficiency was good enough to be included at the Art Institute's first annual Arts and Crafts Exhibition in 1902. When Clara married George Welles, a Chicago amateur silversmith, in 1905, he persuaded her to direct the Kalo shop's full attention to producing metalwork objects. The shop was reincorporated and transferred to their home in nearby Park Ridge. It then was rechristened the Kalo Art Craft Community and entered the first of many idealistic phases. She expanded production to bowls, pitchers, and other hollowware and began to hire many skilled silversmiths, nearly all Scandinavian immigrants of recent arrival. One wonders if, had she remained a leather artisan, the work be as widely collected as the silver from Kalo?

The Kalo alumnae, leather artisan sisters Rose and Minnie Dolese, of nearby Evanston, formed and maintained The Wilro Shop in the Michigan Avenue Fine Arts Building in 1902 and continued their leather work into 1915.

For the most part, though, the leather art of the Arts and Crafts Movement has remained unheralded. When we think of the Forest Craft Guild of Grand Rapids, Michigan, do we first see the simple elegance of hammered copper with a cabochon stone inset across the top of an ooze leather purse? Hardly! Few even know the Forest Craft Guild did such things, unless they've seen the stunning examples presented in Don Marek's *Grand Rapids Art Metalwork—1902-1918* (Heartwood, Grand Rapids, 1999).

Suffering a similar fate are the purses, bill books, book covers, card cases, belts, and bags produced by many artisans over a decade at the Handicraft Guild of Minneapolis. Yet, the pottery, tiles (Ernest Batchelder was director from 1905 to 1909), and pierced and hammered copper is customarily discussed and shown.

In Boston, leatherwork held out into the 1920s before losing its enchantment. That was likely because of one vital leather artisan, Mary Coffin (Ware) Dennett, who, with her sister Clara, another leather artisan, opened a cooperative handicraft shop in Boston. Mary was a prime mover in organizing the Society of Arts and Crafts Boston in 1897 and displayed her leather work in the society's April, 1899, exhibition. As late as 1916, the Society of Arts and Crafts Boston (SACB) listed 37 persons who claimed leather as their medium of primary expression.

Commercially Produced Leather

On the commercial side, Roycroft offered hand-made artistic leather objects as early as 1905 and continued doing so for a decade after the deaths of Elbert and Alice Hubbard on May 7, 1915. By then, master leather immigrant artisans, Louis H. Kinder, Otto Hilt, Frederick C. Kranz, and George ScheideMantel joined first generation, native-born leather artisans John F. Grabau and Herbert E. Kaser at Roycroft, The Cordova Shops, and Kaser's Art Leather Shop. Roycroft offered its fine modeled leather-bound books from the late 1890s until past 1910. Grabau and Kinder also operated their separate bookbinding and leathercraft studios in Buffalo as did ScheideMantel in East Aurora after retiring from Roycroft. As early as 1908 the Cordova Shops, directed by Otto Hilt, produced modeled leather purses, mats, desk sets and other objects. Frederick C. Kranz, a former Roycrofter, was in residence there from 1913 until his untimely death at 50 in 1919. Yet the Cordova Shops and the H.E. Kaser Corp. continued to produce splendid leather goods at least past 1940.

Across the Northeast, commercial leather companies operated with Arts and Crafts and Art Nouveau designs into the very late 1920s. Prominent manufacturers include Arthur L. Reed's Reedcraft of New York City, Bates Brothers of Athol, Massachusetts, Charles K. Cook Company of Camden, New Jersey, and the Ryan Cushing Company of Boston, Massachusetts. The C.F. Rumpp & Sons Leather Company of Philadelphia, the German-owned training ground for

There were many modeled leather articles produced especially for the home, rather than carried on a person. Roycroft, Stickley, Cordova Shops—Meeker, Amity and Wilro Shops all offered home accessories well into the late 1920s. Some continued the craft with the early designs into the 1930s. Collectors will readily find blotters, bookends, pen wipes, portfolios, photo albums, cases and frames, mats of all sizes—the list is rather extensive. One can see how extra-ordinary a collection of these small items delights the eye and how well it assimilates with other decorative metal accessories. Many will be presented in their appropriate sections of the book. The desk is an L& JG Stickley, #235.
Courtesy Ken Nelson and Jessica Greenway of Kirkland, Washington. Photograph by Marissa Natkin, Seattle, WA.

Otto Hilt and Frederick C. Kranz before their migration to Buffalo, continued producing into the 1960s.

Outside the Northeast, commercial leather was the reason for being at the Meeker Company of Joplin, Missouri. In Springfield, Ohio, the Hugo Bosca Company made modeled leather goods in 1911 and is still in business with the fourth generation Bosca heir at the helm. Down the street, Springfield Leather Company produced its "Cameo" line of leather goods in the early 1920s, but the parent company had been making other leather goods since 1904.

Near Chicago were large leather goods factories of Paragon (Gerlach-Barklow Corp. of Joliet) and Volland Leathercraft Company. Around Milwaukee, Enger-Kress (1895- and still producing), Rolf's Leather Company (1915- and still producing) and Amity Leather Products (1915- and acquired by Enger-Kress) flourished with a broad line of leather goods in addition to women's handbags.

In Dallas, Ft. Worth, and Nocona, Texas, the Justin Boot Company, Nocona Leather Company, and the Broncho-Padgett Company delighted women across America with their modeled leather purses, from c. 1914 into the 1950s. Both Justin and Nocona are still producing a variety of tooled leather goods, as well as their namesake boots.

There was no shortage of commercial leather companies producing modeled and embossed purses and other items. Today, internet auctions such as eBay® regularly list several hundred leather articles. Many sellers claim they find their leather offerings at local estate and garage sales. The leather is out there. What is in short supply is information about it. That's why this effort is an important attempt to acquaint the devoted Arts and Crafts collector and the beginner with an almost forgotten segment of the A&C heritage.

Most of the individuals and firms we've quickly mentioned, and many others, will be described in as much detail as we could find as we went to press. What you're reading represents a work in progress. The gathering of information will proceed and hopefully be seen as a call for further discoveries. Perhaps this initial effort will even aid in the uncovering of presently unknown leather artisans of the Arts and Crafts movement. If you discover you have a family link, or hold any leather articles or documents related to the leather of the Arts & Crafts era, please contact the author. It is quite possible to include the new information in a future edition.

An elegant design solution on a Cordova wastebasket

ScheideMantel often "drew" life forms on leather. Helen Ess made this purse showcasing a young woman for his lifelong partner Gladys. *Courtesy Roycroft Arts Museum.*

Reedcraft Leather
envelope purse

Volland Leathercraft of Chicago
was more than a card company

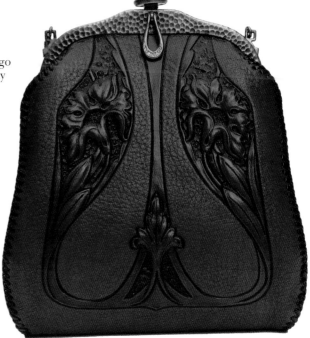

Hugo Bosca worked his
leather magic in 1912

Leather as a Medium for Artistic Expression

At the onset of the Arts and Crafts movement, a talented SAC Boston leather craftsman, Annah C. Ripley, described her notions of how working in this medium furnished fulfillment. Writing in the SAC Boston *Handicraft Journal,* (Vol. II, October, 1903, No. VII) she tells us:

Hand-wrought leather is but a branch of the general Arts and Crafts movement of the present day, and in speaking of leather work we necessarily speak upon principles applicable to the movement in any of its various branches, for, as craftsmen, we all stand similarly related to life, art, work, and the problem of earning our living by the work of our hands.

Legitimate work groups itself under four general styles: Illuminated, or Cordovan leather; Gold-tooling, used principally on book bindings; German embossed leather; and carved or Mexican work. By legitimate leather work we mean a process of decoration which manipulates the leather surface in such a way that the effect produced could not be so obtained on any medium but leather, and becomes so much a part of the surface that nothing can efface it. The same tests should apply to any kind of applied art—china painting, metal work, wood carving, modeling, weaving, etc. Each medium has its own particular advantages, and its own particular limitations. These four styles, considered historically, span many centuries of handicraft, from an undetermined origin to the revivals of the present day—and most modern leather work traces its ancestry to one or more of these old processes.

Cordovan leather is so called because the style reached its greatest perfection in Cordoba, though it was done all through Southern Europe and Morocco during the Middle Ages. The effect is exceedingly rich and brilliant, being obtained by the application of metal-leaf and color in various Arabian and Renaissance designs, the whole surface covered with the impressions of small tools. Many craftsmen are attempting to reproduce these old leathers, most difficult now to obtain, and much as been accomplished toward the revival of this beautiful lost art of old Spain. After hundreds of years' exposure these old leathers remain undimmed, the metal and pigments glowing with the rich, softened luster that age alone can give.

The exquisite gold-tooling with which we are familiar on hand-bound books is an entirely different style of leather decoration. It was introduced into Venice in the fifteenth century and is the most minute and technical of leather processes. The design is sunk in gold, or blind, into the cover of the book with hot tools after the forwarding, or binding, of the book has been completed. Technically it reached perfection in France several centuries ago, and bookbinders of today can only strive to equal, hardly hope to excel, the work of the famous binders of those days. This remarkable high technical standard makes bookbinding one of the most ambitious branches of leather work, and admits of no comparative excellence. It is also one of the most intellectual of the handicrafts, requiring all the refinement and culture one can give it, for though the cover of the book should never illustrate the contents, it should, I believe, interpret, not only the text, but the spirit of the time and country in which the book was written, necessitating most exhaustive research.

On embossed and carved leathers, the design is in relief, thereby reversing the former processes. Embossed leather is molded out from the back while wet, and stuffed with a pulp to hold it in place; whereas carved work is manipulated entirely from the front, more like carved wood. These styles were originally left in the self-color of the leather used, but of late a process of coloring with transparent dyes has been applied with distinct success. This application of transparent dyes, making it possible to preserve the leather texture and a dull finish, is entirely a modern development. Also new is the use of suede-finish sheep and calf-skins which were first perfected for pyrography. Carved leather work, commonly known as Mexican, was introduced into California by the Mexicans, who brought the art up from the south with them, where it traces back several centuries. It is so entirely different from the Spanish styles that it does not seem possible that its presence in California was at all due to the Spanish occupation there, as is sometimes supposed. Old specimens of Mexican leather—carved saddles, bridles, etc—are remarkably beautiful, but the modern work has greatly deteriorated as the result of over-production and commercial opportunity.

Most modern leather work shows then, directly or indirectly, the influence of one or more of these historic styles, however original and individual the result. This individuality, this self-expression in our work, is of vital importance. It is therein that handiwork can never be supplanted.

Before beginning any piece of leather work let the craftsman look at the untouched leather before him and ask himself whether or not he is going to improve it. If not, better to leave it as it is. Let him never forget, in the application of his decorative effect, the material to which he is applying it. Leather is a conservative material and should be conservatively handled: boldly, of course, with certain freedom and originality, but never with glaring, decadent design in the sketchy poster-esque fashion of the day. Let us revere the dignity of its traditions.

In decorating leather or any other surface, one is not free to consider design apart from process. It is not enough simply to paint a flower on leather or trace a stencil. If so, why leather? Design should suggest, not imitate nature, and in applying design to leather one should use some process to accomplish the decorative effect which is distinctly a leather process. These various processes are obtained through the use of tools, metals, chemicals, etc., with more or less originality and success. The commercialism of the day which is content with temporary effects is responsible for much carelessness of process work, but a growing sincerity is noticeable in most of our modern workshops as craftsmen begin to realize their responsibilities not only to themselves, but to the public.

Kaser Art Leather blossoms climb to prominence on this purse

Kaser shows off its Buffalo Nouveau form of this purse flap

Often, as on this purse, Kaser saw that a single flower was all that was required

Leatherwork References

Should you want to trace the history and utility of decorated or artistic leather examine the reference *The Art and Craft of Leatherwork*, by Cecile Francis-Lewis, (The Mayflower Press, Plymouth, Great Britain, 1928). It offers a detailed "show and tell" explanation of every facet of leatherwork; especially that of illuminating a modeled leather surface. The author says: "I have striven to express through the illustrations, the various types of work as interpreted today, which are based on the traditions of the past, rather than to show reproductions of very ancient leatherwork which are to be found in our museums."

Another text, "The Leathercraftsman" by W. E. Snyder (*American Handicrafts*, 1936) will suit the newcomer's understanding as it discusses the importance of selecting the appropriate leather to the task, the proper tools to use, and shows how to braid and lace. It supplies all you may want to know about dyeing, coloring, enameling and Venetian gold and silver decoration. Author Snyder comments: "Because leathercraft is a versatile craft involving drawing, applied design, and modeling, as well as craftsmanship—because of its educational as well as utilitarian qualities—and lastly, because it is an inexpensive craft that requires no costly material or equipment, it is fast becoming recognized as one of the most practical and valuable crafts to teach in schools, hospitals, camps and other organizations."

Leatherwork, by Adelaide Mickel (Department of Manual Arts, Bradley Polytechnic Institute, Peoria, Manual Arts Press, 1927, Peoria, IL), is a practical guide for both teachers and students on technique. Nicely illustrated, it includes plans for everyday personal use and household objects. This text (a 48 page pamphlet) was widely used in vocational schools, rehabilitation centers and summer camps across the nation.

Finally, although not devoted to leatherwork, *The Training of a Craftsman* (H. Virtue & Co. Ltd., London, 1901) gives the flavor of the era and discusses a wide variety of crafts most suited to women. Its author, Fred Miller, challenges the reader: "To the patron I say, Search out for yourself a craftsman to do the particular work you require, and having found him trust him, and ask him to give you of his best; and to the craftsman I say, Before all else be faithful to the best traditions of your craft, and put yourself thoroughly into all you do."

Numerous (out of print) leather and tool company treatises are available and do a fine job of discussing leathercraft, transferring designs, and executing them. One of the more comprehensive is "*Leathercraft—In the New and Interesting Graton & Knight Way*" (Third Edition, self-published by Graton & Knight Co., Worcester, MA, 121pp, 1929). Profusely illustrated, it includes plans for more than two dozen useful objects to make from leather.

Miss Ripley mentions the illuminated Cordova leather walls undimmed and glowing with the metal and pigments after centuries of exposure. A few examples are showcased among America's grand houses and museums of today.

A glorious example is the Isabella Stewart Gardner Museum of 280 The Fenway, Boston, Massachusetts. It was completed as a labor of love in November, 1901, decorated with both European and U.S. artistic treasures the following year and opened to the public in early 1903. Surely, any SAC Boston leather worker now had first hand access to the leather artistry of the past.

Described by Hilliard T. Goldfarb, "The Veronese Room, the first gallery on the third floor, is a dark yet sumptuous space created by an extraordinary wall covering: gilt and painted Spanish (mostly) and Venetian leather of the 17th century. Gardner acquired the more than 500 pieces of leather between 1892 and 1901 in Germany and Italy. " (*Companion Guide and History*, the Isabella Stewart Museum, Yale University Press, 1995)

Of lesser scope but with equal drama and artistic brilliance is the tooled and polychromed leather wall covering in the Breakfast Room of the Biltmore Estate, (completed in 1898) nearby Asheville, North Carolina. In Chicago, Illinois, the Nickerson mansion at Erie and Wabash has a library/parlor adorned with modeled and gilded leather wall panels. More artistic leather wall coverings/locations will be revealed as known.

Artistic leather gets its own
venue at Roycroft in the 1909
Leather Book

More classy work by an experienced amateur leather artisan

Milton Bradley's
alternative to painting
china in 1914

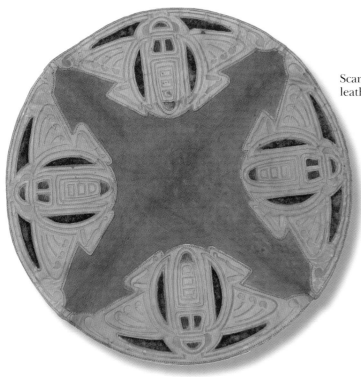

Scarabs were an important
leather design element

Eleonore Bang's multicolored wallet

Early Cordova handbags featured
the stylish braided leather handle

Top of the line modeled leather items from Roycroft in 1912 as advertised in *The Fra*

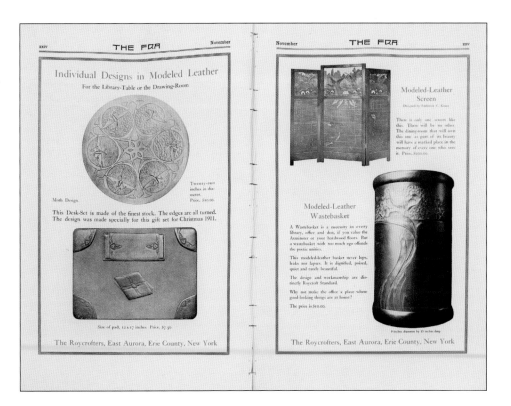

No trinket box was unimportant at Roycroft

Kranz is credited for the design for this Roycroft clock

A shoulder bag needed a long handle

Amity did present an artistic bent on many of its styles

A dragonfly was a popular Cordova purse design element

THE ARTS & CRAFTS MOVEMENT PUTS DOWN ROOTS ACROSS AMERICA

Far more numerous than the communities were the Arts and Crafts societies—sometimes called guilds—that were established at first in the major cities, and quickly spread to even small communities. These functioned as associations of craftsmen (with far more women participants) that promoted the Arts and Crafts and informed, trained, and otherwise aided their members. The societies sponsored lectures by prominent artisans and other experts and provided centers for the exchange of ideas. Many supplied working space, offered regular courses of instruction and operated sales shops to sell members' work. Annual exhibitions of the items and special loan exhibitions promoted the work as well as the public appreciation for the movement as a whole.

—Coy L. Ludwig, *The Arts and Crafts Movement in New York State: 1890s-1920s* (Gallery Association of New York State, 1983)

From English Roots to Boston Beginnings

The intellectual styles and ideologies of the English John Ruskin, William Morris, C.R. Ashbee, and Christopher Dresser were turning over in the minds of American artistic movers and shakers. As early as 1870, a newfound need to control the "arts and visual culture" spread its roots wherever persons of authority (and their ancestor's money) bonded in a mutual beneficial society. Shortly after the U.S. Civil War Boston became the cultural "Grandpere" for defining the direction of what was to become the Arts and Crafts Movement.

As Edward S. Cooke Jr. points out in *Inspiring Reform—Boston's Arts and Crafts Movement* (p. 19):

What prompted such a surge of interest in visual culture in the 1870s? Much of the interest accompanied the city leadership's transformation from an elite to a social class whose members had abdicated a political role, and parlayed the economic success of their ancestors into building non-profit organizations that defined appropriate taste and educated others who formed a community distinct from theirs, and who used their positions of authority to maintain their unassailable status. They were not manufacturing, railroad, or financial entrepreneurs but rather cultural capitalists, linked by common backgrounds, Harvard educations, intermarriage, and board memberships. They stressed their mastery and understanding of artistic genres and styles, the need for suitable leaders to lead and teach others, and the belief that the majority of citizens, although perhaps mechanically skilled, were incapable of creative, imaginative work. To counter what they viewed as popular vulgarities, these Boston Brahmins built institutions that defined visual culture and set the parameters of public discourse about such art. The value put on culture—and control of culture—and the social distinction between mind and muscle provided the defining framework for Boston's acceptance and adaptation of Arts and Crafts principles.

Essentially, the literati of Boston and New England preempted the application of their English counterparts and set themselves apart as the taste makers of the movement. The "main man" of the transformation of visual culture was Charles Elliot Norton, an 1847 graduate of Harvard and friend of John Ruskin. He was a contributing writer on intellectual matters to *Atlantic Monthly* and *The Nation*. He managed to get named a Professor of Fine Arts at Harvard—the first appointment in art history to an American university. (*Inspiring Reform*, p. 20) His bonding with Ruskin and prominence at Harvard set him up to be the filter through which the philosophy of the Arts and Crafts Movement passed. His influence directed the newly cultured aristocracy and served as a catalyst for the formation of Boston area clubs or associations to discuss art, architecture, and design...including the Tavern Club (1884) where he pulled the strings as vice president and later president from 1886 to 1898. (*Inspiring Reform*, p.22)

Seven members of the Tavern Club were also charter organizers of the Society of Arts and Crafts, Boston (SACB) which was organized shortly after an April 1897 exhibition of industrial arts—the first Arts and Crafts exhibition in America—held at Copley Hall. Harvard education or membership in one of the artistic clubs linked most of the founders. The only actual craftsmen involved were two book designers and printers—Henry Lewis Johnson and Daniel B. Updike—and three carvers—John Evans, John Kirchmayer, and Hugh Cairns. Carvers and book designers ranked at the top of the crafts hierarchy in Boston and frequently mingled with the leaders of the Arts and Crafts Movement. The SACB provided an important local forum for discussion and exhibition of high quality handicraft.

Beginning in 1900, the SACB also maintained a sales room in Boston that became known as the "Handicraft Shop." (Ibid p.22)

The intellectual controllers of the SACB, the enthusiasts, were mainly well-educated gentlemen and some wealthy young women. Mostly, they were architects or artists, or college educators.

They sought out skilled craftsmen—many of whom were immigrants—to execute their work. Non-Anglo-Saxon names were plentiful in the membership lists of the SACB, and most belonged to technically accomplished artisans, whom the elite patronizingly assumed were incapable of working by themselves. Such collaboration permitted the making of suitably artistic handicrafts, most of which only the well-to-do could afford and offered further benefits to the cultural elite.
—Inspiring Reform, Edward S. Cooke, Jr., p. 23)

It seemed there were plenty of competent artisan immigrants to go around for the wealthy to supervise at "settlement" houses across metropolitan Boston. Notably, for young women, the Denison House furnished an industry for textile work and the Paul Revere Pottery for those with a talent for decorating ceramics. The process quickly spread to New Orleans and Newcomb College. It serves no purpose to beat up on the intellectuals or wealthy patrons of the movement. It is likely that without their involvement and passion to fund and spread the Arts & Crafts gospel (they did become the exporters of A&C design, ideas through lectures, teachings, books and articles) that there would be far fewer objects for today's collectors of the decorative arts. "A craftsman working in a small shop carrying out the good designs of an educated man would discover the nobility and value of his work, accept his social role with pride, and act as a contented citizen who would not disrupt the social order." (Inspiring Reform, Ibid., Edward S. Cooke, Jr., p. 13)

One of the early members of the SACB was Bostonian Mary Ware, a self-described leather artisan and the only leather worker ever to serve as a SACB jury member (1900-1903).

She studied at the School of Design, Boston Museum of Fine Arts, under Arthur Wesley Dow, Joseph Smith and C. Howard Walker, and she was one of the Society's first directors. She carried the movement to Philadelphia and organized the School for Decorative Design at Drexel Institute at the age of 21. Following this she traveled in Spain and Italy on a pilgrim's quest to rediscover the lost art of producing the Cordova leather wall hangings of the Renaissance. On her return to Boston, she, with her sister Clara (who had been on the same quest only in Germany) opened a shop in Boston where they continued their studies and experiments in the processes. This went on for five years as they ground and mixed pigments and varnishes, cut

their own steel dies, made their color blocks, as well as the designs for their wall patterns. By 1897 they were able to hold an exhibit of gilded leather which made a considerable stir among the art critics and architects.
—The Biographical Cyclopedia of American Women, Vol. II, p.236

In 1900, Mary was married to architect Hartley Dennett and in a few years her family cares made it necessary to give up the all day work at the shop. She developed into a consulting home decorator in active partnership with her husband. Her leather shop then became the Handicraft Shop of Boston where she encouraged skilled craftsmen and trained designers to join forces to maintain a truly cooperative workshop. It was a success both financially and aesthetically and has produced some of the most distinguished silverware made in America. (Ibid. p. 236)

Artistic leather working may have been tolerated in the Society's formative years. Many well known artisans, including Madeline Yale Wynn and Hazel French, were once "fluent" in leather, but their careers blossomed when they focused on painting and "finer" arts, such as jewelry.

As early as 1913-1914, C. Howard Walker, a Beaux-arts trained architect and critic for the Society's jury report said: "The various classes of objects are different in intrinsic merit because of the materials and the skill required in the workmanship. It should be obvious that jewelry and enamels, woodcarving and illuminating can be expressed in higher terms than the usual china painting and leather work and coarse basket making." (Ibid. p. 39)

Even as not being considered a "higher craft" art form, the membership of the SACB in 1916 showed 37 crafts persons who listed "Leather" as their identifier. The largest group of respondents, 143, suggested they be known as designer, with jewelry a close second at 129 members."
—Inspiring Reform, p. 41

Even though many society members began their artistic training on leather, they embraced a new material and discipline. Silversmithing and jewelry-making were logical steps up on the chain of "higher terms." Except for the design and its implementation on book covers, leather work was clearly not considered to be one of the so-called higher crafts.

Basically, good design ornamentation can be represented in nearly any medium whether textile, leather, paper, metal, or clay. The Society of Arts and Crafts of Boston master artisans reached into major cities across the nation. The publication Handicraft, begun in 1901, featured stories across many disciplines from these masters—jewelry making and silversmithing, china painting, and pottery were among the most often presented. In almost every city across America there were "Applied Arts" (meaning artistic expression other than fine art painting or sculpture) schools. There were also hundreds of "private schools" conducted by artisan-teachers who earned a modest living from instructing young adults in advancing specialty crafts such as metalworking, jewelry making, china, and pottery painting.

The Movement Spreads

Many Midwest artisans, educators and social reformers had strong professional and academic ties with Harvard and influential Bostonians.

> With its close ties to English culture, a heritage of college industries and crafts dating back to the 17th century, and its ecclesiastical support for art and education, Boston was well-placed to introduce Arts & Crafts ideals to an American audience. Boston-educated architects, craftsmen, designers and teachers disseminated Arts & Crafts standards of good taste across the country."
> —*Inspiring Reform-Boston's Arts and Crafts Movement*," Marilee Boyd Meyer, Consulting Curator, Davis Museum and Cultural Center, 1997, p. 14

The intellectual leadership founded or taught in numerous summer schools infiltrated societies and guilds, especially in the Midwest in the early 1880s and ongoing until the decline of the movement. In the early 1900s, nearly 25 percent of the SACB members were from the Midwest or South, with a few in the far West.

In the milieu of publish or perish, educators and school founders/directors of the SACB flooded the publishing world and magazine media with scores of technically competent "how to" stories of design and execution. Besides the ego-gratification this had the positive effect of inspiring others to develop "schools" and take up the cause of handicrafts. Early on, the SACB embraced the formation of guilds, similar to the European practices, as a method of establishing high standards for design and workmanship in the respective crafts. Aside from some criticism of a pocket or two of elitism, there is no question that the SACB was the major contributor for the care and feeding of the Arts and Crafts movement. Within 30 years of its 1897 founding it had achieved more than 3,000 members and exhibitors through the nation. Many eastern disciples became mentors to others in communities far from Boston.

New England's pioneer patrons-turned-painters-and-artisans also helped inspire and colonize societies in other regions. Madeline Yale Wynn, an accomplished painter, jeweler, and metal worker helped establish the Deerfield, Massachusetts, and Chicago, Illinois, Arts & Crafts Societies. Her competent colleague, Jessie Luther, a multi-talented metal worker, helped to spread the Arts & Crafts doctrine through her social service and occupational therapy work at Chicago's Hull House. Both women tirelessly taught their craft to the young women and made many lengthy visits over many years in the late 1890s.

Long before establishing the famous tile company in Pasadena, California, Ernest Batchelder had studied and taught at the Massachusetts Normal Art School of Boston with Denman Ross, noted designer. Batchelder established design principals for the Handicraft Guild of Minneapolis in 1904 (although the school had been operating in a quasi-official manner as early as 1883, first as the Minneapolis Society for Fine Arts and continuing as the Handicraft Guild five-week long summer schools through 1909). "His unique design style remained at the HG as his legacy and manifested itself in ceramics, metal work marked by pierced work and the presence of negative and positive design spaces." (*"The Substance of Style,"* edited by Bert Denker, Winterthur Museum, 1996, p.222) Essentially these design teachings were embraced in the appliquéd, cut and modeled leather work produced by the students.

Beverly K. Brandt suggested that "Perhaps its [the SACB's] chief accomplishment was its national stature which prompted similar organizations hoping to further the cause of design reform to model themselves after the SACB. The 1906-1907 annual report states; 'The society is looked to as the center of the movement and as the one to which younger societies naturally turn for guidance and inspiration.'" *Inspiring Reform*, p. 40

Many other societies were already functioning at the moment of this pronouncement, but decrying the importance of the material and the techniques may have sent leatherworking to an early grave. Even if the SACB influence were minimal, it would likely discourage any new leather artisans and would probably cause those experienced in the art form to consider a new discipline of a "higher order."

The coveted silver work of Clara P. Barck and the early "Kalo Girls" in Chicago may owe some of its pedigree to the fact that they were decorating leather as a course of instruction before receiving a decorative design degree from the Chicago Art Institute in 1900. She is reported to have transferred her design skill to sterling with the very tools she used to decorate leather. When she married George Welles (a talented silversmith) in 1905, the Kalo Shop began to produce metalwork exclusively.

Examine the early membership rosters of Arts and Crafts societies or Applied Arts exhibitors at world's fairs and you'll find a predominance of women. This is especially evident among leatherworkers. The Society of Arts and Crafts Boston Exhibition Record, 1897-1927 shows over 90 percent of the artisans involved with leather were women. At the 1904 Louisiana Purchase Exposition in St. Louis, of the nine leatherworkers, only one was a man, and more than 65 percent of all "Allied Craft" exhibitors were women. One contemporary report explained it this way:

> Women seem to have a remarkable faculty for designing. Their intuitive sense of decoration, their feeling for beauty of line and harmony of color insures them a high degree of success.
> —*The Training of a Craftsman*, 1901.

Many leather artisans, then, were young, enthusiastic women (many only in their late teens) who hadn't acquired their full artistic sophistication. Miss Barck was fresh off an Oregon homestead when she enrolled in a design course at the Art Institute in 1898. It is a natural evolution that she, and many other young women like her, continued with what they knew best.

Many of these young girls cut their artistic teeth on textile embroidery, paper illumination, and leather decorating. Most were taught by mothers and aunts to be adept at sewing, embroidery, and drawing while in their early teens. Some found it to be their calling and stayed with it until its importance diminished. Others married and moved on to raising a family. And some saw greater challenges in a new medium where other kindred spirits received great recognition.

Added impetus for the spread of the Arts & Crafts Movement came from numerous magazines published in the era. Gustav Stickley's *The Craftsman* printed numerous instruction for "how-to" turn leather into decorated desk sets, guest books, albums, and portfolios, and bind your own books. In the May, 1910 (vol. XVIII) *The Craftsman* suggested that readers who "possess reasonable skill with the fingers and a feeling for color and design" can make these leather objects at home.

The article "Leather Work as a Handicraft for Home Workers" sweetened the interest with an offer:

> We will be glad to give more detailed instructions for making them [leather hand bags] as well as designs for opera bags, purses, card-cases, book-covers, belts, desk pads, memorandum books, pocketbooks, cigar cases, music rolls, sewing bags, magazine covers, watch fobs, table covers, mats, and other articles both useful and ornamental. We will be glad to send patterns free to any subscriber who is sufficiently interested to write to us for them.

For the fledgling leather artisan there were numerous offers for less ambitious patterns, plus tools, leather, and lacing in *Popular Mechanics* and other magazines.

The principal design and hands-on instruction manuals were *Leather Work* by Adelaide Mickel, Department of Manual Arts, Bradley Polytechnic Institute, Peoria, Illinois, and *Leathercraft in the New and Interesting Graton & Knight Way*. This Worcester, Massachusetts, tannery, established in 1851, was quick to see that thousands of young boys (and tom-girls too) armed with sharp knives could readily hack-up a lot of leather. Since it claimed to be "one of the largest leather companies in the world" it annually had to dispose of 300 thousand hides. The 121 page booklet (Third Edition, 1929) offers thorough and lucid explanations and diagrams for braiding and especially coloring leather. It advises the novice to understand color composition by "studying Coptic textiles, Indian designs, Oriental rugs, as well as Egyptian mummy cases, Greek pottery, and Mohammedan tiles." (p. 33).

Maybe not surprisingly (since the workers had plenty of time) some rather fine leather work was widely produced by the inmates of state prisons. Their finished goods were usually sold at a prison outlet store.

In the first few years of the twentieth century, nearly every major city had in place (or soon would have) an Arts & Crafts society or organization. Recognition and honors were bestowed by the local society during juried exhibitions and these extended all the way to the occasional "World's" fairs in the U.S. For instance, Miss Barck, and founder Kalo "sister artisans" Rose and Minnie Dolese, and Grace Gerow exhibited and sold 16 decorated leather items at the 1904 Louisiana Purchase Exhibition in St. Louis. They also had entries at the Lewis and Clark Exposition in Portland, Oregon, in 1905.

Did the Arts & Crafts Leather Legacy have German Roots?

Although the SACB may have considered itself the standard setter for the movement in America, "probably no region made more of a contribution to the spreading of the gospel than New York State." (Coy Ludwig, *The Arts & Crafts Movement in New York State-1890s to 1920s*, Op. cit.)

Unlike Boston, New York City was a principal port of entry for thousands of German and middle European immigrants who "followed the chain" of those who preceded them from their native regions. More than a few landed at Ellis Island with important knowledge and skills in their own crafts. They made their way to a new home in western New York where language, customs, and food were familiar. Transportation systems (railroads, steamboats, rivers, and canals) were in place early. Electricity from nearby Niagara Falls was a new source of power to speed manufacturing production. Natural materials, wood, clay metals, woven fabric, paper, and lots of leather were readily available.

There was a strong tradition of leather work among the Germans. After all, they wore those manly leather shorts as they performed that slap-happy dance for decades! Leather was boiled and form-fitted to a soldier's chest and became armor in the medieval times. The "picklehaub" helmets of the Kaiser's reign were also decorated leather. The German's even honored their leather artisans with a title, "lederkunstler" and filled a few museums with the decorated objects of the craft. Master bookbinder artisans adorned volumes with modeled and painted leather for kings and popes, and displayed the same craftsmanship on mansion walls and furniture. Peter Behrens, an art nouveau designer, was renowned for using modeled leather on his furniture as late as the Turin, Italy, exhibition of 1901. One of the pre-eminent German firms renowned for this style of artisanship was that of Georg Hulbe of Hamburg.

Hulbe, (b Kiel, Sept. 29, 1851; d Hamburg, Nov. 16, 1917) trained as a book binder and opened a studio in Kiel. After moving to Hamburg in 1880, he had mastered the intricate leather styles from medieval and renaissance to baroque and rococo. In 1886 he got a leg up on competitors when named "Court Purveyor to His Imperial and Royal Highness the Crown Prince" and became a founding member of the Hamburg Crafts Society. His commissions included work for the Emperor Wilhelm I and Empress Augusta. Most notable were chairs for the meeting rooms of the Reichstag and commissions from wealthy Hamburg patrons. His forte was tooled/modeled and often gilded leather design applied to presentation portfolios and almost any furniture; especially chairs, room screens and wall tapestries.

Many Roycrofters were of German descent. Louis Kinder and Frederick C. Kranz were born and trained there and certainly had a strong influence on their colleagues John Grabau, Lorenz C. Schwartz and Axel Sahlin. All the Roycroft designers had access to the English and German decorative arts and graphics design publications that presented the latest work of their counterparts across the Atlantic. The most notable were *International Studio* (English) and *Dekorative Kunst, Deutsches Kunst und Dekoration and Dekorative Vorbilder*. Hulbe's leather artistry was presented in detail regularly in these trendsetter publications, so his fame was quite global. It is very likely that Elbert Hubbard as well as C. R. Ashbee and other English leather designers were familiar with his work. Then too, Dard Hunter included Germany and Vienna on his honeymoon trip of 1908 and could hardly have missed Hulbe's influence. The early (1904) Roycroft three-panel room screens, portfolios and the special armchairs designed and executed by Kranz bear a strong resemblance to the work of Hulbe.

Hubbard, Kranz, and others had numerous opportunities to see Hulbe's work. He took part in the German exhibition at the World's Columbia Exposition of 1893 in Chicago and won a gold medal. His work appeared at the Pan American Exposition of 1901 in Buffalo and at the Louisiana Purchase Exposition of 1904 in St. Louis where he took home the gold once again. His leather was also showcased at the 1900 Paris Exhibition and the International Craft Exposition of 1902 in Turin, Italy.

The Georg Hulbe firm was no small venture. In 1896 his 200 employee workshops included leather artisans, calligraphers and water colorists, engravers and lithographers, plus departments for book binding, hand gilding, leather stamping, picture framing, metalwork and the production and restoration of leather tapestries.

By 1905, the Hulbe publication "*Spezialkatalog*" (leather offerings for sale) showed that the workshops produced more than 200 different leather articles of household and decorative items such as: small chests, club and dining chairs, room and fire screens, luxury household items such as wastebaskets, guest books, stationary portfolios, decorative jewel caskets and boxes, hand mirrors, brushes, purses, cigar cases and wallets, plus special awards for political and military figures. This preceded the first Roycroft catalog devoted to modeled leather articles (1909) by at least four years. It isn't a stretch to imagine that the catalog was quickly being examined by Hubbard and Kranz

and their "we can do that" plan set in motion.

[Data for these details about Hulbe's life and work were contained in a German language exhibit catalog "*Jahrbuch Des Museums Fur Kunst Und Gewerbe*" Hamburg, 1997; supplied by Dr. Rudiger Joppien, Direktor. The translation into English was provided by The Reverend Dennis A. Andersen, Seattle, Washington.]

Fanning the Flames

The wildfire of interest in the development of Arts and Crafts was fueled through the quality and sheer number of movement-related periodicals with roots in the state. Magazines like the *The Craftsman*, published by Gustav Stickley in 1901; *Keramic Studio* published by Adelaide and Samuel Robineau, Syracuse, 1900; and Elbert Hubbard's *The Philistine* (1895); the short-lived *Roycroft Quarterly* (only 3 issues in 1896); *Little Journeys* (1900) and *The Fra* (1908) out of East Aurora, spread the word of the movement.

Stickley untiringly championed plans for furniture and Craftsman houses, presented technical and feature articles about the A&C lifestyle. It directed the reader to participate in one of the many craft societies and furnished reviews of numerous exhibitions and books on the movement. *Keramic Studio* became an important guide for the experienced ceramist with technical articles on clays, glazes, and firing methods, as well as news of artisans, exhibitions, and awards.

The Philistine and *The Fra* had enormous distribution across the nation, were read by influential persons with the social bent and income to further the movement. Many became the driving forces to establish local splinter groups, societies of woodworkers, metal bangers, and finger-poking embroiderers.

Both publications presented the reader with news of the order, success stories of artisans, and (because of the significant readership) carried advertising of manufacturers and consumer goods sympathetic to the cause. Also, the publications often carried illustrations of emerging and famous American artists and offered the products of their company or of the artisan cadre they espoused.

Another influential, widely read magazine with scholarly or educational intent was the *Chautauquan*, published by the Chautauqua Institution in the 1890s at Chautauqua Lake, New York. A series of stories in 1902-1903 by Rho Fisk Zueblin presented the group's commitment to the ideals of the Arts & Crafts Movement. Many of the earliest institutions for training young men and women were in New York, which combined the practical with the academic aspects. These included the Mechanics Institute, Rochester (1891); the New York State School of Clayworking and Ceramics at Alfred, New York (1901); Teachers College of Columbia University, New York City (1897); and the Pratt Institute of Brooklyn in 1887. The grandmother of all the artistic training, first for women's art in 1857, resided at Cooper Union, New York City.

Arts & Crafts on Exhibit

Exhibitions were touchy-feely places where the public could marvel at an object's craftsmanship, be dazzled at its color, hold it, touch it, and order one when they returned home. They also inspired potential artisans to say, "I'd like to try that!" and enroll in a class in an attempt to do so. Other than a few eccentric ones, most artists in any discipline liked the idea that there were people who would pay for their hand-made items. Simultaneously, around the time of the first major Arts & Crafts exhibition in Boston (1897) the American public was dazzled with a series of colossal events; The World's Columbian Exposition in Chicago, 1893, The Pan American Exposition of 1901 in Buffalo and the Louisiana Purchase Exposition in St. Louis, 1904.

The likely impetus for such spectacles was the celebration of our first hundred years as a nation with the Philadelphia Centennial in 1876 that attracted eight million people. Two decades later the Paris Exhibition of 1889-1890, with the Eiffel Tower as its centerpiece, attracted 32 million. In 1901 Italy tried to upstage the French with its Turin Exhibition, and world's fairs were becoming a very big deal.

Not to be outdone, in 1890 the U.S. Congress anointed and partially funded Chicago as the city to hold the World's Columbian Exposition of 1893…a coming of age venue to present the US as a political and industrial power. (This was America's fourth major world's fair in 17 years.)

Within the "White City" at Chicago was an unprecedented collaboration of artists, architects, engineers, sculptors, painters, and crafts artisans in general among the 65,000 exhibits. In its six month run it drew over 27 million visitors from around the world. Notably for the Arts and Crafts in general, and women in particular, there was the famous Woman's Building crammed with objects made by 19th century women from Europe and the U.S. It was designed by 21-year-old MIT graduate Sophia Hayden and filled with women's accomplishments in science, literature, invention, and art. It was intended to showcase the women's clubs of America, but it emerged instead as the very heart of the unstoppable suffrage movement where, finally, women won the right to vote in 1920!

When the poet Katherine Lee Bates visited the fair, she marveled at the White City and went home and wrote "America the Beautiful." Basically, the intermingling of fine art, handicraft art, and manufactured goods, well displayed in the "Manufacturers and Liberal Arts Building," gave a cultural cache to the consumption of goods, and to their producers and consumers. The presence of manufacturing lent credence to the idea that art, increasingly like the rest of American life, could be consumed. Business became a necessary component of high culture and the U.S. fairs to come were designed to achieve cultural parity with Europe and show consumers how many different and well made American goods had become.

The Decline

Those who treasure all things Arts and Crafts should be grateful for what has been saved. Just as the notion was implanted in a person's mind to immerse the home with Arts and Crafts décor, so was the notion to replace it with a contemporary style.

If you examine the "shelter" magazines for the home of the early 1920s, you'll see self-appointed consumer "taste-cops" were clamoring for dramatic changes. Interior design on

the whole had decided that Arts and Crafts was to be dismissed long before the calamitous 5-year depression, 1929-1934.

Homemakers agreed and, like "Puff the Magic Dragon," the Arts and Crafts movement went into the cave. The depression and World War II ensured that it would remain there a long, long time.

Print items promoting the artistic capabilities of the Georg Hulbe Workshops and its awards of the 1890s into the early 1900s. *Courtesy of Faire Lees.*

Much of the inspiration to commercially produce artistic leather articles of utilitarian use is traceable to Germany's premier leather artisan, Georg Hulbe, and his Hamburg workshops. This example, a cylinder wastebasket of the late 1890s, could easily be mistaken as the work of Roycrofter Frederick C. Kranz, for he was familiar with Hulbe's work. Roycroft articles of nearly the same dimensions and sinuosity of the art nouveau, features a stylized iris and appeared in the Roycroft leather catalog of 1909. 9" dia. X 15"h. *Courtesy of Faire Lees.*

The trademark Hulbe workshop galleon imprint. Note the initials GH on either side of the mast. *Courtesy of Faire Lees.*

THE ALLURE OF DECORATED LEATHER

From attics, basement trunks and storage boxes, once prized purses are being rediscovered. Unearthed alongside vintage textiles and a shoebox of ancient photos the leather treasures of generations-removed are finding new admirers.

Within internet chat rooms, live auctions and eBay® too, the availability of Arts & Crafts leather objects appears to be increasing. Almost exponentially, there are more willing buyers for a pristine modeled leather bound Roycroft book or purse. Longtime collectors grumble that the rush of more buyers is driving up the prices. Such activity in turn spurs a more careful search of an elder's estate sale. The upward spiral of interest is enhanced annually as more and more potential collectors become educated about the leather goods and the artists and commercial firms that were responsible for the design and production. And that is the purpose of this book.

Broadly defined, decorated, and designed leather is that which is modeled or tooled, colored or painted, and even burned. Some is layered in different colors in a pleasing appliqué of different smooth and suede types of leather. One important characteristic is that most often its maker worked with a love of the craft's period design and used quality materials in its assembly.

All manner of dramatic table mats or large settle and chair throws and pillows were composed of multi-color leathers, usually glued and nearly invisibly sewn. Designs varied from ones with straight line designs most often associated with Arts & Crafts, to the free-flowing and sinuous floral forms of the Art Nouveau. Regardless of the style, many possess uniqueness for the absorbing designs, harmony of colors of leather used, and the exceptional skills required to assemble one.

The Purse

All of these techniques were employed by both skilled "sole proprietor" artisans and those in commercial firms. Most usually, the skilled solo artisan sewed and glued the leather, and hammered and attached any metal elements, to combine into a finished object. An example of this difference would be one-off purses made at the Handicraft Guild of Minneapolis, the Wilro Shop of Chicago, or Forest Craft Guild of Grand Rapids. At the latter firm, when producing a purse, the artisan usually employed suede "ooze" lambskin leather, hand-stitched or machine-sewn with a design element of hammered and pierced/cutout metal, usually copper or brass, and often combined with an inset semi-precious cabochon at the top. If the object was not equipped with a fold-over flap, the leather was slit in numerous places around the top and a drawstring threaded through the slits in order to effect the closing.

Purses made at Roycroft, Cordova, Bosca or any of the other quality manufacturers used a metal frame closure that required a special clamp to install. The completed top leather edges were laced before being inserted into the continuous slot of the frame. The hand tool crimped the frame edges close and tight over the leather. The handle would receive the same lacing treatment along its edges after the two flat pieces of leather first were glued and sometimes machine stitched. Note: Very early (1904) purses often had handles braided from 5 or more thin leather strands into a leather "rope." Connector fittings were either combined at the ends of the braided strands or inserted into a metal ferrule connector on the ends so it could be attached to the purse frame.

Generally, the leather purses were smaller in the early 1900s for two reasons: 1) In manufacturing, smaller meant lower cost. Readily available "scrap" leather, leftover from primary manufacturing of bookbinding, or turning out shoes, boots, gloves or luggage, could be used. 2) The fashion trend of the times. A decorated leather purse was a "new look," an unproven departure from a belt-hung Chatelaine cloth, mesh, or beaded pouch bag that was still in common use. A woman didn't need to carry much. It may include a door key, comb, calling cards, coins for the trolley or automat, and if she was very daring, rouge and face powder. A leather purse at the lower price range of $2.50 far exceeded the typical cloth purse priced at thirty-five cents.

The 1909 Roycroft leather catalog offered a truly small, palm-sized (5-1/2 x 4-1/2 inches) modeled leather handbag in an oak design with leather lining, and three outside pockets for $15.00. The larger (8 x 5 inches) lily-of-the-valley design, leather lined handbag, with one inside pocket plus a modeled leather change purse was $18.00, while a worn-at-the-waist Chatelaine bag of gray ooze calf with belt and silk-lined was $8.00. This was an expensive fashion statement for the working girl, yet it was of little concern to a woman of means who was accustomed to silk or fine Italian beaded handbags, and who was in a position to have "a purse for every ensemble."

Essentially, the well-made, modeled leather handbag appealed to a rather narrow spectrum of price-conscious women who may have placed more value on sustainability than on the fashion of the moment. As Evelyn Haertig points out:

> A plausible theory is that the leather purse was the work horse of purses and it was used on a daily basis. They seem to remain in the memory of an astonishing number of elderly ladies, much like Whiting and Davis metal mesh purses. A serviceable bag that would hold together longer than your face seems a wise investment. Granny would approve.
> —*More Beautiful Purses*," 1990, Gallery Graphics Press, Carmel, CA, 93923

Even before World War I concluded, a woman's needs for access to more items had increased. Whether hand-modeled and machine-stamped, the leather purse had been established as a necessary appointment in a woman's wardrobe, and there were nearly 300 thousand women entering the work force annually. That's a good reason to make a lot of purses. Other manufacturers with some market clout, Amity, Bosca, Enger-Kress, Justin, Meeker, Nocona, Paragon, and Volland, as well as Cordova, Kaser, and Roycroft emerged with larger multi-line offerings. Major mail order retailers such as the Sears, Roebuck and Company and Montgomery-Ward offered a wide variety of styles and some colors, black being most prominent, in their stores and catalogs. Sizes of handbags increased and

there were dozens of designs. The Roycroft leather catalog of 1914 offered its hand-modeled fuchsia design in a size of 8"w x 10-1/2"h with leather lining, inside pocket, and coin purse for $12.00. Its quite stylish envelope style bag in Colonial design had a top handle, was surprisingly lined with moiré silk, and was fitted with change-purse, mirror, notebook and pencil in an accordion shaped size of 8"w x 3-3/4"h for $7.50.

Across the board, leather purse makers increased the size by at least 20 percent. Modeled and stamped leather purses of nearly 8 x 10 inches were produced by most companies. The envelope-shaped "clutch" version with multiple lined pockets and a telescoping sliding strap became more prominent.

Still, these flat and rather stiff leathers were not as expandable as the conveniently pouch-shaped fabric versions. Even larger purses were hard-pressed to contain the daily needs of the working woman of the 1920s, such as a compact, handkerchief, car key, even cigarettes.

The Dynamics of Change—1917 to 1929

Never before in America had so many life-style altering events happened in such a brief moment and women were especially affected. America joined the war in Europe and mobilized four million young men and women in the conflict. In the space of 19 months (April, 1917, to November, 1918) more than 300 thousand Americans were killed or wounded in World War I. On the heels of this shock was the catastrophic flu epidemic of 1918-1919 that caused the death of over 500 thousand Americans and 22 million worldwide. The mobilization of the nation's industrial might combined with the epidemic, which hit returning soldiers hardest, caused women to step forward to fill the jobs of men. In addition, the need of business for "lady typewriters" (stenographers and clerks) now employed over 300 thousand new women by war's end.

Tens of thousands of new women annually entered the workforce. Although it had taken more than two decades to achieve, the 8-hour day, 48-hour work week did come to pass and women did win the hard fought federal right to vote on June 4, 1919. There were now over 8 million women employed in gainful occupations at offices, shops and factories.

Women's fashion changes, which had been slow to evolve over the past decade, accelerated with the new lifestyle of disposable income, greater social interaction, especially with men, and the advent of some leisure time. The street-dragging hobble skirts and calf-high leather shoes were passé. Skirts had crept up to calf height and the high top shoes gave way to fashionable pumps. Even during the economic downturn of 1920-1921, women's fashions steadily evolved. Hemlines crept ever upward and the authoritative women's magazines began to feature styles of turned-down hose, powdered knees, and shingle-bobbed hair. More women kept their own apartments, many drove automobiles, and even smoked cigarettes.

So what does all this have to do with the modeled or decorated leather purse that was adored a decade earlier? New handbags that complimented the working woman's ensembles were available in colored and patterned fabrics. A woman could readily find shoes and a handbag that matched in chic smooth and colored leather. And there was room to spare in the handbag to carry money, lipstick, combs, keys, gloves, and cigarettes! Even the more mature woman, working or at home, recognized her old standby—the brown modeled leather purse that served so well—was ready for the closet shelf or bottom bureau drawer, just in case. After all, it was so well-made and held such fond memories.

The purse manufacturer that didn't respond to new fashion trends was on the edge of being discarded as the decade of the 1930s opened. The additional economic shock of the 1929 stock market crash and the lean years of the Great Depression (that continued through 1935) would finish off all but the cash loaded makers with broader product lines that could ride it out.

Surprisingly, there were a few of these organizations that did just that. Roycroft lost its chief and cash cow, Elbert Hubbard (and wife Alice) on May 7, 1915, but survived under the guidance of the son Elbert "Bert" Hubbard until 1938. However, its leather production in the latter years had dwindled to a few items such as billfolds, letter and cigarette cases.

Nearby, the Cordova Shops that began in 1908 kept up the fight until 1941. The H. E. Kaser Company endured into 1942 and listed Fred Kaser, leather worker in the Buffalo City Directory. In the Midwest, the Bosca Company of Springfield, Ohio, founded in 1911 by Hugo Bosca, survived by a succession of mergers with other leather goods and purse makers. It is still a premier leather goods manufacturer and retailer.

Among the most carried purses by the working woman were those of the largest manufacturer, The Meeker Company of Joplin, Missouri, which evolved its diverse modeled and stamped line of leather goods from 1908 until 1959. The Justin Leather Goods Company of Ft. Worth, Texas, had its roots planted deep as a cowboy boot maker with the first Justin boots made in 1879. It began making leather purses at the close of World War I and continued with a line of purses into 1965. Amity Leather Products, perhaps the world's largest producer of personal leather goods, ceased manufacturing in West Bend, Wisconsin, during the late 1990s. It moved its headquarters to nearby Brown Deer and eventually dissolved into bankruptcy. The company's product names were purchased by Texas-based Tandy Brands in 1998. The ubiquitous frame maker, the J. E. Mergott Company (JEMCO) of Newark, NJ, served dozens of purse makers from 1889 into the late 1950s.

Most historians and devotees of this unique movement in America cite the date of 1916 as the final curtain in a grand show. Elbert Hubbard was gone. Gustav Stickley had declared bankruptcy. Their main voices, the magazines so widely read by several hundred thousand, were silent. The fact that a few of the disciples carried on is some tribute to the legacy of these and other forgotten artisans, who made the decorated and modeled leather so desirable today.

Making a Purse

The leather purse was the first purse to be entirely commercially made, commencing between 1880-1900. However, they involved so much handwork it is difficult to view them as a machine-made product.
—*More Beautiful Purses*, Evelyn Haertig, Gallery Graphics Press, 1990, p. 95

As the twentieth century progressed more machines were used in the leather making process. But even when aided by labor-saving machines, most of the decorated leather purses and the dozens of other personal articles still required many hand steps for completion. The following was obtained in conversations related to the procedures typical for working leather and fashioning a purse. Information was supplied in interviews with Mrs. Dorothy Samples, Nocona, Texas, a retired Justin Leather Company purse designer; Mrs. Eddie Kelly, Justin Brands Inc., Ft. Worth, Texas, who began as a piece worker, retired as a fashion coordinator and later served as Corporate Archivist; and Mr. Jim Wear, Laramie, Wyoming, an active harness maker and leather artisan.

Mrs. Eddie Kelly: "Even with an embossed but naturalistic floral pattern, the designer and artist had to consider that their leather 'canvas' would contain several elements. If the decision was to produce a purse other than straight across at the top, an appropriate metal frame would be required. In any case, the cost, appearance, decoration, and finished color of the frame were important elements. The size of the finished product also dictated the size and closure method of the frame.

Other questions to be resolved included: What would a woman like to carry in the purse? This helped fix the style and size. Would the art on the leather have more appeal to a young or old woman, city or rural? Would a regionally identifiable flower design, say, the Texas bluebonnet, also appeal to the women of the Northeast US?"

Mrs. Dorothy Samples: "Once sketches of the design were approved, a full-scale 'cartoon' or realistic drawing/design sheet was made so that the die makers could reproduce the metal master. The proper grade and color of vegetable-tanned leather and the quantity was determined and the purse leather/shape was stamped out on a machine known as a 'Klicker' press. Now, the softer suede leather lining was selected and its corresponding shapes needed were stamped out on the Klicker press too. There usually had to be small pockets hand-sewed on each side of it to retain a mirror or coin purse. Those leather covered mirrors were made to order from a specialty leather producer and we made the pockets to fit the ready made mirrors and purses. If background design color was part of the design, it was applied by the girls with artists' brushes and sealed. The outer leather pieces were ready to be hand-lined and hand-laced to the gussets with the appropriate color lacing. Typically, the lacing pattern was the loop stitch. It was attractive, durable and covered the edges of the leather more completely than other forms of lacing. After this, the leather was given a lick of transparent wax and buffed with a soft rag before being packaged. All of these hand worked steps went into purses that wholesaled for $3.50 apiece."

Mr. Jim Wear: "Leather artisans preferred material known as 'vegetable-tanned' (a tanning agent usually made from tree bark and preferably oak) instead of the harder and faster to produce method that used 'chrome-tanned' chemical salts. Leather pieces would be soaked in a clear water bath until the air bubbles ceased rising from the pores. It was then allowed to drip dry a short time and stored in an air tight container. When ready to be worked by hand or embossed, the piece (now darkened and quite pliable) was laid flat and allowed to dry.

When it was judged to be just right to accept and retain a pattern (it would nearly return to its original color) it would be positioned in a press and the intaglio pattern was die-stamped on the grain side surface. On some designs with pronounced raised elements, a second die and pressing was required. This was applied to the underside, known as the flesh side. In some instances, the now raised design required filler that would harden in order to preserve the integrity of the uplifted design. The filler would be concealed by the suede lining. Once the piece was impressed it was ready for the perimeter lacing slits to be punched with a thonging chisel. It looks like a fork and produced evenly spaced slits to accept being laced with fine kangaroo hide strips. A similar procedure was required to produce the gussets at each side."

Laced handles were customarily 12 to 14 inches in length so the top of the handle arc would be about five to six inches above the frame. Most were two thicknesses of leather often tapered at attach points. The one-inch width pieces, some even decorated with a design, were skived [thinned] at the edges, cemented together, punched and loop-stitch-laced to match the style of the bag. Later on, edge-laced handles were replaced with machine-sewn ones.

Most of the metal frames, even decorative and hammered ones, were steel and brass. Especially fancy frames were plated in copper, silver, nickel, gold, or gun-metal blued. Many purse makers used frames made by JEMCO (the J. E. Mergott Company) of Newark, New Jersey.

The Metal Frame

If you've wondered how they got the leather to remain in the frame there was a special trick. Most frames were two parts in one! There is a thin metal U-shaped channel (known as a sheen) of the same contour shape as the outer frame, which also has a channel in which it will fit. The leather top of the purse was tucked into the groove of the sheen with a blunt edged tool called a stuffer or pusher. Once inserted, about 3/16" on both sides, frame-closing pliers were used to squeeze together this inner U-shaped channel so that it tightly gripped the leather.

Once the two sides of the sheen were secured over the leather, it easily slid into the channel of the outer frame. Commonly, at the hinge on each side there were small (1/32") holes. Corresponding tiny pins/rivets were inserted and aligned with

hole in the sheen. These could be cemented and inserted or hammered on the penetrating end of the pin to ensure it didn't work loose.

For one part frames, a heavier duty toggle action pliers with wide smooth jaws were used to squeeze the U-shaped channel of the frame itself closed on the leather. When working with one-piece frames, a piece of leather was folded over the frame to avoid marring the metal with the pliers.

The handle D-ring clips were crimped to the frame attachment points, the mirror and coin purse inserted in the inside pockets and the closing mechanism tested to assure that it operated smoothly.

Essentially, a typical purse included: 1) The primary leather piece that became the front and back, sometimes with a design on both areas; 2) a gusset piece at each side; 3) suede leather pieces with pockets installed to hold a coin purse and mirror and used to line the interior; 4) a hinged metal frame; and 5) a laced leather handle with reinforced ends fitted with D-ring fasteners to attach to the ears on the frame."

The Frame Makers

The J.E. Mergott Company with the factory in Newark, New Jersey and a sales office in New York City, is mistakenly credited for making more leather purses than all the companies combined. Its frame acronym is JEMCO™ (often in a diamond-shaped outline) stamped on the inside of the frame along with patent dates. The fact is that JEMCO™ never made a leather purse!

The J.E. Mergott Company of Newark, NJ reveals its identifiable diamond trademark—Jemco— verifying it as a maker of metal frames, not leather handbags. *Courtesy Bag Lady Emporium.*

JEMCO

This Trade-Mark
inside of a
HANDBAG FRAME
assures you of

Finest Materials
First Class
Workmanship
Authentic Style
Handsome Finish
Long Service
Customer
Satisfaction

THE J. E. MERGOTT COMPANY
Office and Salesroom
200 Fifth Ave., New York City
Plant
Newark, N. J.

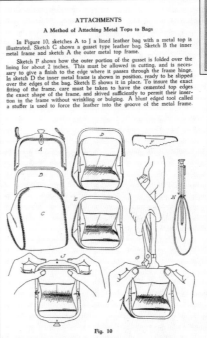

ATTACHMENTS
A Method of Attaching Metal Tops to Bags

In Figure 10, sketches A to J a lined leather bag with a metal top is illustrated. Sketch C shows a gusset type leather bag. Sketch B the inner metal frame and sketch A the outer metal top frame.

Sketch F shows how the outer portion of the gusset is folded over the lining for about 2 inches. This must be allowed in cutting, as is necessary to give a finish to the edge where it passes through the frame hinge. In sketch D the inner metal frame is shown in position, ready to be slipped over the edges of the bag. Sketch E shows it in place. To insure the exact fitting of the frame, care must be taken to have the cemented top edges the exact shape of the frame, and skived sufficiently to permit their insertion in the frame without wrinkling or bulging. A blunt edged tool called a stuffer is used to force the leather into the groove of the metal frame.

Fig. 10

73

Here's how a metal frame is mated to the top of a leather purse during assembly. *Courtesy of Jim Wear, from the Lester Griswold of Colorado Springs, CO catalog of 1922.*

It flourished as a metal frame maker for purses, fabric, beaded, wire, and woven mesh in 1878 at 19 Green Street, Newark. It later moved to 10 Ward Street and incorporated with the company name per above. After a fire in 1905 a new 4-story factory of nearly 100,000 square feet was constructed at Jelliff Avenue. In 1912, with 600 workers, it produced the majority of bag, purse and pocketbook frames you'll see on purse manufacturers across the U.S.

In a May, 1929 advertisement in *Harper's Bazaar* the company proclaimed itself to be "The Largest Producer of Ladies' Hand Bag Frames." It also made other metal specialties such as match safes, cigarette cases, and desktop novelties, usually of plated steel and brass. In 1912, the founder's son, Louis F. Mergott served as president. The firm continued in business until January 4, 1950, when it was acquired by the Fedder-Quigon Corp. It still continued to supply frames into the mid-1950s.

Most frames produced by JEMCO during the Arts and Crafts era were held closed by a simple catch often stamped "Turnloc." The closure device, a ring or decorative tab, could be rotated 180 degrees to release the frame and the bag could be opened. When rotated 180 degrees either way as the frame halves were held together, the purse could be locked. Curiously, while most Jemco frames are steel and plated, the ring or decorative tab is non-magnetic, usually brass. The device and the word "Turnloc"™ was a registered trademark of the J.E. Mergott Company.

The August Goertz and Company frame makers were established in 1881 in Newark, New Jersey, and it never made a leather purse either. Principals were August Goertz, Edward Wester, and Edward Knecht and it incorporated in 1904 with Mr. Goertz serving as President. In 1912 a new 90,000 square foot factory was located on Morris Avenue near South Orange Avenue. According to the publication, *Newark, the City of Industry, 1912*, "The goods manufactured consist of every kind of purse, bag and pocketbook frame, both cheap and costly, and are made from various metals, including copper, nickel, silver and gold plate, aluminum, etc. Besides purse frames, the company produce a large line of metal specialties, brass products, trim for fancy leather goods, advertising novelties. Many decorative, artistic designs made in gold and silver plate is patented by Mr. Goertz and was his own invention."

[Both the J.E. Mergott Company and August Goertz & Company information was obtained from the 1912 reference *Newark, The City of Industry, 1912*, published under the auspices of the Newark, New Jersey, Board of Trade.]

Leather for Man & Home

We've seen how women's fashion dictated the need for a purse. Remember, a dress of 1916 (or a decade later for that matter) had no pockets of any substance and a purse was required for personal needs. A man's suit had the equivalent capacity of two women's purses in his pockets! A business suit, replete with vest, furnished nearly a dozen pockets where personal objects of all sizes could be concealed with no discernable bulges.

Typically, professional dress may have required a business card case, an envelope-style bill-case to hold folded documents, a billfold with coin purse, and all would fit in an inside coat pocket. The really fashion-conscious male may have also carried a small leather-covered memorandum pad notebook (and contained pencil) to jot down thoughts, perhaps a leather cigar or cigarette case, a comb in a leather case, a pen wiper, and even a leather cover match case. On his office desk (and at the home desk) might be a leather-covered ensemble of a blotter, ink well, paperweight, document portfolio, letter knife opener, scissor case, letter holder, photo frame or case, and even leather-covered bookends on a leather mat. All of these objects were available from larger leather companies and were among the many popular items in the Roycroft 1915 Handmade catalog.

For a moment in time, modeled leather items had ascended from bungalow to mansion status. Modeled leather achieved some cultural parity—that is, it was a desirable decorative element in the homes of both the wealthy and those of modest means. It's likely to have occurred as a result of the continuing reinforcement by Elbert Hubbard in the advertised offerings in *The Fra* and *The Philistine*. These two publications monthly reached nearly two hundred thousand homes—plus pass-along to other readers—resulting in nearly half-a-million reminders to add accessories of modeled leather to their homes. To this can be added the testimony of a few hundred thousand users and the hundreds of allied arts and crafts manufacturers and their employees. Those intensely dedicated people left a significant paper trail for those who followed, especially Gustav Stickley and *The Craftsman*, Adelaide Robineau and the *Keramic Studio*, Elbert Hubbard and *The Fra*.

The same modeled leather purse, personal, desktop, or home items that were acquired by the wealthy were within reach of the working folks of modest means. Consider the brilliantly designed and executed Roycroft moth-design, 22-inch diameter modeled leather table mat. For only 10 dollars it could serve beneath an exquisite Tiffany dragon-fly, glass-shaded lamp on a foyer table, or enhance a modest piece of art pottery on a generic oak sideboard. Modeled leather had achieved status. As the Roycroft 1915 catalog pointed out, "These mats come in shades (meaning color tinted) to harmonize with the fine woods used in library-tables and mantels."

Besides Roycroft modeled leather mats and bookends and photo frames in numerous sizes, the homeowner could have a sewing basket, desk set, cuff-link box, collar, glove and tie cases, portfolios (similar to a flapped briefcase) hand mirror, manicure set, music rolls and cases, laced-edge clocks and even modeled leather pillows of 20 x 20 inches.

Other companies offered these and different home accessories such as paneled screens, fireplace screens and portieres (room divider curtains). When given reasonable care, leather objects survive just fine when tucked away in trunks and boxes. There was a lot of it made and awaiting discovery.

COLLECTING A&C LEATHER...ESPECIALLY A PURSE!

When even seasoned collectors of Stickley, Roycroft, or Rookwood are asked, "What Arts & Crafts decorated leather objects do you collect?" most are apt to say, "I hadn't really thought about the leather." When they learn that the internet's electronic classifieds are presenting the collector with vintage leather articles, their interest piques. Internet auctions such as eBay® or Yahoo®, and dealer websites now offer all things A&C. In spite of its fragile nature, decorated leather of the 1900s is emerging to augment established furniture and pottery collections. Artistic leather offers an affordable entrée into the A&C milieu for the new collector.

A notable exception are the Roycroft rarities—the exquisite modeled leather bound, hand-colored, and illuminated books. Such volumes always have been prized since their offering in the late 1890s. As early as the 2005 Grove Park Inn Arts and Crafts Conference (Ashville, North Carolina), long-time and devoted Roycroft book collectors Richard Blacher, Paul Johnson, and Boice Lydell noticed the collecting opportunities brought about by the internet. They confirmed that although the internet may furnish more competitors for a unique and luxuriously bound volume (hence a higher price), it may create an awareness to rediscover an ancestor's legacy of books.

As with any new area of collecting, some guidelines are needed. What follows are some suggestions for the leather collector.

Condition, Condition, Condition!

Experienced collectors demand and deserve near perfection for a top dollar item. So should you. Broken laces/stitches, rips in the leather, severe stains anywhere, missing leather handles (usually replaced with a chain or a silk cord) broken or missing tab or "turnloc" latches, sprung frames are all serious detractors.

When you hear or see phrases "some stitches broken," or "easy to repair," "find a ring at the hardware store," "missing the turn tab," let it go and look to the next one. It's unlikely a leather craftsman in your area has touched one of these and may charge $40 or more an hour to attempt the repair. There is no spare parts wrecking yard for these.

Generally, if you're at a dealer's booth and can handle a modeled leather purse you're better prepared to assess the "buy/don't buy" decision than on the internet. When you're searching eBay® or other web sites you need to keep the following in mind and ask questions of the seller. (You sellers would be wise to cover these in the description.)

• **The Lacing**

You want as few breaks as possible (one may be acceptable if it can be glued and tucked back in, two together is reason to question it, three or more together, leave it). The handle got most of the wear and its laces are most likely to break first. Also, it often cracks or breaks where it joins the metal connector. Scuffed lace color can be restored. Walk away from one with a broken handle.

• **The "Turnloc" Tab**

The idea is that by rotating the turnloc tab 180-degrees (a half-turn) the purse frame can be opened. When shutting the frame you reverse the turn and the frame is now locked and stays closed. These are often broken and non-operable. If the tab is missing you'll see a hole in the frame. Even if the purse was nearly perfect in lacing, design, color, etc., would you want to display it so your friends could say: "what's that hole there?"

• **The Frame**

If a magnet sticks tight it's steel. If it doesn't it is likely brass or copper that has been plated. Steel will rust but the others won't. Many will bear the stamped name "Jemco" in a diamond with some dates. This is the J. E. Mergott Company frame maker's mark, not the mark of the purse manufacturer. See that the frame closes evenly, Are all the decorative jeweled or applied elements (if any) still in place? Jeweled cabochon ornamentation is nearly impossible to replace. Has it been spray-painted to simulate the original plating? Some plating wear is acceptable, but spray painting isn't. If this area is perfect, especially around where the fingers would rotate the "turnloc" tab, it is likely the purse hasn't had much use.

• **The Leather**

Expect the leather to be firm but supple. If it appears too limp and dark it may be soaked with some conditioner. If it feels stiff or brittle, it often can be softened with special oils we'll talk about in another place, but never use Neatsfoot® oil! Can you live with a small dime sized stain or scratch if it's right in the middle of the design? If the purse has a clear Roycroft, Cordova Shops, Kaser, or Bosca brand in it you may want to learn to do so, especially if the design is crisp and vivid. Severe scratches can be blended with colored leather waxes.

• The Interior

Most purses are lined with a suede-like skin known as "ooze" leather. The thin sheepskin or calfskin was immersed in a vat of oak bark, sumac, and slurry of mud. Under some heat and small pressure the cooking mixture was forced through the skin, that is, it "oozed" through, hence the tanner's term. It became uniquely soft and pliable and was dyed the ubiquitous dull green or sometimes brown. Its primary use was for purse lining and backing on leather mats.

If it is stained, ripped, or moldy, pass it by. If it merely has a slight odor, this can be greatly reduced by filling it with kitty litter and letting it sit for a month. Very small tears can be refastened with leather cement. Some stains, ballpoint pen for instance, can be reduced by rubbing with a ball of white bread. You can release most inside residue by carefully brushing it with a fingernail brush or tooth brush and vacuuming the interior.

• The Handle

No catalog we've ever seen shows a worthy, branded purse with a chain handle. This is usually a replacement when the original leather handle has broken. Look for zero-defect on the lacing. By the late 1920s and early 1930s purses, the handle had changed from being edge-laced and was usually machine-sewn. If the thread has pulled from this type of fastening it may be quite difficult to find the same size needle and thread and have it resewn.

• The Accessories

Mirrors weren't always signed or stamped with the maker's mark, but many were. Most have deteriorated somewhat but that is to be expected. Change purses that were original to the purse were occasionally signed or marked in the same manner as the purse. It is especially desirable to have a matching mirror and change purse, or other items. It is even more desirable to have the original packaging, box, tissue wrapping, and sometimes a "guarantee" card.

How to Care for Your New Find

Some collectors are loathe to clean the dirt from or apply any dressing to a leather article. They store the item in a dry, cool place out of sunlight. However, many collectors choose to present their leather as a coordinated display, or in concert with other period items, like a modeled leather table mat beneath a copper table lamp on a table, with perhaps a leather photo holder alongside. If so, you may want to consider the following leather treatment process, verified by a longtime collector. Test all procedures on an inconspicuous part of the leather before proceeding. The author and publisher assume no responsibility for the result, positive or negative.

First, examine the purse for loose or broken lacing. Glue any loose ends with leather cement, tuck these into the original position and let dry several hours. If the black lacing is horribly scuffed it can be reclaimed. Acquire some black liquid leather dye and use a fine artist's brush to carefully apply it to the scuffed lacing, being careful to not run into the brown leather. Use corn starch on a dampened cloth to remove leather burns and dark spots. The corn starch adds luster to the leather. If no broken laces are found, clean the surface by applying a generous coating of virgin olive oil and let dry overnight. The leather will temporarily darken, but it will return to the original color. The next day buff the surface and frame with a soft cotton cloth and you will see the dirt transfer to it.

Depending upon the leather's dryness a second coating of olive oil will help to soften, preserve, and even out the color. If applied, let dry overnight and buff again with a soft cloth. A discarded toothbrush and Q-tips® are ideal to remove grime from the metal frame design and also remove the greenish corrosion sometimes seen at frame joints or metal closure snaps. Be careful, for this residue can be smeared into the suede leather lining. If that has already happened, brush with a clean fingernail brush and vacuum out the residue. Once the leather has been buffed an appropriate colored or neutral paste polish/wax can be applied. Let this dry for an hour and polish with a soft cotton cloth or brush. Sometimes, it serves to apply a second coat and polish as usual with a buffing cloth.

There is an optional step that was furnished by Richard Blacher, a longtime Roycroft fine leather book collector. The leather preservative/restorer is known as the "Fredelka Formula®." It's an easily applied rich cream that furnishes a rich patina and doesn't leave an oily or sticky finish on the article. Let this dry several hours and buff again with a soft cloth or brush. It's available from University Products, The Archival Company of Holyoke, Massachusetts, website: universityproducts.com).

MASSACHUSETTS

Boston: Cradle of the Nation—
Birthplace of U.S. Arts & Crafts

Academicians may quibble or split hairs on when and where the Arts and Crafts movement made its U.S. debut, but those in the know point to Boston. The year; 1897, the month and day; April 3, the place; Copley Hall. The preparation for this event was months earlier, but it was in Boston that 100 invited artisans presented nearly 400 original art examples we know as "works of Arts & Crafts."

 ## The Society of Arts and Crafts, Boston

"The extremely successful exhibition organized by Henry Louis Johnson, a craftsman printer, and a group of prominent Bostonians, stimulated widespread interest and resulted in the incorporation of the Society of Arts and Crafts on June 28, 1897."

—*The Society of Arts and Crafts Exhibition Record, 1897-1924*, Ulehla, Karen Evans, Boston Public Library, 1981

With a who's who list of prestige and wealth behind it (the first president, Charles Elliot Norton, also presided over Harvard University) success was ensured. As the show closed, plans were being laid for the next event that would offer a juried selection of handicraft work from across the nation. Membership in the Society of Arts and Crafts (SACB) was encouraged, but the work of many non-members was accepted for this exhibit. "In 1899, the second exhibit at Copley Hall comprised over 3,000 examples of fine arts. A few of the notable features included: photographs by Alfred Steiglitz, illustrations by Maxfield Parrish, designs by Louis C. Tiffany, and wall hangings of modeled and gilded leather by Mary and Clara Ware. Large exhibits of jewelry, metalwork, wood carving, modeling, printing, bookbinding, engraving, pottery and stained glass made up most of the show." (*SACB Record*, p.5)

Public acceptance and favorable media attention encouraged the SACB to open a gallery/salesroom at 1 Somerset Street in Boston as a permanent exhibition space. Leather artisan, Mary Ware Dennett permitted Society members to exhibit and sell their goods through her and sister Clara's shop. The gallery then assumed its name, the "Handicraft Shop" of Boston. Oddly enough, Dennett was the only leatherworker ever to serve as a SACB jury member (1900-1903). As the success of the show spread, many artisans outside the Boston area applied for membership.

Over the organization's 30-year span (1897-1927) some 98 leather artisans shared society membership. Although Elbert Hubbard wasn't listed, some Roycrofters were. Noted metal worker Walter U. Jennings identified his SACB craft first as a leather worker. So did Roycrofters Frederick C. Kranz and John Grabau, and Cordova Shops of Buffalo leather worker John Eifert. And there's a name familiar to modeled leather purse collectors, Colombo Bosca. He was founder of the leather company still producing high quality leather goods today in Springfield, Ohio.

The primary level of *Craftsman* includes designers, as well as persons practicing some branch of applied decorative art. Candidates were required to specify the particular crafts under which admission was sought. Also, they were required to submit evidence of his or her qualifications, preferably in the form of original craftwork, photographs, or drawings of work... The title of *Master* was conferred only by the council of the Society upon only one designated as a *Craftsman* and who clearly established a standard of excellence. This annual fee was $3.00." —*SACB Record*, Karen Ulehla, p.3

For the first time, the artistic output of distant artisans with unique designs and styles was available in Boston. As membership increased so did the needs for more gallery and exhibit and sales space. "By the fifth annual meeting in January, 1902, membership had increased to 278 and sales from the gallery amounted to $4,000.00. The technical journal *Handicraft* began publication and featured the styles and works of members in a wide variety of disciplines. In September, 1904 the Society moved to 9 Park Street, where it remained into the twenties. With the move came an immediate increase in sales and craftsmen were urged to produce more handicrafts. In 1905 the organization achieved financial independence for the first time as sales exceeded $37,000. "(*SACB Record*, Karen Ulehla, p.5).

The next year, an adjoining store was acquired and the SACB occupied the entire street floor of Ticknor House and had a needed shipping entrance.

To commemorate the SACB's tenth anniversary, a third major exhibition was held in February, 1907, at Copley Hall. Society archives revealed that the event attracted international attention with favorable reviews from critics and editors of the consumer and arts journals of the day. At this event, various arts and crafts organizations from around the U.S. met as invitees of the SACB. They returned to their cities as members of the National League of Handicraft Societies. Twenty-three new organizations were formed at this show, all basically modeled after the SACB.

The nation's economic setback, later that year, did affect the society's sales for the next 18 months. By late 1909, the Handicraft Shop was recovering with sales of $6,000. Again, craftsmen were asked to increase their output. By 1916, sales had grown to $106,000 and there were 897 members across the nation. Overall, the society had over 3,000 members and exhibitors. It was largely responsible for laying the foundation of the Arts and Crafts Movement that affected the lives of countless persons across the nation.

Arts & Crafts Achieve Parity with the "Fine Arts"

The right place and time for this breakthrough came at the Louisiana Purchase Exposition—commonly known as the St. Louis World's Fair of 1904. For the first time at an international exhibition, the applied arts were segregated from machine-made goods and would be shown and treated as equal with painting and sculpture-the "fine" arts.

"The visionary behind the display of Applied Arts was Halsey Cooley Ives (1846-1911) director of the St. Louis School of Fine Arts and former chief of the Art Department at the World's Columbian Exposition held in Chicago, 1893." ("Worthy and Carefully Selected," Beverly K. Brant, *Archives of American Art Journal,* vol. 28, #1, 1988.)

Ives had attempted to implement this concept in Chicago but met with indifference of American artisans who failed to submit work. He reached out for the one person who knew the Arts and Crafts scene and had the orga-

nizational experience to bring collections together. The man to implement Ives's idea was Frederick Allen Whiting (1873-1959) who temporarily left his job as secretary of the SACB and assumed the role of superintendent of the Applied Arts Division. With Whiting on board, Ives was able to convince Exposition administrators that a new day for American craftsmen had come. A complex classification system was developed stressing commonalities among those objects within the same building. Within the Palace of Fine Art, the unifying factor among all exhibits was that "art was the predominant feature and that each object was the original work of the artist, not a reproduction by another hand nor the result of any mechanical process." (Beverly Brant, p. 5)

"Essentially, all art work—whether on canvas, in marble, plaster, wood, metal, glass, porcelain, leather, textile or other vehicle of expression—is equally deserving of respect in proportion as it is worthy from the standpoints of inspiration and technique." Its intent was to correct unjust conditions that had prevailed in the art world, such as the segregation of artists from craftsmen. "By inviting contributions from American art workers, administrators for the Palace of Art acknowledged publicly the progress made by the design reform movement." (Beverly Brant, p. 3)

The Exposition ran for eight months—May through December—and was seen by twenty million people. Approximately 200 American craftsmen (of which 95 were women and 35 others Native Americans) would exhibit 1,100 examples of art workmanship.

Whiting had little time to contact artists and assemble their work and had to rely on personal contacts and design educators he had met while at SACB. He selected Ernest Batchelder as his "picker" to round up "possibles" in California and other Western states. At the time (May, 1904) Batchelder was president of the Pacific Manual Training Teachers Association in Pasadena. He wrote Whiting that he was familiar with potential candidates and his short list "Represents, with possibly two exceptions, the workers who are at all prepared for a display of handiwork: Isabel Austin, a leatherworker from Santa Barbara; May Mott-Smith Byrd, a jewelry maker from San Francisco; Elizabeth Burton (Santa Barbara) who modeled, painted and inlaid leather with shell; Charles F. Eaton (Santa Barbara) who modeled and trimmed leatherwork with metal; and Douglass VanDenburg, a metal smith from Los Gatos." (Beverly Brant, p. 9)

As it evolved, there were 69 artisans represented in the Applied Arts category. Perhaps the list of "foremost" would have been greater, but many artists were unaware of the possibility of exhibiting at this event and were not prepared to send anything. "Charles F. Eaton was initially surprised to even learn of the exhibition. Robert Jarvie (Chicago metal smith) knew about the exhibit but chose not to contribute as he was unenthusiastic about the pieces he had planned to send." (Beverly Brant, p. 9)

In a report to Ives, Whiting was justifiably proud of his SACB exhibitors as he noted "Approximately 208 craftsmen participated altogether, including painting, sculpture, etchings and engravings and applied arts. If the Native American craftsmen (who were admitted by special invitation) are eliminated from the total, the domination of the applied arts division by SAC members is especially evident. Of the 182 craftsmen remaining, eighty were members." (Beverly Brant, p. 9)

At the closing tally, C.T.D. Fox, the superintendent of the Exhibitor's Bureau of Sales, reported to Ives (January 9, 1905) that all goods sold in the American exhibit totaled $80,400. His breakdown shows paintings with a value of $70,000; sculpture $2,000; engravings and etchings, $900; and applied arts $7,500. Items exhibited and purchased in the applied arts section included all types of silver, bookbinding, jewelry, bronze, copper, illuminations, typography, porcelain, china painting, pottery, textiles, and leather.

The leatherworkers (whose items were purchased) included Clara P. Barck of Chicago, Illinois, and Rose and Minnie Dolese of Evanston, Illinois. Fair goers purchased 13 leather objects from the Dolese sisters with a value of $165.00. Other leather articles purchased were made by Grace Gerow of Chicago, Illinois; Florence Ward of Evanston, Illinois; Charles Frederick Eaton of Santa Barbara, California; Elizabeth Eaton Burton of Santa Barbara, California; Ruth Raymond of Chicago, Illinois; and Magda M. Heuermann (no address).

The SACB's Enduring Legacy

From World War I up until the dawn of the nation's economic collapse, the SACB survived and even thrived during hard times. "In 1922 the Handicraft Shop rang up sales over $152,000 and membership had increased to 1,100. Shortly before Christmas of 1923 the Society opened a midtown Manhattan salesroom. Even with a loyal clientele it had trouble meeting expenses. A 1927 move to larger quarters on lower Madison Avenue helped defray costs. Still, the operation wasn't profitable and the New York City showroom was closed January 6, 1928." (Beverly Brant, p. 9)

The final hurrah—a grand show of the Society was held at the Boston Museum of Fine Arts in March, 1927. Membership at the time had reached 1,269. That the SACB remained vital and influential for 30 years is a tribute to the sincerity and truth of the crafts it nurtured and the personal dedication of the members.

Mary Ware Dennett, 1872-1947
Boston, Massachusetts

Renowned in mid-life as a women's rights suffragette and militant advocate of birth control and sex education, Mary Ware Dennett of Boston, Massachusetts, earlier established herself as a major influence in the art of decorated leather before she won the right to vote.

This talented teenager and so many of the artistically versatile young girls at the turn of the 20th century deserve more recognition. Even though they began their artistic careers as leather workers, biographies of women artisans most often don't include the intense dedication and contributions they made to the craft. This is mentioned as a plea, a "heads-up" to the descendants of the women who were touched with genius. Since many regularly documented their work, it is possible their drawings, notes about their processes, and thoughts on life as they matured still exist— entombed in a trunk or shoebox in the attic. Please, if you had a talented relative, look for such items. Get them in the hands of a curator at the local historical society or nearest museum.

Those who study Mary Ware Dennett are fortunate. The Arthur and Elizabeth Schlesinger Library on the History of Women in America, Radcliffe College Institute, and the Hollis Catalog of Harvard University library have a large collection of materials. These document her development of gilded leather, her design teachings at Drexel

Institute in Philadelphia, and Arts and Crafts leatherwork associated with the Society of Arts and Crafts Boston. It contains an extensive collection on her involvement in sex education, birth control, peace movement, and social injustices.

Mary Coffin Ware (Mrs. Hartley Dennett in 1900) was born April 4, 1872, in Worcester, Massachusetts, to-well-to-do parents George Whitefield and Livonia Coffin (Ames) Ware. Her father, a wool merchant, died in 1882, when she was only ten, and the family of four children moved to Boston. She attended public schools, then enrolled in Miss Capen's School for Girls in Northampton, where she exhibited an inordinate early talent for drawing and design. The School of Design, connected with the Boston Museum of Fine Arts, was her choice for advanced study. Under the direction of Joseph Lindon Smith, C. Howard Walker, and Arthur Wesley Dow from 1891-1893, her tapestry and leather designs consistently won top honors. Professor Charles Elliot Norton of Harvard was laying the groundwork for the founding of the Society of Arts and Crafts of Boston and Mary Ware became an enthusiastic, outspoken advocate of the movement. She was selected to carry the message to Philadelphia and at age 21, organized the School for Decorative Design at the Drexel Institute and

A portion of Dennett's methods to duplicate embossed art leather of the Renaissance. The leather was silvered and otherwise colored and the pattern was made by the imprint of a wooden block, carved in relief, upon the dampened leather in a hand press. The process had application as wall covering and for covering furniture in leather. Sample dimensions: 24" square. *Courtesy of the Schlesinger Library, Radcliffe Institute, Harvard University.*

served as director for three years—1894-1897. She, along with her sister Clara, then traveled across Spain and Italy on a pilgrim's quest to rediscover the lost art of producing Cordova leather wall hangings, an important art form in these countries during the renaissance. Mary Ware had long admired the designs and had collected remnants of these leathers. A citation in the *Biographical Cyclopedia of American Women* (Volume II, p. 236) states: "She hunted in vain for some craftsmen who might still be carrying on the work. None were to be found. Machine-made, thoroughly commercialized imitations were all that modern Europe could show. She did, however, find some ancient descriptions of the process of making the Cordovan leathers which were first published in Venice in 1564."

On her return to Boston, she and Clara (who had been on the same quest, only in Germany) opened a studio where they continued their studies and experiments in the leather process. They ground and mixed their own pigments and varnishes, cut their steel dies, made their color blocks, as well as the designs for their wall patterns. Their gilded leather was featured in the SACB's 2nd Exhibition of 1899 and made a considerable stir among the art critics and architects.

One of the period art magazines, *Brush & Pencil*, reported:

There are few kinds of handicraft in which union of arts and crafts is more evident than in the gilded leather made by the Misses Ware, of Boston. These young ladies have revived the art introduced by the Moors into Spain in the eleventh century, which afterward became one of the great and famous industries of the country. Many cities of Spain grew wealthy by making gilded leather, and Cordova surpassed all others, both in quality and quantity. So superior was it that it received the name of Cordovan leather. A sixteenth-century author, writing upon the gilded-leather industry of Cordova, says that: "It brings great wealth to the city, and gives to its principal street a beautiful aspect. As the leathers are exposed to the sun, now gilded, now colored and tooled, and as they are spread upon great tables to dry, truly it is a beautiful sight to see the streets thus hung in such splendor and variety. The industry declined with the general decline of art in Europe, and became extinct toward the end of the last century, and might have been forgotten had it not been for the leather which remained to speak of what had been.

During their life in Venice, the Misses Ware became interested in the lost art, and determined to revive it. When they sought information upon the subject, they found very little had ever been written concerning it and that only in the vaguest manner. Using the books as blind guides, they experimented and after years of trials and failures succeeded in discovering how to gild leather. The process is very slow, as it was then. Every step must

be taken by hand, and requires the greatest patience and exactness. The leather is made from goat-skins, which are imported. It is covered entirely with silver leaf. On this the colored pattern is printed by hand blocks, a varnish is applied which turns the silver to the color of gold, and finally the surface is tooled by means of small dies.

The result is indescribably beautiful in life and light, shade and texture, and cannot be rendered by any know process of reproduction. The leather has almost a velvety texture in appearance, and the gold, delicately tooled, adds a strikingly rich effect. Gilded leather makes the finest hangings for the walls of public buildings, hotels, and theaters, and for special apartments in private residences.

Simultaneously, the sisters opened their studio to other artisans and were instrumental in helping to form the Society of Arts and Crafts of Boston. Mary served as artistic decorator of the shop and was one of the Society's directors. This leather shop became the Handicraft Shop of Boston where skilled craftsmen and trained designers joined forces to maintain a workshop on a truly cooperative basis. Some of the designers had been her students at Drexel.

Dennett worked on large surfaces and articles such as wall hangings for interior decorations, screens, chests, and coats of arms.

Please consider that in the U.S., in the late 1880s, the art of tooling, gilding, and decorating leather as practiced in England and Europe was a new art form. Elbert Hubbard of East Aurora, New York, had visited the Kelmscott Press book binding studios of William Morris and returned with examples, but the shops of Roycroft had not begun to produce the fine modeled leather books so cherished today. It would be another decade before Roycroft really acquired talented leather artisans from Germany and established a department to produce the modeled leather articles such as women's handbags, table mats, music cases, and a myriad of tooled leather personal items.

Even Gustav Stickley saw some merit or interest in what would emerge to become known as Americanized Art Nouveau or Wiener Werkstatte modeled leather designs. Early issues of *The Craftsman* regularly carried features on the emerging art form.

Mary Ware Dennett described in some detail the history of the gilded leather art and the manner in which she and her sister Clara refined their processes as a guide to other modern craftsmen.

In the July, 1903, issue of *The Craftsman*, Stickley permitted Mary Ware Dennett great freedom in describing her passion.

There was a very beautiful sort of gilded leather made that was not tooled at all, but was embossed and painted. It was a later production than the tooled leather. The pattern was made by the imprint of a wooden block, carved in relief, upon the dampened leather after the silvering was done. This was done by a hand press. The Dutch did especially beautiful work of this sort. The finest specimens of tooled leather are those where the pattern is printed in one color—or at least very few colors, whereas the embossed leather permits the widest range of color, and in many cases, gains thereby. There have been several attempts in Europe, and at least two in America, to imitate the fine old tooled leather by machinery. Such efforts must always fail, for no machine can give the spirit and vitality of hand tooling. The modern work also has shown the fatal error of imitating the effects of time. The result has been merely to dim, and not to glorify the color. However, no truly great work of this kind can be expected to come from the modern factory system. The beauty of the old work corresponds exactly with the relative justice of industrial conditions and the freedom and responsibility of the craftsman.

Perhaps surprisingly, there was a demand for this art form. Dennett was fairly pragmatic about her specialty.

The criticism has many times been made that this is not a craft worth reviving, since gilded leather is distinctly a luxury, and could only be bought by the very wealthy; that it smacks of royalty and state apartments and the like; and has small place in a democratic country. However, there are so many public and semi-public places where so glorious and permanent a wall-covering would be right and proper, that there seems to be a real place in life for the "*guadamacilero*"—(Spanish for leather gilder).

While few examples of the gilded leather art exist today, it can be seen as a wall covering in the breakfast room at the Biltmore Mansion Estate in Asheville, North Carolina, and the Isabella Stewart Gardner Museum of Boston, Massachusetts.

It was also in the early days of *The Craftsman* that Stickley began promoting the concept of tooled or modeled leather produced by the home craftsman. From 1903 to 1911 numerous articles appeared, possibly driven by the 1903 detailed description of "The Art of Tooling Leather" by Katherine Girling.

The art of tooling leather ought to commend itself to amateurs. It is not expensive. It demands a firm touch, but not great strength. It is not a noisy craft, like that of working in metal work. It is not trivial. It is a noble old art. A beginner may feel his way along with surprising satisfaction, yet in it, an artist may find scope for his highest powers.

In January, 1900 Mary Ware was married to Hartly Dennett, a Boston architect. Their eldest son Carleton was born that year, and with her husband she established a house decorating business. Another son, Devon, was born in 1905. A Schlesinger Library biographical document show that Hartley had an affair with a client, Margaret Chase, and left Mary and the children to live with Mrs. Chase and her husband, a prominent physician. Mary sued for divorce and was awarded custody of the children in 1913.

It was around this time when she took up several active roles in the National American Woman Suffrage Association; the American Union against Militarism/Women's Peace Party. Her leather artisan career was put on hold as she continued to champion social inequalities and civil liberties issues. In 1915, with Jessie Ashley and Clara Gruening Stattman, she founded the National Birth Control League. It was later reorganized into the Voluntary Parenthood League (VPL) with Mary Ware serving as its first director and as editor of the *Birth Control Herald* a national publication. Her intense participation in these quests, and the authorship of a pamphlet "The Sex Side of Life," banned as obscene by the U.S. Post Office, landed her in jail for a moment. She persisted, and was finally vindicated, and kept up this work for more than a decade. When the U.S. entered the War in April, 1917, she became an organizer for the People's Council, a radical anti-war group, and a board member of the Women's Peace Party.

In 1926, at age 52, she abandoned the time consuming social issues, resigned as director of the VPL and returned to leatherwork as, she said, "My Salvation." She was joined and assisted in this renewal by her son Devon. One major work from this late period was a large chest of modeled leather was enhanced with gilding and colored pigments. The chest was adorned with a design of two entwined Chinese dragons in strong repousse and was signed on the back (wall-side) with the initials MD and DD and the date 1934.

She remained active in the fight for sex education for young people and maintained a "voluminous correspondence" with members of Congress. Mary Ware Dennett died at age 75 in a nursing home in Valatie, New York, in 1947.

Dennett never lost her passion for carving leather. This chest, adorned with two entwined Chinese-style drag-ons, was carved on all sides except the bottom. It was gilded and enhanced with colored pigments and signed on the wall side with initials MD and DD, for Mary and her son Devon, who assisted her in 1934. Dimen-sions: 32"w x 18"h x 16"d. *Courtesy The Schlesinger Library, Radcliffe Institute, Harvard University.*

The chest's lid featured the dragon's heads, modeled in deep relief and gilded and enhanced with colored pigment. Dimensions 32"w x 16"d. *Courtesy the Schlesinger Library, Radcliffe Institute, Harvard University.*

Dennett designed and modeled on leather the seal and motto of the Society of Arts and Crafts Boston. Dimensions: 18"dia. *Courtesy the Schlesinger Library, Radcliffe Institute, Harvard University.*

Tooled, polychromed and gilded peacock on a portion of leather wallcovering. It is reminiscent of early 1900s work by Mary Ware Dennett or Elizabeth Eaton Burton. Image of 12"w x 14-1/4"h was cut from a larger section. *Courtesy of Faire Lees.*

Eleonore E. Bang, 1873-1958
SACB leather artisan 1912-1927
Newton, Massachusetts

Eleonore Bang was another of the irrepressible and enthusiastic immigrants who arrived in America endowed with artistic abilities and perseverance. Early records show she and husband, Armand C., were 30 when they arrived at Ellis Island, August 7, 1904, as Danish citizens.

As they searched to find a place to make their contributions in America their sons, Paul (1906) and Franz William (1908) were born in New York City. After a short time in Virginia, their journey brought them to Roxbury, Massachusetts, where Society of Arts and Crafts Boston reviewers found her wood carving and leather art worthy enough for her invitation to membership. By 1917 she and the family were in the Boston suburb of Newton, where she remained until her death 41 years later.

From the foreword in her well-received book *Leathercraft for Amateurs*, published by the Beacon Press Handicraft Series in 1927 (and available on the internet) it is apparent that Eleonore had made a career choice of showing both the young and adults the personal satisfaction that could be achieved through the carving of wood and leather.

A member of the Fellow Crafters Guild, later to be affiliated with Boston University, she was instrumental in preparing an occupational therapy program—using leather crafting—for World War I returning veterans, many wounded in battle and recovering in the Boston area. She expanded the curriculum to train others who would teach the process to school children and to adults within therapy organizations across the nation.

She saw the process of leather work as both practical and artistic, with useful possibilities.

Of the various handicrafts, leather work holds forth special claims upon the interest of an ambitious worker because of the simplicity of the processes, the inexpensiveness of the equipment and the practically noiseless and therefore non-irritating nature of the work. Yet leathercraft affords at the same time, an outlet for individuality and artistic expression in developing articles of beauty and of enduring value.

She also designed items for wood carving, all two-dimensional, and remained as an active exhibitor in the SACB. She was elected a craftsman member in 1925 and achieved a mastership in 1939. Her practical and humanitarian contributions prompted the Danish Government to bestow the high honor of knighthood and pronounce her as "Dame Eleonore Bang."

A cluster of her surviving artistic leather articles and a few carved wood examples were discovered in Minneapolis. These reflect remembrances of both Danish and Icelandic culture and were likely produced around 1918.

Leather mat with sinuous sea serpent suggestion, 8-7/8" dia. *Courtesy Gordon Hoppe and Steve Schoneck.*

Carved, gilded and painted table mat, 8" square. *Courtesy Gordon Hoppe and Steven Schoneck.*

Geometric notebook cover, 6-1/4"w x 8-1/4"h. *Courtesy Gordon Hoppe and Steven Schoneck.*

Even before Roycroft, Cordova, and Kaser, the Buffalo area had become a haven for skilled leather artisans. As a major graphics arts center (164 printing houses in 1905) fine illustrated books were being produced at Gies & Company, Peter Paul, A.T. Brown printing, and at the Roycroft Print Shop in East Aurora. Then too, many expert bookbinders maintained home studios where they designed and re-bound special books for private collectors. Notable Roycrofters Louis H. Kinder, Peter Franck, Axel Sahlin, Lorenz C. Schwartz, John F. Grabau, Dard Hunter, Walter U. Jennings, and many others were skilled in the design and execution of tooled bindings. These were often inlaid and decorated with gold, silver, ivory, multiple dyed leathers and cabochon stones. There were active trade organizations such as The Buffalo Guild of Allied Arts, The Guild of Book Workers of New York, and The Buffalo Graphics Arts Society, where the art of luxurious book design and binding was exalted. The point is, the nation's foremost leather artisan talent ever assembled resided in the Buffalo/East Aurora area. There was a ready pool of master designers to journeyman leather workers for Roycroft, Cordova, Kaser, and others to draw from. Perhaps that was why there is very little difference in the high quality of workmanship on leather articles produced at any of these companies.

Roycroft, 1905-1936
East Aurora, New York

"Not how cheap, but how good"
—Fra Elbertus Hubbard Motto

Longtime Roycrofter Felix Shay suggests in his biography, *Elbert Hubbard of East Aurora* (Wm. H. Wise & Co., New York, 1926) that Fra Elbertus was tiring of his sales position with the Larkin Soap Co. and the bustling big city of Buffalo (80,000 in 1893). He retired to the village of East Aurora, 15 miles from the Buffalo train station. Shay says he settled in this "buckwheat town" because he loved horses. East Aurora just happened to be headquarters for trotting horses in western New York. Hubbard, really a country boy at heart, started raising them on a few acres of meadow. Shay mentions that Hubbard confided to him that, while saddling his favorite mare Garnet, he had "an idea to become the finest book publisher in the nation, [which] would become a reality within a decade." That was 1895 and type was being set for the first issue of the *Philistine* at an East Aurora print shop.

Hubbard was a rapt admirer of hand-made books, and a student of the history of books and printing, from the timeless efforts of the ancient monks through the early Venetians, the Elzevirs, Plantin, Samuel and Thomas Roycroft, Ben Franklin, down to William Morris and his Kelmscott brethren. When he saw the William Morris establishment where they made just a few beautiful things, his business brains clicked, and he realized that in America an institution built along similar lines was sure to prosper. Morris supplied the inspiration, and the Sixteenth Century English printers, Thomas and Samuel Roycroft supplied the name—"The Roycrofters"—which was eventually to identify Hubbard's American Craftsmen.

The word "Roycroft" means King's Craft or a King's Craftsman. It also denotes the King's country place or farm—so Hubbard got the pleasure of a double meaning from his selected catch-word."
Elbert Hubbard of East Aurora, Felix Shay

As the Charles F. Hamilton (*Head, Heart and Hand*, p. 97) points out: "The historic roots of the Roycroft Modeled Leather Department, formed in 1905, may be traced back to the origin of the Roycroft Bookbinding Department."

Photo frame holding Elbert Hubbard, c.1905, 8-3/4" x 11-1/2" stylized art nouveau design.
Courtesy Roycroft Arts Museum.

THE NORTHEAST

After visiting William Morris at his Kelmscott Press in Hammersmith, England (1896), Hubbard was even more convinced he could produce books equal to those at Kelmscott. He had an idea to become a publisher, but was without a proper facility or the craftsmen to make the journey happen.

Essentially, Elbert Hubbard's goal was to equal or exceed the finely bound books from English and European publishers. To that end he recruited Louis Kinder (who learned the craft in Leipsic, Germany) in 1896 to head the bindery and begin training of apprentices. Albert Lane, author of *Elbert Hubbard and His Work*, wrote in 1901 that "People liked Roycroft work…and the Little Man from Leipsic began to work miracles in levant (leather)."

Reading for enjoyment was a widespread pastime in America in the early 1900s and finely produced books of world class authors were greatly appreciated. A library of fine books became a status symbol among the learned.

Hubbard went on to gather what was perhaps the greatest bookmaking talents ever assembled in the U.S.

They thrived on the Roycroft campus of East Aurora, New York, near Buffalo. The style of leather artistry on book covers became known as "Buffalo nouveau," quite a daring departure for 1900 America that was shaking off the snow of Victoriana.

His publishing success attracted a mercurial Chicago cartoonist, graphic designer, and illustrator, William Wallace Denslow, to make a visit to the Roycroft campus and furnish cartoons for the *Philistine*. Beginning in 1898, Denslow was a summer-long visitor and contributor to the publication, often satirizing Fra Elbertus in his cartoons and producing special illustrations for the leather bound classics. In 1900, he achieved nationwide notoriety for the imaginative characters for L. Frank Baum's *Wonderful Wizard of Oz* (they had met on the campus in 1898). Roycrofter Dard Hunter, a truly renaissance illustrator and craftsman, also became a legend in his time and known for his "one man does all" design and bookmaking.

Roycroft imaginative modeled leather limited edition books were being offered before Frederick Kranz arrived in 1903. Rather suddenly, the designs transcended mere title enhancement. Assembled here are some modeled leather covers from the collection of Boice Lydell, the owner of the Roycroft Arts Museum of East Aurora. If you'll notice the designs of "Contemplations," "A Dog of Flanders," and "Friendship, Love and Marriage" are book-matched, or mirror images, if you divide the design vertically at its center. *Courtesy Roycroft Arts Museum.*

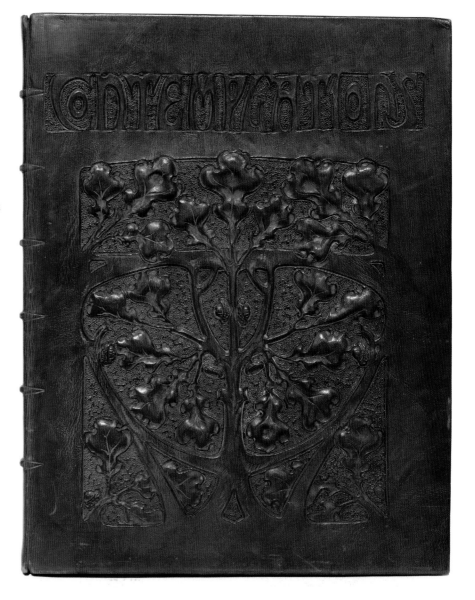

White hyacinths modeled book cover. *Courtesy Roycroft Arts Museum.*

Examine the *"Man of Sorrows"* boxed edition for its nearly careful ecclesiastical feeling of crosses at top and bottom and the ring of thorn foliage along the sides. At bottom center is the proud, rather vertical chop mark—the conjoined initials of Frederick Kranz. *Courtesy Roycroft Arts Museum.*

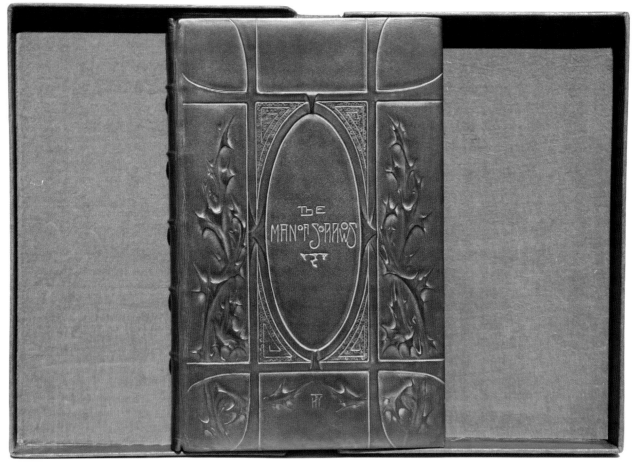

Hubbard had been a business partner in the Larkin Soap Co. of nearby Buffalo and was familiar with the many metropolitan printers. (In 1900, the Buffalo municipal industrial report shows 101 printing firms with 1,100 employees.) Along with this substantial printing industry, Buffalo was a major hide tanning center. Niagara area tanneries supplied an enormous number of finished leather skins for leather goods manufacturers along the northeast corridor from Boston to Philadelphia. The German language journal *Buffalo und sein Deutschum* [Buffalo and its German Community] showed that one tannery in 1877, Schoellkopf & Company (established by Jacob Schoellkopf) processed 2,000 sheep hides daily.

An antiquarian book collector knows that vellum is made from sheep or goat, and is an ideal material for fine book pages. The nation's demands for leather goods was growing almost exponentially around 1900 and Buffalo was ideally positioned to meet the growth. The Schoellkopf factory became the largest tannery in the world as it expanded to over half a million square feet and could daily turn out 12,000 sheep skins. Buffalo was the largest horse and cattle market in the nation and there were three nearby slaughterhouses processing animals and tanneries producing leather hides for all sorts of leather goods. Its Lake Erie docks served 100 cargo ships daily and there was regular passenger ship travel to Detroit. Seventeen rail lines ran through the city (and it was an easy commute to East Aurora). Abundant electrical power would soon be produced at Niagara Falls, less than 16 miles from the city center for the hundreds of new businesses that made Buffalo their headquarters. In 1890, Buffalo's population was 254,495. New European immigrants were migrating to Buffalo after spending a year in New York City, Philadelphia, or Baltimore. This, combined with births of children from the 1843 wave of landed immigrants (primarily German, Irish and Polish), helped Buffalo grow at the rate of 20,000 people annually.

By 1900, the attraction of German immigration to Buffalo showed that more than half, or 175,143 of the city's population of 350,286, were German. They directed major firms in virtually all business categories, such as banking and finance, brewers and distillers, manufacturing, transportation, electric power production, etc. There were two German daily newspapers, the *Buffalo Volksfreund* and the *Buffalo Tribune & Free Press*. Many immigrants came already skilled and most of Buffalo's skilled workers were German—shoemakers, masons, tailors, cabinet makers, blacksmiths, clockmakers, and bookmakers. Even with a large Irish and Polish population the whole fiber of the city had become German."
—*High Hopes: The rise and decline of Buffalo, New York*, Mark Goldman, University of New York Press, Albany, 1983

Elbert Hubbard likeness bookends with leather impressed from a master die and hand finished, 4-5/8"w x 5-7/8"h. *Courtesy Roycroft Arts Museum.*

Because of this, Hubbard didn't have to look too hard to find seasoned and highly skilled typesetters, printers, leather book binding artisans and artists when he established the Roycroft printing shop. Nor did he want for high quality vellum material for the luxuriously bound volumes. Additionally, the young German-American men and women were imbued by parents with a dedicated work ethic and were generally well educated. The list of Roycrofters compiled by Marie Via and Marjorie R. Searl, (*Head, Heart and Hand,* pp.164,165) is abundant with names of German descent.

His choice of German-born (Leipzig) Louis H. Kinder to start the Roycroft bindery (1896) set in motion the qual-ity standard to be achieved and the attraction of artisans to fulfill the need. Typical of the young artists trained early by Kinder were Lorenz C. Schwartz and John F. Grabau of adjoining Buffalo. Both men came to work already skilled as leather artisans. Mr. Grabau's May 20, 1948, *Buffalo News* obituary mentions that he apprenticed at the Peter Paul and Walter Brown bookbinding and printing shop in Buffalo and was a "grown man with a wife and daughter" (26 years old) before becoming an assistant manager and foreman at Roycroft. In 1907 he opened his own studio at 429 Parkdale Avenue, Buffalo. During the next 43 years Grabau won master bookbinding awards across the nation and international acclaim.

Elbert Hubbard praises the leather artistry of German craftsmen and its application in the Roycroft leather shop. February, 1911. *Courtesy of Faire Lees.*

THE ROYCROFT
Modeled=Leather Binding
By Frederick C. Kranz, Master Leather=Worker

HE Germanic Museum at Nuremberg, Germany, possesses a number of bindings from the Four-teenth and Fifteenth Centuries. Their covers are decorated with a lost or forgotten technique, and it was not until the latter part of the last century that any attention was paid to these rare old specimens of bookmaking. However, today we know that the fine old form of decoration of the bookcover was Leather-Modeling. Where the art originated, no one knows.

The fact is, that the Egyptians had some way of decorating leather by incising and staining it; and further, in the Ninth Century, in several towns along the Rhine, a similar technique was used for the decoration of belts and scabbards. But the books in the German Museum represent a standard of the craft that must have taken centuries to develop.

Modeled Leather was so highly estimated in the Middle Ages that men like Lucas Cranach, Hans Holbein and Albrecht Duerer found pleasure in expressing themselves through this art and by assisting less talented workers in the development of beautiful designs.

But the terrible wars in the Seventeenth Century, which made a vast desert out of Germany, killed the flourishing industry like so many others ❧ ❧

It was not until Professor Brinkmann, from the Hamburg School of Industrial Art, called the attention of some friends to the lost art, that a few craftsmen took up anew the study, and today Leather-Modeling has reached a standard of perfection never before attained.

❧ Sure enough there are still a few who are skeptical concerning the use of Modeled Leather as a bookcover; a few who maintain that handtooling and gilding are the only mediums for book decoration, and a few who criticize the use of calf and cowhide which are chiefly employed in modeling.

But to produce good work, the best material is just good enough. And the cowhide used by The Roycroft Leather-Workers is made for us in England by the most reliable tanner. Our American calfskin is sumac-tanned especially for our use—and better was never made.

By 1901 some 60 persons were involved in book production and a new wing on the original print shop was needed to satisfy the growing demand. More leather bound books meant that more leather materials began to accumulate.

As consumer demand grew Hubbard set out to recruit yet another experienced leather designer and modeler. Philadelphia had long been the home turf of the C.F. Rumpp fine modeled leather goods company (established in 1850). This firm served as a talent magnet for kindred German-born leather artisans, including the leather artist Frederick C. Kranz.

Elbert Hubbard had a knack for recognizing the work of inspired genius, and adding the talent to the Roycroft family. In 1902 Hubbard was wooing the artist Alexis Fournier out of Minneapolis to head up and re-install the Roycroft Art Gallery. (*Head, Heart and Hand*, p. 122).

Fournier suggested that Hubbard meet with him in Chicago to see an exhibition of his paintings at the Art Institute of Chicago. Simultaneously, the Art Institute had assembled its "First Annual Exhibition of Original Designs for Decorations and Examples of Art Crafts having Distinct Artistic Merit."

The show ran from December 16, 1902 to January 11, 1903. Its participants read like an Arts & Crafts "Who's Who" with works of well known companies, L.C. Tiffany, Grueby-Faience, Rookwood, Van Briggle; silversmiths Arthur Stone and Mary Knight of Boston; and unknown metalsmiths Albert Berry of Auburn, Rhode Island, and R. R. Jarvie of Chicago.

Now, this exhibition was a big deal for the nation's Arts & Crafts community. It was especially important for those of Chicago and the upper Midwest. The most current examples of furniture, textiles, pottery, tiles, china painting, metal working, and, of course, leather bookbinding examples were available for examination and purchase. It was such a success that it became an important annual exhibition until its demise in 1922.

The show attracted the very best work from artisans across the nation and would have surely taken the better part of a year to organize. News of this event would certainly have reached East Aurora. It is most curious that although there were distinguished examples of the book designer, binder, and printer's art, there was not a single entry in this, or any other category, from Roycroft.

Hubbard was no stranger to the Chicago Arts & Crafts scene and would have been implored to examine the exhibit out of sheer curiosity. He must have been impressed with the quality and quantity of assembled artisan's work. Among the 751 hand-wrought articles were dozens of fresh-to-the-market modeled leather items, ranging from spectacular screens to elegantly simple card cases.

In 1901, few in America had ever thought that a market could be created for modeled leather articles. This likely was also the first opportunity that Hubbard would have had to examine the dramatic California style modeled leather, combined with metal and sea shells, and exhibited by Frederick C. Eaton of Santa Barbara who furnished 26 articles.

There were also three ambitious, large sculptured/modeled leather screens plus a modeled Atlas cover on display. These were submitted by Frederick C. Kranz, Designer, 226 N. 4th Street, Philadelphia, Pennsylvania.

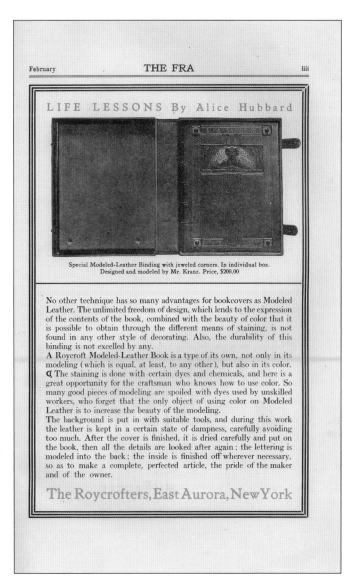

Modeled book covers for *Life Lessons*, February, 1911. *Courtesy of Faire Lees.*

Correspondence with Kranz's great-granddaughter, Mrs. Marilyn Burch of Stuyvesant, New York, related that Frederick Christian Kranz was born January 26, 1869, in Klingnau, Switzerland but lived his early life in Nurtingen, Germany until emigrating to America in 1890. He married Henrietta Wilhimina Winheller in Philadelphia in 1896 and Marilyn's grandfather, Karl Wilhelm Kranz was born there in 1897.

Kranz was with the C.F. Rumpp leather company that had just opened a major sales/showroom at 509 Atlas Block, 35 Randolph Street, Chicago. Rumpp may have encouraged its leading leather artisan to enter in order to call attention to its stock of leather goods at its newly opened Chicago showroom.

It is not known whether Hubbard was aware of the scope of Kranz's leather artistry before this exhibition or if they had arranged a rendezvous at the Art Institute. Whatever the case, in the space of a few months after the Chicago exhibition, Fournier had set up his easel on the Roycroft campus and was painting the mural around the great hall, and Kranz was organizing the newly formed modeled leather department that would soon require the talents of a dozen leather workers.

Kranz would later describe the modeled leather technique in an article in *The Fra*, Vol. VI, No. 45:

> No other technique has so many advantages for bookcovers as Modeled Leather. The unlimited freedom of design, which lends to the expression of the contents of the book, combined with the beauty of color that it is possible to obtain through the different means of staining is not found in any other style of decorating. Also, the durability of this binding is not excelled by any.
>
> A Roycroft Modeled-Leather Book is a type of its own, not only in its modeling (which is equal, at least, to any other), but also in its color. So many good pieces of modeling are spoiled with dyes used by unskilled workers, who forget that the only object of using color on Modeled Leather is to increase the beauty of the modeling.
>
> The background is put in with suitable tools, and during this work the leather is kept in a certain state of dampness, carefully avoiding too much. After the cover is finished, it is dried carefully and put on the book, then all the details are looked after again; the lettering is modeled into the back; the inside is finished off wherever necessary, so as to make a complete, perfected article, the pride of the maker and of the owner.
>
> —Frederick C. Kranz, Master Leather-Worker

With the experienced 34-year old Kranz on board in 1903, Hubbard could now foresee a market for high end artistic leather articles.

The artistic versatility of the Roycroft book designers and the interpretive capability of the women who illustrated and illuminated the pages were soon applied to other mediums of metalwork—copper, brass and silver—and other leather objects. Many of the illustrative floral embellishments within a Roycroft book were transformed to their leather placemats, bookends, purses, and desktop accessories. Many were adorned with art, probably stimulated by the work of Adelaide Robineau and the art pottery that appeared in the *Keramic Studio* magazine.

Simultaneously, these objects were promoted in the Roycroft produced magazines, the *Phillistine*, *Little Journeys*, and *The Fra*, and also featured in nationally distributed literary and homemaking magazines. The decorated books and other leather items were personally promoted by Fra Elbertus Hubbard on his lecture tours across America.

In 1905, the *Roycroft Catalog* presented the first modest group of leather offerings, watch fobs, coin purses, bill cases, etc., as "Roycroft Catalog of Some Things Made By The Roycrofters At Their Shop Opposite the School House in East Aurora." It announced that:

> Our Modeled Leather Department is under the immediate direction of our Mr. Frederick Kranz who is thoroughly familiar with all kinds of repousse, modeled and incised, stained and illumined leather work that is produced in this country and in Europe.

The Roycroft Inn

The Phalansterie

CONDUCTED by the Roycrofters in connection with the work at the Roycroft Shop. Twenty-four Out-of-Door Sleeping Rooms with In-Door Dressing rooms attached, Electric lights, Steam Heat, Turkish baths, Running Water, Art Gallery, Chapel, Camp-in-woods, Library, Music Room, Ballroom, Garden and Wood Pile.

There are Classes and Lectures covering the following subjects: Art, Music, Literature, Physiology, Nature-Study, History, Right-Living, Daily walks and talks a-field—Trips to the Woods, Lake, Roycroft Camp, etc., etc.

Page Number Twenty

Leather Work

OUR Modeled Leather Department is under the immediate direction of our Mr. Frederick Kranz, who is thoroughly familiar with all kinds of repoussé, modeled, incised, stained, & illumined leather work, that is produced in this country and Europe.

Single panel fire-screens, and three-panel screens from	$25.00 to $250.00
Chairs	$25 to $125.00
Table mats	$1.50 to $5.00
Desk pad, blotter and pen-wiper	$2.00
Music Rolls	$4.00 and $5.00

Special books, guest books, family trees, bound with monograms, coat of arms, and special designs.

Page Number Twenty-One

First mention of Roycroft's leather department and the establishment of Frederick Kranz in this catalog: "A catalog of some books and things made by the Roycrofters at their shop opposite the school house in East Aurora—1905 & 06." It has a Dard Hunter designed cover and a few black & white photos. *Courtesy of Faire Lees.*

At the same time, more books were being produced, which meant more leftover materials of both limp and fine leathers. Some were used to fashion large 20 x 20 inch stuffed "lounge" pillows, covered with goat or sheep skin that were the first leather offerings. A plain one was $5.00 and one with modeled design sold for $10.00. These would have been an ideal complement for the new mission style settles and rockers being churned out across the country. The smaller pieces turned up as decorated bookends, book markers, pen wipes, small mats, boxes, and many other objects presented in the earliest leather catalog.

The praise of the new line was consistently offered in the annual book catalogs and demand was such a that the new Leather Department was given a home in 1907. It was moved from a corner of the bindery to the second floor of the Furniture Shop.

Hubbard and Kranz didn't waste a moment to tempt the faithful. By mid-1908 Kranz and his leather workers had developed enough offerings—32 separate hand-modeled leather articles—to warrant a page in the catalog. Most offerings were personal and many were unisex. However, many were designed as decorative but practical accessories for one's living space and office. There were desk sets, blotters, stamp boxes, portfolios, bill books, photo cases and frames, fire screens, and wastebaskets. Prices ranged from twenty-five cents for a matchbox to $100 and up for a scenic, three-fold screen large enough to serve as a room partition. There were another 11 articles made in "velvet" leather. These were unadorned ooze leather and some were offered in colors. The work baskets and waste baskets and portfolios would have had rigid cardboard or thin wood support forms beneath the leather skin.

Sueded, laced edge, 20" x 20", pillow with corner tassels. *Courtesy Roycroft Arts Museum.*

Another interior view of the Roycroft Inn—its reception area in 1905. *Courtesy of Faire Lees.*

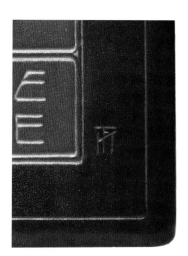

Kranz's initials appear at the bottom right of the letter E of "Marriage" in the modeled leather version by Henry D. Thoreau. *Courtesy Roycroft Arts Museum.*

Frederick Kranz, the German designer and master leather worker. Kranz arrived at Roycroft, married with a growing family in 1903. He remained until he was offered ownership in the established Cordova Shops in nearby Buffalo in 1915 and met a rather early death at age 50 in 1919. *Courtesy Roycroft Arts Museum.*

Some modeled leather work in progress, but never used. Here's another version of *"A Man of Sorrows"*, with a profile of Christ attributed to Frederick Kranz. Next is an exemplary rendering of a dragon fly and lotus flower; likely for a purse. Lastly is a young maiden for a book cover of *"Elbert Hubbard's Writings"* attributed to George ScheideMantel. *Courtesy Roycroft Arts Museum.*

Unique Fra Elbertus photo album with dramatic repousse poppy design, 7-3/4"w x 11-3/4"h, ca 1905. *Courtesy Roycroft Arts Museum.*

One-of-a-kind writing portfolio, 8-1/2"w x 11-1/2"h, rendered by Frederick Kranz for Alice Hubbard. Note the conjoined AH monogram amidst the acorn and oak leaf design. Likely produced before 1905. *Courtesy Roycroft Arts Museum.*

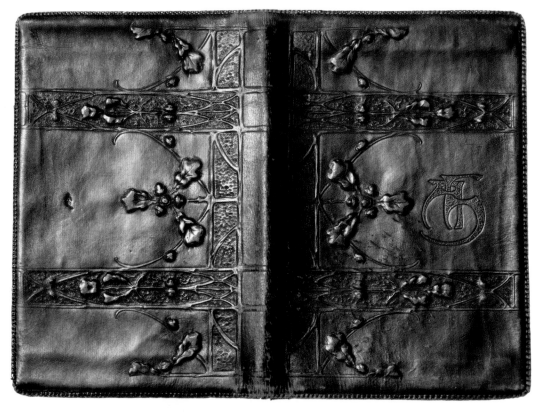

Examples of Frederick C. Kranz's leather artistry for modeled leather covers of: *The Complete Writings of Elbert Hubbard*, Vols. I and II. *Courtesy of the Elbert Hubbard Roycroft Museum of East Aurora, NY.*

By 1909 the activity had earned a special, 6" x 8" black and white, 36-page catalog (with a cover designed by Dard Hunter), *"The Roycroft Leather Book…Being a Catalog of Beautiful Leather Things made Roycroftie by Hand by Roycroft Artists."* Here Hubbard bragged about the Rhineland's competency in leather: "The Germans lead the world in craftsmanship, just as they have in musical composition. The Roycrofters imported the Germans—The Teutons did the rest!" This reference was to Kinder and Kranz. Hubbard continued, "They have taught this wonderful Art to a score or more of Roycroft boys and girls, so now we believe we are producing the best work in this line in America."

He continues to help the reader make a distinction favoring Roycroft:

> Modeled Leather is simply a high grade of heavy leather, decorated by hand. The staining of the leather also plays an important part in the Art. Modeled leather is non-breakable, lasts four hundred and forty years, and is individual, peculiar, distinct and highly artistic. Do not confuse this work with "stamped leather"—that is something else.

With a commitment in print (through *The Phillistine* and *The Fra*) and praise from Hubbard's mouth for the new leather

Fine example of repousse work on complex design. *Courtesy of Jessica Greenway.*

department, Hubbard and Kranz identified a broad product range for 1909. There are 26 basic leather lines with many variations shown (such as a different flower/foliate pattern. Purses alone included children's, saddle (fold-over), men's, women's and small coin versions, all with some modeling even if limited in scope. These ranged in price from 75 cents for children's styles to $10 for five pocket lady's purses.

There were also card cases, cigar cases, bill books, wallets, jewel boxes, writing cases, photo frames--- standing and folding, napkin rings, book marks, scissor and knife cases. A stunning envelope glove case in brown calf with a free form grouping of nasturtium in bold repousse was offered for $15. There was one metal framed, modeled leather handbag with three variations, the largest being 8-3/4" width, by 5-1/4" height for $20.

> Every piece of work we send out is done by hand and shows the loving mark of the tool, and the firm yet gentle touches of the human hand. Being done by hand according to original designs, the production is limited—there are no duplicates. Just bear this in mind when buying for presents. Glassware and Pottery have a short life because the Law of Gravitation is always lying in wait for them, but leather lasts. For Christmas Presents these unique and individual articles are always in good taste. They suggest that which is beautiful in color and proportion—they symbol the useful and lasting.
> —Elbert Hubbard, *The Roycroft Leather Book,* 1909

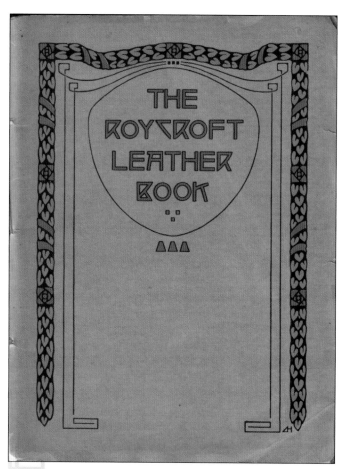

Roycroft recognized the leather department in 1909 with its separate catalog devoted to modeled leather articles. *Courtesy of Faire Lees.*

It is evident that, at age 40, designer Kranz was a master of artistic styles.

Early Roycroft mark and design on this simple, compact paper money billfold. Open the fold to insert currency and it is 8"w x 2"h. When folded it measures 4"w x 2"h. *Courtesy of Faire Lees.*

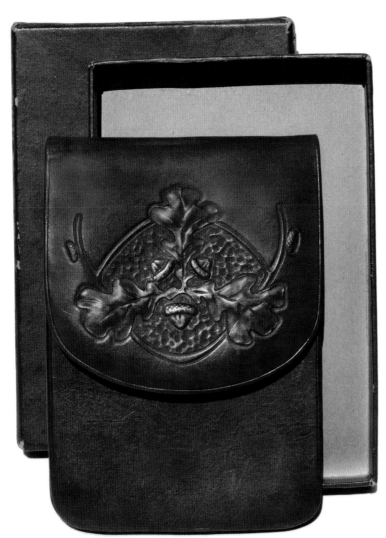

A man's wallet with oak leaf and acorn design unused with box, 4"w x 4-3/4" l. *Courtesy Roycroft Arts Museum.*

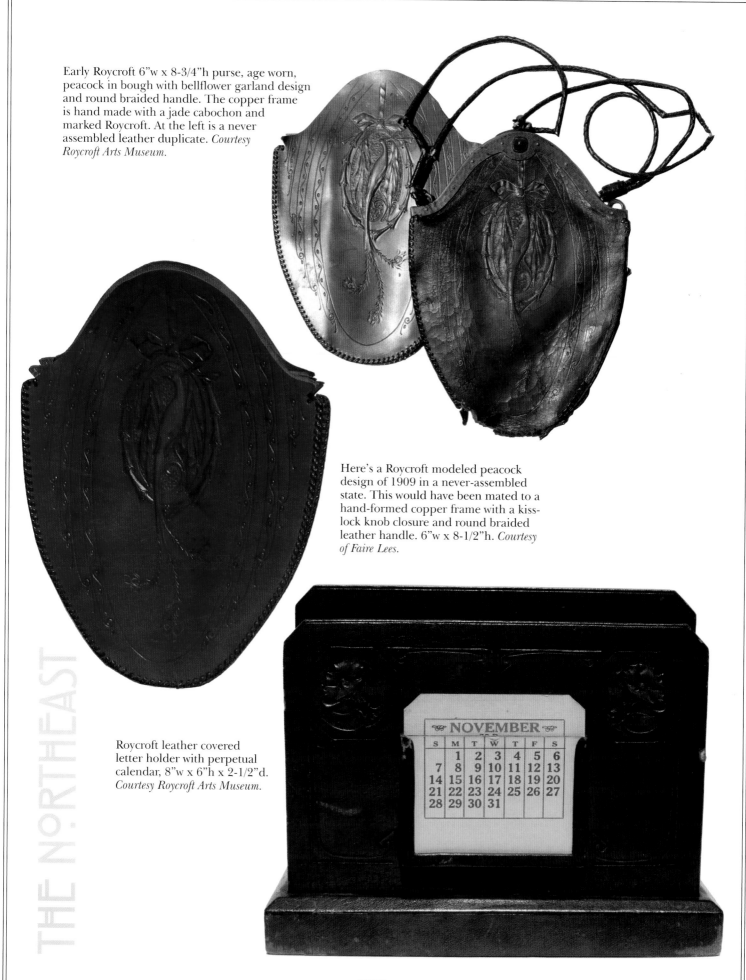

Early Roycroft 6"w x 8-3/4"h purse, age worn, peacock in bough with bellflower garland design and round braided handle. The copper frame is hand made with a jade cabochon and marked Roycroft. At the left is a never assembled leather duplicate. *Courtesy Roycroft Arts Museum.*

Here's a Roycroft modeled peacock design of 1909 in a never-assembled state. This would have been mated to a hand-formed copper frame with a kiss-lock knob closure and round braided leather handle. 6"w x 8-1/2"h. *Courtesy of Faire Lees.*

Roycroft leather covered letter holder with perpetual calendar, 8"w x 6"h x 2-1/2"d. *Courtesy Roycroft Arts Museum.*

One of his most glorious articles was a signed purse presented in *The Fra*, November, 1911, Vol. Vlll, No. 2, pg xxi . It featured a hand-hammered copper frame, with trimmings of silver and set with cat's-eyes cabochons and sold for a rather astonishing $35. Hubbard devoted a full page to this beauty and carefully couched his appeal:

Roycroft modeled-leather bags are distinctive, durable and in good style. Only the highest quality material is employed in the making of these bags and the name of Herr Frederick C. Kranz associated with leather-work is always a guaranty of superfine workmanship. This is undoubtedly the most exquisite bag the Roycrofters have ever offered to a discriminating public. This bag is made of English calf and the lining is a soft-toned ooze calf, lovely in the extreme. The frame is of hand-hammered copper,

with trimmings of silver. It is set with cat's eyes. The bag is hand-laced with strips of goatskin, remarkably tough-fibered. The hand-braided handles are also of goatskin. There is an inside pocket, fitted with coin-purse to match the bag. Size, 9 x 10-1/4 inches. Price, Thirty-five Dollars.

The same ad was repeated in *The Fra,* July, 1912 with a few copy changes. The reference to "Herr" Kranz, was Americanized to just Frederick Kranz. This may have been one of the first attempts at political correctness in an effort to minimize the German heritage of Kranz and other Roycrofters. This opus in leather must have created some demand, but for a less costly version. The bag was now offered in three sizes: 6-3/4 x 9 inches, ten dollars; 7-1/4 x 10 inches, twelve dollars; and 7-1/2 x 11 inches, fifteen dollars.

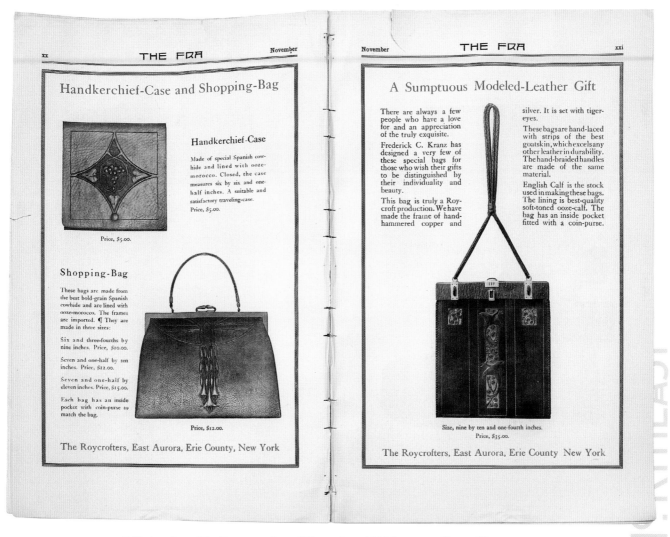

Offering from *The Fra* magazine of November, 1911 is among Roycroft's most elegant leather articles. Shown are Kranz designed handbags. *Courtesy of Faire Lees.*

(continued on following page)

Modeled-Leather Conveniences
Glove-Case

4½ x 15½ inches. Price, $15.00.

Manicure-Case
Open, 6 x 10 inches.

Closed, 3½ x 6 inches.

These cases are fitted with the best instruments that can be bought. Price, $10.00.

Jewel-Box
Depth, one and one-half inches; Diameter, four inches. Price, $6.00.

The Roycrofters, East Aurora, Erie County, New York

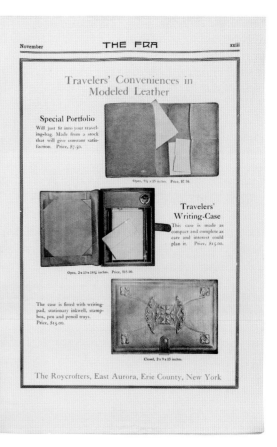

Travelers' Conveniences in Modeled Leather

Special Portfolio
Will just fit into your traveling-bag. Made from a stock that will give constant satisfaction. Price, $7.50.

Open, 9½ x 15 inches. Price, $7.50.

Travelers' Writing-Case
This case is made as compact and complete as care and interest could plan it. Price, $15.00.

Open, 2 x 13 x 10½ inches. Price, $15.00.

The case is fitted with writing-pad, stationary inkwell, stamp-box, pen and pencil trays. Price, $15.00.

Closed, 2 x 9 x 13 inches.

The Roycrofters, East Aurora, Erie County, New York

Individual Designs in Modeled Leather
For the Library-Table or the Drawing-Room

Moth Design.

Twenty-two inches in diameter. Price, $10.00.

This Desk-Set is made of the finest stock. The edges are all turned. The design was made specially for this gift set for Christmas 1911.

Size of pad, 12 x 17 inches. Price, $7.50.

The Roycrofters, East Aurora, Erie County, New York

Modeled-Leather Screen
Designed by Frederick C. Kranz

There is only one screen like this. There will be no other. The dining-room that will own this one as part of its beauty will have a marked place in the memory of every one who sees it. Price, $200.00.

Modeled-Leather Wastebasket

A Wastebasket is a necessity in every library, office and den, if you value the Axminster or your hardwood floors. But a wastebasket with too much ego offends the poetic unities.

This modeled-leather basket never lops, leaks nor lapses. It is dignified, poised, quiet and rarely beautiful.

The design and workmanship are distinctly Roycroft Standard.

Why not make the office a place where good-looking things are at home?

The price is $10.00.

9 inches diameter by 15 inches deep

The Roycrofters, East Aurora, Erie County, New York

Kranz employed the rectilinear motif adorned with squares and right angles in the Wiener Werkstatte-(Vienna workshop) manner. However, much of his design work favors the use of negative open space combined with the curvilinear, sinuous, and flowing foliage shapes of the Art Nouveau (the 1909 cylinder Iris wastebasket is a prime example). On personal items such as a portfolio, or even a small memo pad or purse, stylized plant forms (wheat, grapes, lily of the valley) are laid out to form an "eye trap" for a potential monogram.

With such a pledge to the many thousands of loyal and affluent followers, Hubbard knew they had to perform. He mentioned the "score" (20) and more of leather artisans trained or apprenticed under Kranz. Many of these were young women already trained in design fundamentals and skilled as painters, illustrators, and illuminators in their own right. Now they were being cross-trained to use a knife and modeling tool with leather as their canvas.

Emerging leather artisans often appeared from other career paths. As a young boy, Charles Youngers fed paper into presses at the print shop. George ScheideMantel began his career as a bellboy at the Roycroft Inn, left to work on the railroad, and later became an apprentice to Kranz (who divided his time between Roycroft and the Cordova Shops from 1913 until he made a clean break in 1915). ScheideMantel was considered a fine artisan and a rapid learner under Kranz. When Kranz did finally leave Roycroft in the fall of 1915, his job was offered to ScheideMantel.

Another talented German-American Roycrofter was Otto Hilt of Stuttgart, Germany. He received his education in artistic leather work there before landing in New York City in 1904. The publication *Buffalo and its German Community* of 1912, tells us that: "Mr. Hilt first applied his artisanship for three years at C.F. Rumpp & Sons of Philadelphia, the oldest and most renown leather wares business in America." Kranz also worked at Rumpp. The next four years (1909-1913) were partially spent with the Roycrofters in their modeled leather department, and simultaneously serving as technical director of a new modeled leather goods business, The Cordova Shops of Buffalo, in 1908.

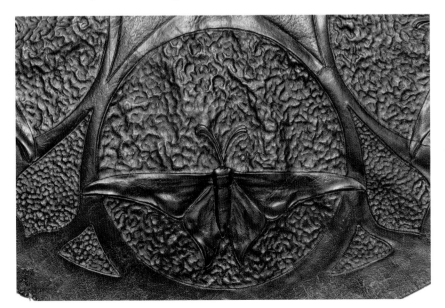

This dramatic moth design pattern was attributed to "Herr Kranz" in advertisements in *The Fra*. It was available only in 18, 20, and 22 inch diameter as was its other insect counterpart, the dragonfly. Both required much repousse modeling (from the back side) and in 1912 the 22" diameter sold for ten dollars. *Courtesy Roycroft Arts Museum.*

Telescoping cigar case with wheat heads by Frederick Kranz, 3-3/4"w x 5" l. The design was adapted to a similar style but smaller configured match case and was used on other small articles. *Courtesy Roycroft Arts Museum.*

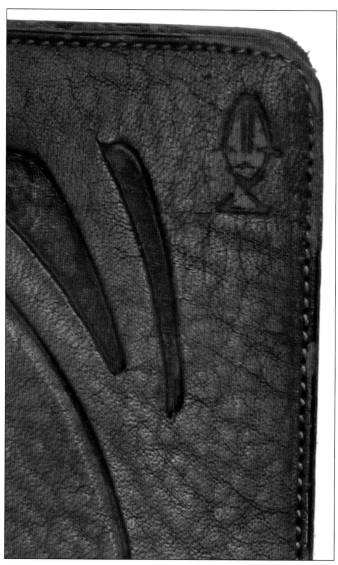

A leather artisan's memorandum records a shop-mark of Frederick C. Kranz on the sueded side and stylized doodles on the working side. The article resides in the ScheideMantel workshop in the Elbert Hubbard Roycroft Museum of East Aurora, New York. It is not impressed with either the Roycroft or Cordova Shops identifying mark. *Courtesy of Faire Lees*

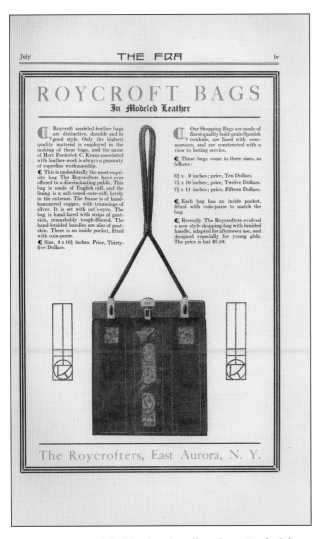

ROYCROFT BAGS
In Modeled Leather

❧ Roycroft modeled-leather bags are distinctive, durable and in good style. Only the highest quality material is employed in the making of these bags, and the name of Herr Frederick C. Kranz associated with leather-work is always a guaranty of superfine workmanship.

❧ This is undoubtedly the most exquisite bag The Roycrofters have ever offered to a discriminating public. This bag is made of English calf, and the lining is a soft-toned ooze-calf, lovely in the extreme. The frame is of hand-hammered copper, with trimmings of silver. It is set with cat's-eyes. The bag is hand-laced with strips of goatskin, remarkably tough-fibered. The hand-braided handles are also of goatskin. There is an inside pocket, fitted with coin-purse.

❧ Size, 9 x 10½ inches. Price, Thirty-five Dollars.

❧ Our Shopping-Bags are made of finest quality bold-grain Spanish cowhide, are lined with ooze-morocco, and are constructed with a view to lasting service.

❧ These bags come in three sizes, as follows:

6½ x 9 inches; price, Ten Dollars.
7½ x 10 inches; price, Twelve Dollars.
7½ x 11 inches; price, Fifteen Dollars.

❧ Each bag has an inside pocket, fitted with coin-purse to match the bag.

❧ Recently The Roycrofters evolved a new style shopping-bag with braided handle, adapted for afternoon use, and designed especially for young girls. The price is but $3.50.

The Roycrofters, East Aurora, N. Y.

The ultimate modeled leather handbag from Frederick Kranz, July, 1912. *Courtesy of Faire Lees.*

The years 1909 to 1915 were especially dynamic ones at Roycroft. The mercurial, near-genius designer Dard Hunter (a Roycroftie since 1905) and Karl Kipp, head of the Copper Shop, collaborated to produce a group of copper articles with the geometric élan of the Viennese Sezession and the Archibald Knox Glasgow School. For a moment in time the expected shapes of the past century received modern lines and forms. These were dramatized with German silver, applied jade cabochons, and silver overlay. Prominent yet subtle hammer marks became a decorative element as well as proof that the article was the work of a craftsman and not that of a machine operator. Out of this collaborative excitement came a rather unique line of modeled leather handbags. Frames were made from copper, (likely by Kipp) hammered with a pronounced vertical design, and trimmed in German silver. The planished frame was set with cat's-eyes jade and agate cabochons, held fast in German silver mountings. Kranz's repousse modeling of a calla lily formed a simple vertical design element to compliment the frame. The leather was English calf, hand laced with strips of goatskin. The hand-braided handle (much like a cowboy's lariat) was also of goatskin.

With thousands of visitors attending Hubbard's lectures and touring the Roycroft campus, the "carry home" sales of modeled leather and copper articles virtually doubled each year (1909-1915). By 1913 there were now 500 people on the Roycroft campus with a large percentage at work in the copper shop and furniture department. A monumental order of 400 pieces of furniture and over 700 pieces of copper light fixtures, including some very large chandeliers, American beauty vases, and other copper articles had been received in 1912 from the Grove Park Inn in Asheville, North Carolina.

The offerings of copper and leather articles had been broadened and *The Philistine* and *The Fra* monthly presented multiple pages advertising them.

LECTURE PLATFORM, SALON, ROYCROFT INN, EAST AURORA, N. Y.

Roycroft Inn of East Aurora, New York, showing salon and lecture platform. The side chair on the dais in this 1905 postcard is featured among the Roycroft artistic leather images. *Courtesy of Faire Lees.*

THE NORTHEAST

Especially made to grace the speaker's platform in the Roycroft campus salon. Four of these unique arm chairs present leather panels that were artistically designed and executed by Frederick Kranz. These were offered to the general public with "modeled and embossed leather" as early as 1906 in a Roycroft Furniture catalog. Dimensions: 37-5/8"h x 24"w x 25-3/4"d. The close-up view presents a panel 22-1/4"w x 18-1/4"h. Such chairs may be examined both at the Elbert Hubbard Roycroft Museum and the Roycroft Arts Museum in East Aurora, New York. *Courtesy Roycroft Arts Museum.*

More useful items from the Leather Shop, March, 1913. *Courtesy of Faire Lees.*

THE SALON, ROYCROFT INN, EAST AURORA, N. Y.   53837-C

Another view of the reception area at the Roycroft Inn in 1905. *Courtesy of Faire Lees.*

Close-up of heroic styled rose design frieze of 18"h x more than 108" (9-feet) length. It was created by Frederick Kranz, likely in 1904-05 to decorate the wall of Alice Hubbard's office. A major section of some eight feet is intact and on display in Boice Lydell's Roycroft Arts Museum in East Aurora. *Courtesy Roycroft Arts Museum.*

But in 1915 an event shocked the Arts & Crafts industry, especially the Roycrofters, and the nation as well. Elbert and Alice Hubbard were killed, along with 123 other Americans including Alfred Vanderbilt, on May 7 when the British *SS Lusitania* was sunk by a German submarine.

This event became a rallying point for retribution by much of the nation's media and certainly sowed a seed for the public's distrust and hatred toward Germany and even Americans of German descent. It was still burning when the U.S. entered World War I in 1917. Gustav Stickley may have felt this anti-German backlash, although he had declared bankruptcy two months before the Lusitania incident. The trendsetter voice of Elbert Hubbard, *The Philistine* magazine, sadly declared its farewell issue July, 1915 in deference to Fra Elbertus and its subscribers were transferred to *The Fra*.

Even though Frederick Kranz's designs produced best-selling articles it appeared either he, or the Hubbards, were tiring of one another by 1915. Consistently, Kranz had produced dramatic pieces for their personal use, such as Alice's personal portfolio bearing her monogram; or the stunning modeled leather frieze of 13" x 91" from Alice Hubbard's office.

While it is generally acknowledged that Franz left Roycroft sometime between 1913 and 1915, the details have been a bit hazy. In *Roycroft Collectibles*, Hamilton tells us that Kranz "had left Hubbard's employ and had formed his own Cordova Shops specializing in fine modeled leather goods" in 1913 (p. 11).

Head, Heart and Hand suggests that Kranz was dividing his time between working at the Roycroft and operating the Cordova Shops. "When Kranz resigned from the Roycroft in 1915 to devote all his time to his own shop [meaning Cordova] ScheideMantel was offered, and quickly accepted, the vacated department head position, with supervisory responsibility for eight to ten workers" (p. 100).

Interestingly, the mid-year 1915 Roycroft catalog, *Hand Made At The Roycroft Shops, East Aurora New York*, seems to indicate that Kranz was still involved with Roycroft. It pays tribute to the now gone Hubbards and lists Felix Shay as Editor of *The Fra*, and then, on page 31, presents "Fritz Kranz, Master Leather Worker," including a rare photograph of him. The text suggests Kranz is responsible for all the items shown for it says:

The Modeled Leather Department is under the direction of Fritz Kranz, Master Leather-Worker who furnished a new "mission statement": "The Masters of Old, modeled the leather from the top side, and sometimes the work was beautiful, and sometimes the tool slipped. The Roycroft Master plans to the smallest detail and makes his design before the leather is cut.

"Formerly, the artist had to cut in the outline of the design; now we do not injure the surface of the beautiful leather. We get our results by raising the ornament from the back. Not alone will the exquisite designs and the execution of the same satisfy you—the marvelous coloring, too subtle to describe, will call forth your admiration."
—Fritz Kranz, Master Leather-Worker

This certainly doesn't sound as if the man in charge, Elbert (Bert) Hubbard II, intended to sack him.

Further research revealed that the "Cordova Shops, Inc., Designers and Makers of Cordova Leather Goods" were founded in Buffalo in 1908. The German language business directory of 1912, *Buffalo und Sein Deutschtum*, offers a faithful English translation (by Susan Kriegbaum Hanks at www.archivaria.com) of numerous German run businesses in Buffalo in 1912. It reveals that "The Cordova Shops at 36 West Huron produce everything which can be made of leather and everything from the facilities is hand-crafted." Essentially, the products are very similar forms to those produced at Roycroft.

Leather artistry is at its best when the subtle work blends seamlessly across the surface. This is Roycroft's first glove case, featured in the 1909 leather catalog. The carefully laid out design is of nasturtiums. Fully opened it will hold four pair of kid leather\opera\dinner gloves, for it extends to 14-1/4". Closed dimensions are 13-1/2"w x 5"h. *Courtesy of Faire Lees*

As to its founding members, the story reports:

The technical director of this wonderful enterprise is a born German, Mr. Otto Hilt of Stuttgart. He received his education in artistic leatherwork in Germany and he acquired his many years of experience in the first businesses in this field. In 1904 he came to the United States where he first worked for 3 years in Philadelphia for Rumpp & Sons, the oldest and most renowned leather wares business in America. Then for 2 years he was with the Roycrofters in East Aurora and he was one of the founders of the Cordova Shops in Buffalo, grown from 2 workers in 1908 to 50 workers today, where he is a partner and the technical director."

Though there is no mention of Kranz in the report, in a 1913 listing of "New Incorporations" published in *New York Times* the following item appears:

Special to the *'New York Times'*, Albany, May 22, 1913. The following companies were incorporated today: Cordova Shops, Incorporated of Buffalo, leather, metal goods and bookbinding; $175,000. Wilbur F.S. Lake, Otto Hilt, Frederick C. Krantz [misspelled last name] East Aurora.
—ProQuest Historical Newspapers

So, there is hard evidence of a date in 1913 that Kranz became officially a principal of Cordova Shops. The Buffalo City Business Directories for 1914 and 1915 were examined. The directory showed Cordova Shops with a new location of 237 Elm St., Buffalo, with a Mr. A.B. Brown serving as President and a Mr. John Efert as Secretary-Treasurer, and listed the firm as a manufacturer of modeled leather goods. No other names were mentioned.

The Cordova Shops catalog of 1915 makes no mention of their new leather master. Could it be the omission was out of deference to their Roycroft colleagues and the recent deaths of the Hubbards?

The likeable Kranz did not have much of a chance to work his magic at Cordova Shops. He died rather suddenly January 20, 1919, at age 50. His early years' legacy of inspired design had already been embraced at Roycroft.

Among those who followed Franz in leather work was Walter U. Jennings, most renown for his metalwork and jewelry design and craftsmanship. He was an accomplished leather artisan and produced a number of articles and book bindings prior to Kranz's departure. His skill is attested to by his inclusion in membership of the preeminent Society of Arts and Crafts of Boston. This was a designation of competency given only those designers and decorative arts workers who proved themselves worthy to an SACB review panel. Jennings was admitted for the years 1914-1918 as a craftsman—leather worker and metalworker of 279 Oakwood Avenue, East Aurora.

Kranz, himself, was listed by the SACB as a craftsman-designer for the years 1914-1917, with an address at Cordova Shops, 237 Elm St., Buffalo.

This spectacular and intricate design embracing stylized moths and trillium made its way to even an everyday useful item such as this 3"w x 7"l blotter. The reverse side in ink contains the message attributed to Frederick Kranz. The article resides in the ScheideMantel workshop in the Elbert Hubbard Museum of East Aurora. It is not impressed with either the Roycroft or Cordova Shops identifying mark. *Courtesy Roycroft Arts Museum.*

Card cases and purses for men
and women, November, 1911.
Courtesy of Faire Lees.

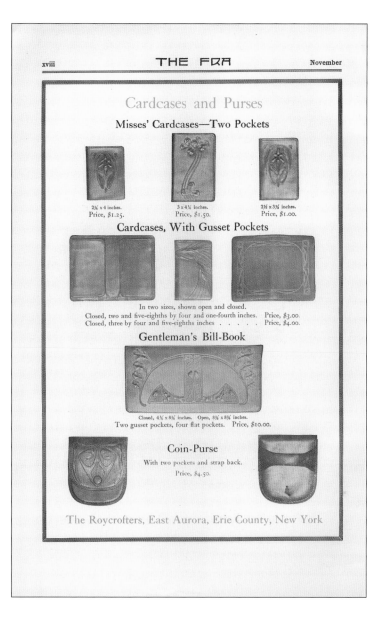

Cardcases and Purses

Misses' Cardcases—Two Pockets

2¾ x 4 inches.
Price, $1.25.

3 x 4¼ inches.
Price, $1.50.

2⅝ x 3⅝ inches.
Price, $1.00.

Cardcases, With Gusset Pockets

In two sizes, shown open and closed.
Closed, two and five-eighths by four and one-fourth inches.   Price, $3.00.
Closed, three by four and five-eighths inches . . . . .   Price, $4.00.

Gentleman's Bill-Book

Closed, 4¼ x 8¾ inches.   Open, 8¾ x 8¾ inches.
Two gusset pockets, four flat pockets.   Price, $10.00.

Coin-Purse

With two pockets and strap back.
Price, $4.50.

The Roycrofters, East Aurora, Erie County, New York

Roycroft handkerchief case, 5"w x 5-1/2"h with single
floral element in octagon surround. *Courtesy Roycroft Arts
Museum.*

Typical Roycroft bill pocket to hold paper currency, 3-1/2"w x 1-7/8"h. *Courtesy Roycroft Arts Museum.*

Even diminutive everyday articles were offered modeled leather protectors. Here the acorn and oak leaf design is 2-7/8"w x 4-1/2" l. *Courtesy Roycroft Arts Museum.*

Worthy leather scraps found a playful purpose in softballs and medicine balls and were featured in the Roycroft catalogs after 1911. *Courtesy Roycroft Arts Museum.*

Roycroft music roll with sliding handle, size open, 15" x 16". *Courtesy Roycroft Arts Museum.*

Roycroft leather mat in stylized fuchsia design, machine-sewn suede backing, impressed Roycroft mark on suede back, 18" dia. *Courtesy of Jessica Greenway.*

Leather mat of stylized Dard Hunter rose design, machine-sewn backing with Roycroft orb impressed into suede back, 18" dia. *Courtesy of Jessica Greenway.*

Close-up of Roycroft mat showing Dard Hunter rose design. *Courtesy of Jessica Greenway.*

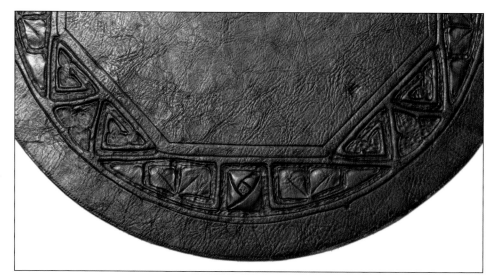

Roycroft produced table mats in many shapes and sizes. This bellflower design repeats at each end of the oval 8-1/2"w x 6"h lined version. *Courtesy Roycroft Arts Museum.*

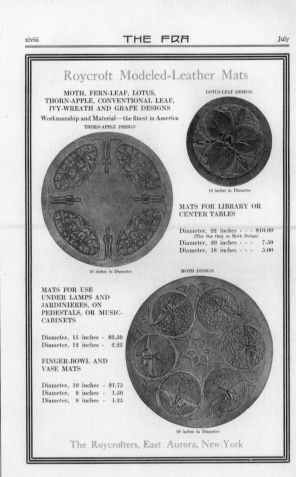

Roycroft Modeled-Leather Mats

MOTH, FERN-LEAF, LOTUS, THORN-APPLE, CONVENTIONAL LEAF, IVY-WREATH AND GRAPE DESIGNS

Workmanship and Material—the finest in America

LOTUS-LEAF DESIGN

THORN-APPLE DESIGN

MATS FOR LIBRARY OR CENTER TABLES

Diameter, 22 inches - - - $10.00
(This Size Only in Moth Design)
Diameter, 20 inches - - - 7.50
Diameter, 18 inches - - - 5.00

18 inches in Diameter

MATS FOR USE UNDER LAMPS AND JARDINIERES, ON PEDESTALS, OR MUSIC-CABINETS

Diameter, 15 inches - $3.50
Diameter, 12 inches - 2.25

MOTH DESIGN

FINGER-BOWL AND VASE MATS

Diameter, 10 inches - $1.75
Diameter, 9 inches - 1.50
Diameter, 8 inches - 1.25

22 inches in Diameter

The Roycrofters, East Aurora, New York

A primer for using modeled leather mats. July, 1912. *Courtesy of Faire Lees.*

All Roycroft mats were suede-backed with sewn edges, such as this 10" mistletoe design. Many were given a subtle second color or dye tone. Others were finished with burnished gold. *Courtesy Roycroft Arts Museum.*

THE NORTHEAST

Larger sized mats, 16" diameter or greater, were often elaborately modeled examples of an ivy wreath, thorn apple, fern leaf, acorn and oak leaf, lotus and many other well recognized bits of foliage. These usually sat beneath a large oil lamp or pottery vessel on a hall or library table. *Courtesy Roycroft Arts Museum.*

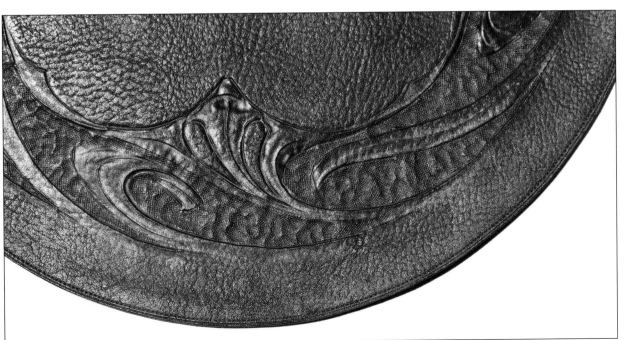

Elaborately modeled oak leaf and acorn foliage on large Roycroft mat, 16"w x 12"h. *Courtesy Roycroft Arts Museum.*

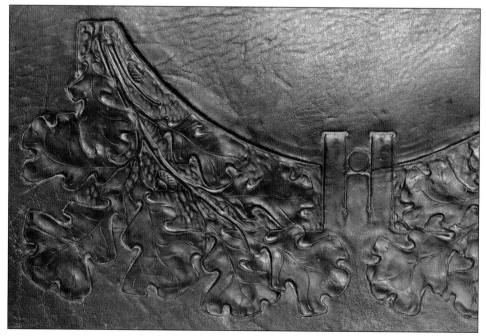

One of the most popular choices in large diameter was this 20" grape design. *Courtesy Roycroft Arts Museum.*

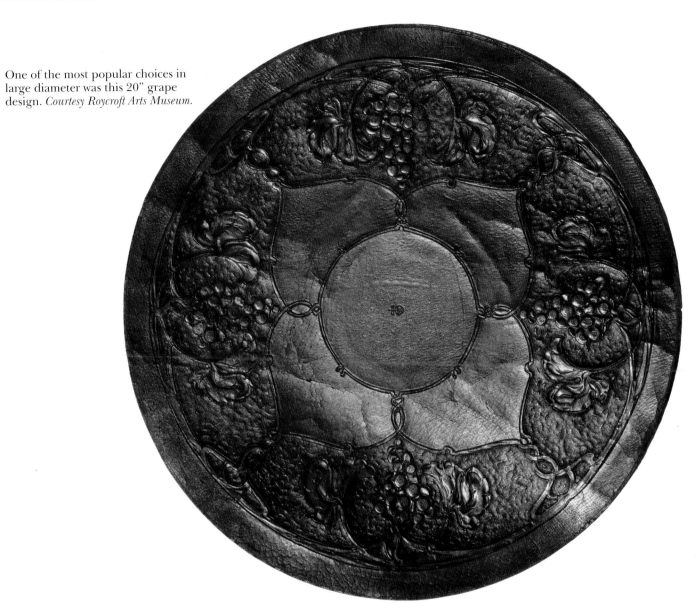

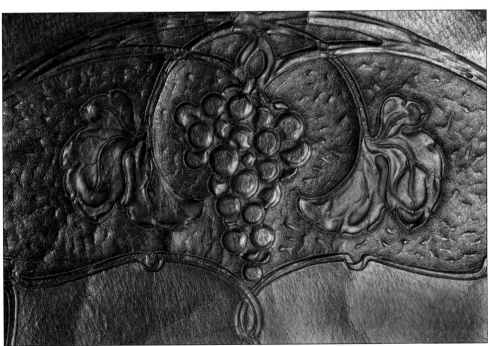

Gifts for Christmas, November, 1911. *Courtesy of Faire Lees.*

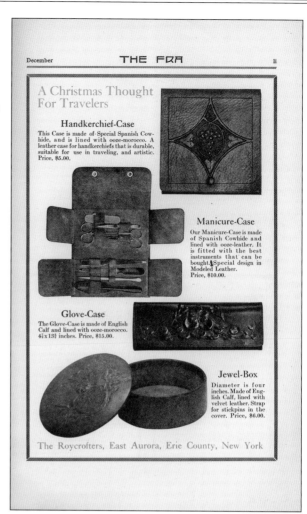

More Roycroft items for Christmas of 1911, from a November issue of *The Fra. Courtesy of Faire Lees.*

Roycroft napkin ring, 1-3/4"
diameter with green dye tint.
Courtesy Roycroft Arts Museum.

Roycroft 4-3/4" diameter
x 1-1/2" d jewel box with
modeled design lid. *Courtesy
Roycroft Arts Museum.*

Wheat head design on Roycroft pen
wipe 4"w x 2-7/8"h. *Courtesy Roycroft
Arts Museum.*

Roycroft mantel or desk clock with wheat design, laced edges all around, 4-1/4"w x 5-7/8"h. *Courtesy Roycroft Arts Museum.*

Roycroft Manicure Case, stylized Gingko leaf design, 4-1/2"w by 3-3/4"h; opens to 9-1/2"h. *Courtesy of Jessica Greenway*

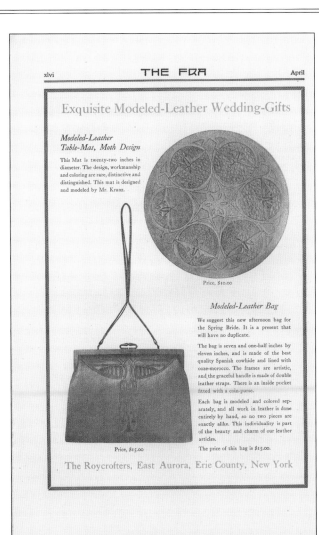

Exquisite Modeled-Leather Wedding-Gifts

*Modeled-Leather
Table-Mat, Moth Design*

This Mat is twenty-two inches in diameter. The design, workmanship and coloring are rare, distinctive and distinguished. This mat is designed and modeled by Mr. Kranz.

Price, $10.00

Modeled-Leather Bag

We suggest this new afternoon bag for the Spring Bride. It is a present that will have no duplicate.

The bag is seven and one-half inches by eleven inches, and is made of the best quality Spanish cowhide and lined with ooze-morocco. The frames are artistic, and the graceful handle is made of double leather straps. There is an inside pocket fitted with a coin-purse.

Each bag is modeled and colored separately, and all work in leather is done entirely by hand, so no two pieces are exactly alike. This individuality is part of the beauty and charm of our leather articles.

Price, $15.00 The price of this bag is $15.00.

The Roycrofters, East Aurora, Erie County, New York

Gifts for the Spring Bride, April, 1912. *Courtesy of Faire Lees.*

Detail of Roycroft pen wipe, 2 piece; mark on bottom piece, stylized morning-glory and leaf design. 3"w by 7"h. *Courtesy of Jessica Greenway*

Even women's belts received imaginative modeled leather closures as well as a subtle modeled design along its entire length. *Courtesy Roycroft Arts Museum.*

Personal accessories for men and women, September, 1913. *Courtesy of Faire Lees.*

Original teal blue dye highlights this carnation design. A rarity for Roycroft on this 7"w x 8"h laced-edge hand-bag. *Courtesy Roycroft Arts Museum.*

Roycroft purse, flower, and leaf design, leather covered snap button, interior coin purse; featured in 1925 Roycroft Copper and Leather catalogue. 7-1/2"w x 6"h. *Courtesy of Jessica Greenway*

Roycroft small clutch purse, 4-1/4"w x 7-1/2"h, stylized repousse rose with foliage and machine sewn seams. *Courtesy Roycroft Arts Museum.*

One-of-a-kind specialties attributed to Frederick Kranz, November, 1911. *Courtesy of Faire Lees.*

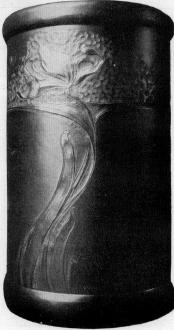

A classic iris executed in the sinuous art nouveau manner adorns this 15" tall x 9" diameter wastebasket produced at Roycroft. Once again, the design is credited to "Herr Kranz". In November, 1911 it was offered for ten dollars. *Courtesy Roycroft Arts Museum.*

The Roycroft simulated tooled leather cover of its 1914 catalog also held the first full-color views of its hand-modeled handbags and other leather goods. *Courtesy of Faire Lees.*

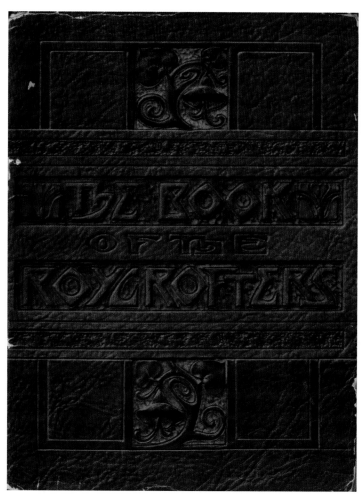

First modeled leather appears in full color in the Roycroft catalog of 1915. *Courtesy of Faire Lees.*

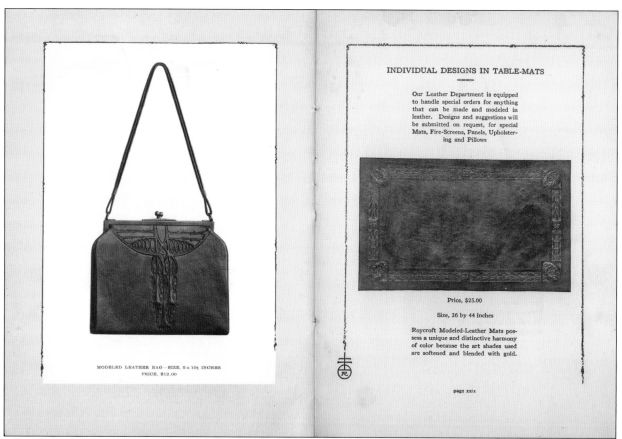

MODELED LEATHER BAG—SIZE, 8 x 10¼ INCHES
PRICE, $12.00

INDIVIDUAL DESIGNS IN TABLE-MATS

Our Leather Department is equipped to handle special orders for anything that can be made and modeled in leather. Designs and suggestions will be submitted on request, for special Mats, Fire-Screens, Panels, Upholstering and Pillows

Price, $25.00

Size, 26 by 44 inches

Roycroft Modeled-Leather Mats possess a unique and distinctive harmony of color because the art shades used are softened and blended with gold.

page xxix

Listed as a Kodak album in the *Roycroft 1919 catalog of copper, leather and books,* it was available in two sizes. This larger version is 11-3/4"w x 8-1/4"h with an 8x10 inch mounting area. *Courtesy Roycroft Arts Museum.*

The Roycroft catalog of 1915 featured unique modeled leather work by Frederick Kranz. The chair on page 53 is shown among the images in the Roycroft section. *Courtesy of Jessica Greenway.*

Typical modeled leather frame used to hold a Roycroft motto card. 5" x 7" sight area. *Courtesy Roycroft Arts Museum.*

Post-Elbert Hubbard days often featured smaller ad offerings during the spring and summer of 1916. *Courtesy of Faire Lees.*

George L. ScheideMantel, Kranz's successor at Roycroft, listed himself as a designer and leatherworker, 1915-1916, Cordova Shops, 237 Elm St., Buffalo. This is at the time he is purported to have been overseeing the Roycroft Leather Department. ScheideMantel may have been able to ensure that the Kranz designed leather articles flowed from the workers in the leather department, but his personal designs are somewhat removed from what we recognize as either "Arts & Crafts" or "Art Nouveau" styling. He headed the Leather Shop from 1915 until 1918 when he opened a design studio of his own in leather art and bookbinding in his East Aurora home, now the Elbert Hubbard Roycroft Museum at 3630 Oakwood Avenue.

Awareness of modeled leather articles was further broadened in 1916 when Bert Hubbard made alliances to establish Roycroft Departments in large city department stores. Leather goods, metalwork, books, mottoes, and stationery could be purchased in 61 cities, including Lord & Taylor in New York, Marshall Field in Chicago, and Bullocks in Los Angeles. In October, 1918 *The Roycroft* volume 3, no. 2 listed 149 branch stores. [Note: *The Roycroft* publication replaced the monthly *The Fra"* discontinued in August, 1917. It lasted until March, 1926. In June, 1926 a slightly larger 6" x 9" magazine titled *The Roycrofter* was issued every other month and continued into September, 1932.]

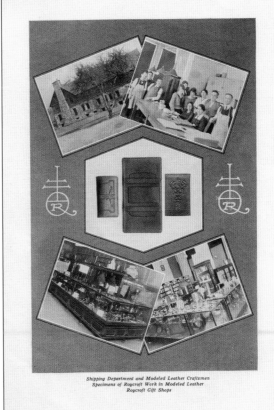

Shipping Department and Modeled Leather Craftsmen
Specimens of Roycroft Work in Modeled Leather
Roycroft Gift Shops

As late as the *Book of the Roycrofters* of 1926 there was still a good show made to support its modeled leather department. In actuality, it was virtually defunct by then. *Courtesy of Faire Lees.*

Signed ScheideMantel artistic leather of rose blossom stem design as a gift to a neighbor, 11"w x 4-1/2"h. *Courtesy of Jessica Greenway.*

This hallowed ground was the lifelong home of Roycrofters George and Gladys ScheideMantel, built in 1910 at 363 Oakwood Avenue in East Aurora, New York. It was gifted to the Roycrofters by Gladys on her 100th birthday and became the Elbert Hubbard Roycroft Museum in 1987. It contains important examples of most of the articles produced by the Roycrofters, including some marvelous examples of artistic and modeled leather. *Courtesy Elbert Hubbard Roycroft Museum*

In an interview with historian Boice Lydell, Roycroft leather worker Helen Wilson Ess recalled her work and the processes used in the Modeled Leather Department under the direction of George ScheideMantel, around 1918.

The girls would model leather by wetting the surface to make it soft and pliable. Then a paper pattern would be laid over it and traced out with a dull knife. Or, if a lot were needed at once, a heavy patterned cardboard was placed on top of the leather and a light pattern would be stamped on it. When the pattern was removed, the outline was scored with a sharp knife. The lines were then opened from the front with a modeling tool.

The areas to be raised were molded out by holding a zinc bar on the front while modeling from the back, to raise the desired designs into relief. Next, the back indentations were filled with a glucose-sawdust mixture. The designs were then smoothed out from the front and backgrounds were pounded and stamped, using metal tools with designs on the ends and a leather-headed hammer. As the glucose-sawdust mixture dried, the high area would remain in relief.

Next, the leather had to be stained. This was done in a small room in a corner of the Leather Department by Jerry Youngers, Carl Ewald and Otto Wagner. Days later, the almost-finished products would go back to the girls for lacing the seams. An awl would be used to punch holes around the edges of the article, and the leather lacing, with a paste-hardened end, was woven in and out of the holes. That finished the product.

Each girl had her own marble slab to work on and her own tools. We usually turned out two or three pieces a day, and would do different designs and articles each time, if possible."
—Helen Wilson Ess, Retired Leather Worker

[Note: To contribute to Mrs. Ess's recollection, there was a number of additional hand-work steps required to complete a typical Roycroft handbag of 1918. For example, once her modeled work on a leather piece was complete, its inside edges were skived (a 3/8" bevel applied). Then an ooze leather liner would be glued to it. This liner usually had at least one pocket for a mirror sewn in, sometimes two. At each purse end was a gusset, not modeled, that would be cut, skived and lined. All the leather would then be colored/stained and finished before holes would be punched around the perimeter in preparation for lacing. The article was typically laced with the edge loop stitch since it is ornamental and covers the edges of two thicknesses of leather more completely. Once lacing is completed, a metal closure frame could be fitted on the top leather edges. A small amount of adhesive/glue would be applied in its slot or groove that would be carefully fitted over the exposed leather top edges and snugly crimped in place. A final touch was the handle, either a round 4-strand braid, or a flat leather strip, doubled and sewn and most often punched and laced with the same edge loop stitch.

Roycroft clutch handbag with sitting nude female amidst garden foliage. Overall, 10-1/4"w x 6"h with decorative side bands. Monogram is that of Helen Wilson, the last leather worker. Design is likely that of George ScheideMantel. *Courtesy Roycroft Arts Museum.*

Often the braided style was threaded through the loop/ears on the frame and hand-plaited in place. The flat style handle usually had some sort of a metal D-ring connector at each end that was sewn and laced in during its assembly. These could be made up in advance and by slightly spreading the metal connectors it could be quickly attached to the loop/ears of the frame. A very special Roycroft purse (often a pear-shaped version) usually had the more stylish braided handle. However, the 1909 *"Roycroft Leather Book"* shows purses with a variety of handles. There is also a handle of 1" width leather, sewn the entire length along each edge, without any edge loop lacing.]

Even with the turnover of artistic talent at the Roycroft shops, the years following World War I were still productive, although the production of leather goods was uncertain. Bert Hubbard continued to add dozens of new "Roycroft Departments" in major and even secondary cities across the U.S. In *The Book of the Roycrofters* of 1921, leather goods were being touted as strongly as ever. The workers who made the leather, books, and copper articles were given photographic prominence. Charles Youngers was shown as Superintendent of Bindery and Modeled Leather. The bindery photo presented 25 workers (nine were women) while there were 11 in the Leather Modeling Department and six were women. Despite the heavy promotion, by late 1923 Edith Cole and Helen Wilson Ess were the only remaining leather workers and were being directed by Karl Kipp in the Copper Shop.

By late 1925, the Leather Department had been phased out, yet the November, 1926 *Roycrofter*, vol.1, number 3, carried a personal message from Bert Hubbard. It reminded the faithful reader, "The following pages show many of these Roycroft hand made things in handwrought copper and richly modeled leather. The list has been compiled with the idea of making your Christmas shopping easy for you and eminently satisfactory in every way. "

By then there were Roycroft Departments in 329 shops and stores across the U.S. The dwindling selection of leather articles offered for "ladies" included one 7-1/4" x 9" handbag for $27.50; a 4-1/2" x 8" under arm bag for $18.00, two small coin purses, and a card case. Those for the "man" included a 7" x 9" Kodak album for $10.00, a billfold (three fold) with 4 pockets and identification card for $12.50, two other standard billfolds, one in pigskin with a greyhound side profile view modeled in high relief, and a cigarette case for 20 cigarettes.

In his message for the Christmas 1926 issue of the *Roycrofter*, Hubbard matched the eloquence of his gifted father with what he must have felt was both a tribute to his fellow workers and a premature eulogy for the company.

There is an apostolic succession in art as well as in religion. Whether The Roycrofters have improved on the work and ideas of William Morris and John Ruskin is not the question. In any event The Roycroft Shops have succeeded, in degree, since their founding by Elbert Hubbard, thirty years ago. Today they are known the world over as the home of a community of workers living in an atmosphere in which their souls may grow—a group of men and women who print and bind books and fashion unique and beautiful things from sheets of copper, with 'Head, Hand and Heart.' And the result is a beautiful and useful thing, very, very carefully done.

—Elbert Hubbard II

Modeled Leather in 1928

While the number of leather artisans and the product selection had dwindled by 1928, Elbert Hubbard II was struggling to fulfill a diminishing need. In the *Book of the Roycrofters* of 1928, there is a photo on page 36 titled "Modeled Leather Craftsmen." It shows 11 workers, six of whom are women. It is the identical photo used in 1921. Another photo shows three modeled leather articles—a card case, a wallet, and a woman's clutch purse. All have a superficial degree of modeling or styling with laced edges. Two other photos show views of retail store display cases (locations not identified) that are filled with Roycroft metal and leather goods. Potential modeled leather buyers are reassured with a "business as usual" story that harkens to the literary enthusiasm of the main man Elbert. The son's message:

Today, the Roycrofters stand as the pioneers of the revivalists of a lost art. They model and decorate leather as the Berbers did—they excel the productions of the old Cordovan quadamacilliros or leather modelers.

Roycroft modeled leather artists are not mere theorists; they are practical craftsmen and would fulfill one of the requirements of the ordinances of Cordova which required that an applicant for license for leather modelers and decorators must prove himself in presence of examiners able to make his colors and design with them, make a canopy of fringe as well as a cushion of any style or size demanded of him, and show his skill with his trade tools. Nor shall he explain merely by word of mouth the making of articles, but make them with his very hands in presence of overseer of the craft."

The noble Roycroft accomplishment was not going to be allowed to roll over and die so long as Bert Hubbard maintained the quest. However, the 1929 depression and hard times across the nation made this 1928 catalog the last one with an extensive offering of Roycroft modeled leather.

Roycroft's Last Gasp—Art Textileather! 1936

After a run of some 28 years producing glorious modeled leather articles, the booklet titled *Roycroft—A catalog of books and things handmade at the Roycroft Shops* could muster but three insignificant leather articles. This 40 page catalog has a terra-cotta colored card stock cover with text in blue ink, and measured 8-7/8" width x 5-7/8" height. It bore no date, but on page 25 in the copy description of the Roycroft diary was a qualifying sentence: "Calendar for 1935 and 1936."

On page 18 are three rather dull leather offerings; a small mottled cowhide key case, a small mottled leather cowhide billfold, and a traveling book carrier of limp suede lamb with a silk lining. All had only stitched rather than laced edges.

Instead of even a limited selection of hammered copper lighting fixtures are two quite hideous lantern-style shades; a 9-1/4" tall cheese grater and a 7-1/8" tall milk pail of light gauge steel with copper plating. Both are designed to cover a hanging bulb.

Perhaps the most unkind cut of all is an ersatz leather writing portfolio of 10" width x 16" height. Its cover bears two blind-stamped horizontal bands with a three inch tall stamped orb and cross trademark centered on the cover. Its grainy-patterned appearance is that of a mediocre duo-tang peche report cover. And the final insult in an attempt to give this $2 item some legitimacy by reminding the reader it is made of "Art Textileather."

Keeping Roycroft Alive Today

The Roycrofters At-Large Association (RALA) emerged from the spirit of early Roycrofters. They sought to extend a bond of fellowship to men and women who embraced the Roycroft ideals wherever they lived. The "Roycroft Renaissance" cadre adheres to the standards of quality, productivity, and fraternity that established the Roycroft at the forefront of the American Arts & Crafts movement. It is composed of artisans and crafts persons whose work has been deemed worthy of the highest standard of quality.

"Roycroft Renaissance" masters include furniture makers, wood workers, metal smiths, jewelers, fine art painters and illuminators, screen, block and letterpress designers and printers, tile makers, potters, weavers and sculptors. Annually, a few worthy artisans from across the U.S. are reviewed and accepted in this RR family. The organization is a perennial exhibitor at the Grove Park Inn Arts & Crafts Conference, Asheville, North Carolina and holds seasonal lectures, demonstrations, and classes on the Roycroft Campus, East Aurora, New York. It maintains a web site at www.ralaweb.com.

Gordie Galloway, of Cheektowaga, New York, in one of the artists continuing the Roycroft tradition into the present.

Since I was a kid I wanted to design and make something with my hands. As a boy I'd always wanted a wallet with a bounding buck deer on it and couldn't find one. My first commercial job was as a mold and die maker. Twelve years later, in 1980, I finally bought the tools and leather and made one. The leather hobby spiraled out of control since all the people at the plant wanted me to make something in leather. In 1990 I made leather working a full time career. The Arts and Crafts work of master designers intrigued me. I concentrated on the styles established by Dard Hunter and Frederick Kranz and was named a Roycroft Renaissance craftsman in 1992.

As he spoke, his hand deftly modeled rose petals on his interpretive work, a 19" x 48" sinuous derivative of the Frederick Kranz frieze of English roses. The Kranz 1904 original (a 9-foot section can be seen in Boice Lydell's Roycroft Arts Museum in East Aurora, New York) hung above Alice Hubbard's desk in the print shop tower.

Galloway maintains a showroom for his modeled leather articles in a corner of the Roycroft Campus furniture shop. His skills are often called on to restore and recreate the leather work on original Roycroft and Stickley furniture.

Over the years Galloway's "head, heart, and hand" have produced a variety of items for the home; large circular and rectangular table mats with images of dragonflies, lotus flowers and lily pads. In 2005 he produced a series of three, 20" x 50" modeled leather runners for an original Roycroft sideboard, dresser, and vanity. In addition, his artistry is regularly applied to women's hand bags, men's wallets, notebook covers, book marks and a variety of monogrammed personal articles.

Here, leather artisan Gordie Galloway shows collector Faire Lees a finished example of his interpretation of English roses. It is from the 1904 work by Frederick Kranz mentioned earlier, a 19" x 48" wall frieze. The finished design has received several dye colors and shading, then protected with a transparent wax.

Leather suitable to the task was selected and the design lightly traced and outlined on the grained side. A swivel knife is used to incise the design, usually 1/16" deep into the leather.

A modeling tool is used to slightly depress the incisions left by the swivel knife.

Some of the rose forms have been incised, and the lower blossom has received some shading.

Now, a pear shading tool depresses the area inside the petal and supplies contour relief and shading.

Cordova Shops of Buffalo, 1908-1942
Buffalo, New York

Among collectors of artistically crafted leather articles, the Cordova Shops work is considered equal to Roycroft. Surprisingly, it is far more available through internet auctions and often found in far better condition.

Although the corporate mark changed slightly over the years, it is readily recognized with the artistic capital letters C and S of the Cordova Shops. This is usually burned in the ooze-suede interiors and impressed in the smooth leather. It is rarely absent. *Courtesy Faire Lees.*

Cordova Shop customer sales room of 1912. Presented in *Buffalo und sein Deutschtum, 1912.* Translation by Susan Kreigbaum-Hanks; online at archivaria.com/BusDHistory. *Courtesy of Susan Kreigbaum-Hanks.*

The company's origins parallel those of Roycroft for it was founded in November, 1908 twenty miles away in Buffalo, New York. The German language business journal of 1912, *"Buffalo und sein Deutschum* (Buffalo and its German Community), furnished enthusiastic praise for this new company that had grown from 2 to 50 employees within four years and where "the experienced artisans work the leather into wall decorations, fire screens, table covers, desk blotters, purses for ladies, correspondence baskets, cushions, picture frames, photo albums and many specialty items."

A century of leather artistry. Among Cordova Leather Shop's first offerings, c.1908, this pouch style handbag has an early kiss-lock closure combined with a Turnloc style locking mechanism. The 1/2" wide brass frame projects the recognizable "bat ears" loops for attaching the handle. Its handwrought design sports a floral motif on the Turnloc front and an owner's 1-1/4" height hand-cut conjoined monogram on the rear. 8"w x 8"h. *Courtesy of Faire Lees.*

The Cordova Shops catalog of 1914 featured this whimsical grasshopper over a daisy design. Hand-laced edges and a hand-braided strap conceal the purse's metal "birds mouth" frame opening. Dimensions are 7-5/8"w x 10"h and this style would have been among the first produced at Cordova. The actual purse can be seen in George ScheideMantel's workshop. *Courtesy the Elbert Hubbard Roycroft Museum.*

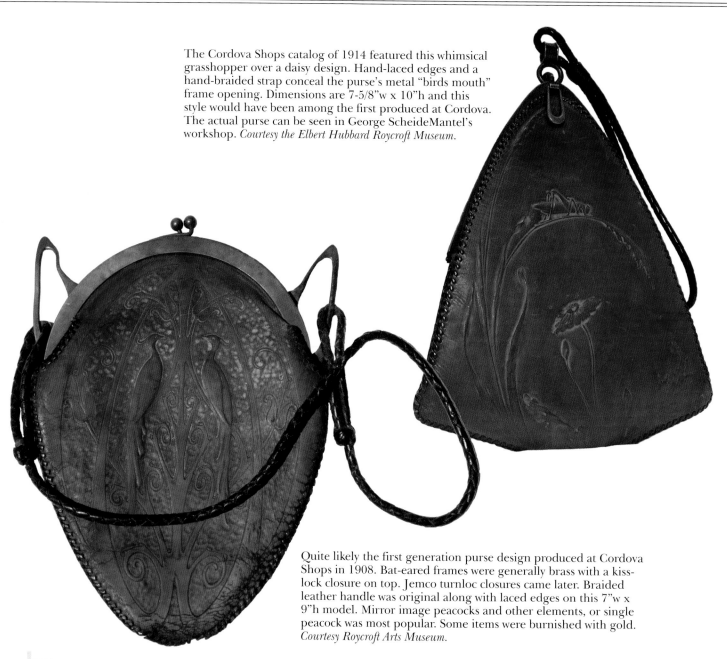

Quite likely the first generation purse design produced at Cordova Shops in 1908. Bat-eared frames were generally brass with a kiss-lock closure on top. Jemco turnloc closures came later. Braided leather handle was original along with laced edges on this 7"w x 9"h model. Mirror image peacocks and other elements, or single peacock was most popular. Some items were burnished with gold. *Courtesy Roycroft Arts Museum.*

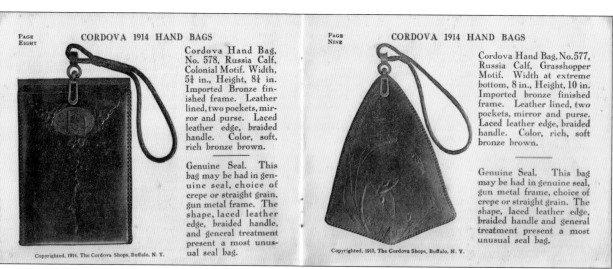

The breadth of the Cordova Shops leather offerings in 1914. The pear-shaped handbag on the right page features a grasshopper on a bending stem, designed in 1913 for the Cordova Shops by George ScheideMantel. *Courtesy of Jessica Greenway.*

One of the Cordova Shop founders, German-born Otto Hilt, became its technical director in 1908. *Courtesy Susan Kreigbaum-Hanks.*

One of Cordova's 1909 purse designs with a concealed birds-mouth metal frame opening. Dimensions are 6"w x 10"h with a rose motif modeling on one side, full perimeter lacing and a round braided handle. The diamond-shaped escutcheon holding the handle is hammered copper, pinned and riveted through the interior. Some version designs were finished in burnished gold. *Courtesy Roycroft Arts Museum.*

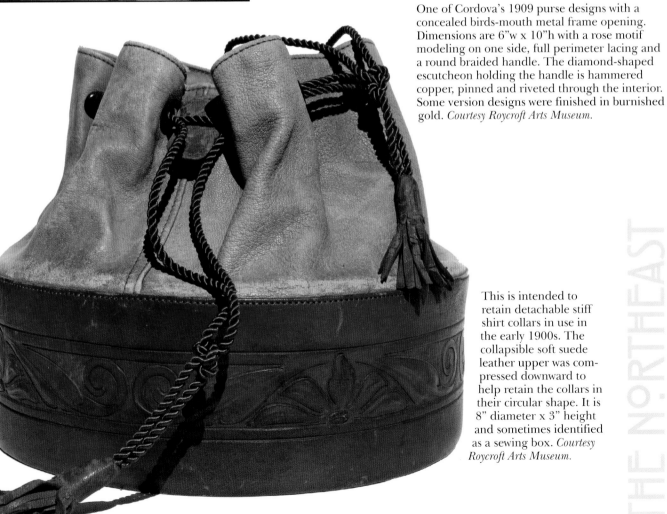

This is intended to retain detachable stiff shirt collars in use in the early 1900s. The collapsible soft suede leather upper was compressed downward to help retain the collars in their circular shape. It is 8" diameter x 3" height and sometimes identified as a sewing box. *Courtesy Roycroft Arts Museum.*

THE NORTHEAST

Card case and note pad with the trademark Cordova stylized square rose blossom; inspired by Frederick C. Kranz. Lined in calf, 2-3/4"w x 4-1/2"h. *Courtesy of Faire Lees.*

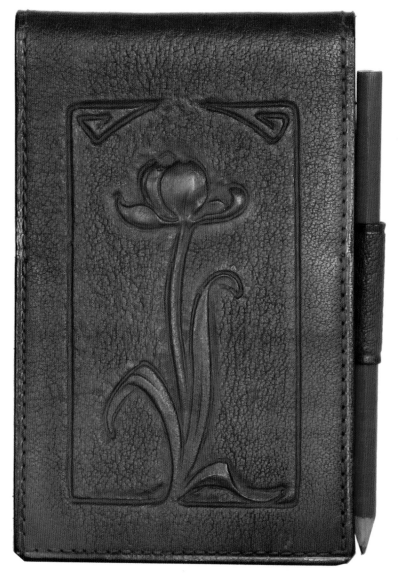

A simple and sweet woman's notebook with attached pencil. 2-1/2"w x 3-3/4"h and a tasteful floral design. *Courtesy of Faire Lees.*

Cordova wastebasket of 14" height and nearly 10" diameter with a dogwood garland design. Leather over built-up paper and wood hoop rims and wood bottom. Interior is an impregnated black fabric. Roycroft also produced similar designs as early as 1909. *Courtesy Roycroft Arts Museum.*

The sinuous art nouveau designs swirl around this massive 14-1/2"w x 19-1/2"h leather photo holder. On its reverse are permanent tabs with eyes for wall hanging. It seems this application was unique with Cordova for not one from Roycroft or any other maker has been seen. *Courtesy Roycroft Arts Museum.*

In 1912, Cordova operated from the Bowen Building, 36 West Huron Street at Pearl. As business grew the company moved to 237 Elm Street in 1915. Not as well known as the Roycroft campus, Cordova relied on sales through major retailers. Its 1911 price list offered "3% cash discount with order, net 30 days to parties known to us or furnishing references." In these early days it eclipsed Roycroft in sheer numbers and sizes of modeled leather articles. Its round lamp and table mats, with six floral variations, ran in size from six to 42 inches. It even offered an octagon mat, 5-foot across with a "4-seasons" design for a whopping $350. Rectangular mats in rose, ivy and teasel ran from an 11" x 16" to 57" x 33", priced from $5.50 to $60.

The next generation, c. 1912, Cordova purse featured an exposed brass frame that was usually plated. The applied burnished gold is still visible at the low spots on this wisteria design. The braided handle was still popular, even though strap leather handles, laced along the edges, were appearing. This purse measures 6"w x 10"h. *Courtesy Roycroft Arts Museum.*

Cordova's deluxe artistry on leather handbags. *Everybody's* magazine, 1912. *Courtesy of Jessica Greenway.*

Considered as a desk or mantel timepiece, this seven inch tall clock was a favorite gift item. Its design is the easily recognized pine cone and branch hallmark of Cordova. *Courtesy Roycroft Arts Museum.*

Cordova, as well as Roycroft, produced extraordinary designs on household articles such as this 19" x 19" settle pillow. The open circle could contain the owner's monogram when requested. *Courtesy Roycroft Arts Museum.*

Cordova offered several dramatically modeled music satchels or rolls often used as document cases. This survivor measures 14-1/2"w x 6-3/4"h in this configuration. *Courtesy Roycroft Arts Museum.*

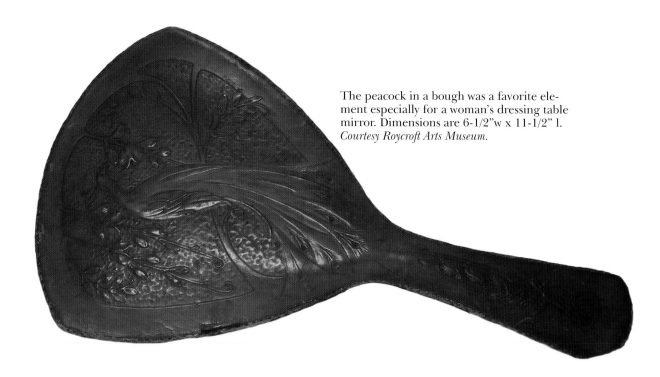

The peacock in a bough was a favorite element especially for a woman's dressing table mirror. Dimensions are 6-1/2"w x 11-1/2" l. *Courtesy Roycroft Arts Museum.*

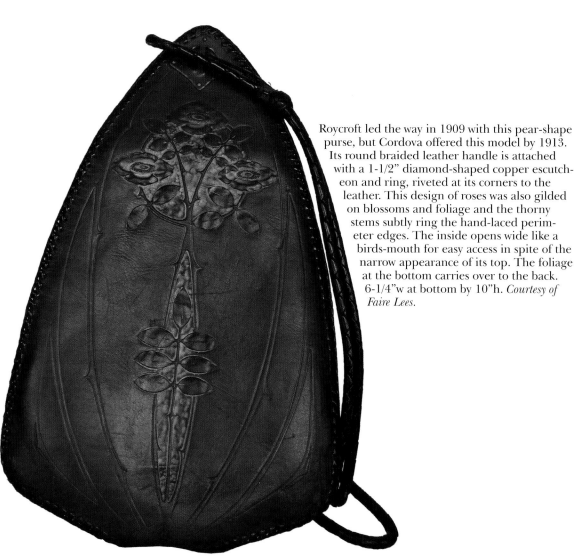

Roycroft led the way in 1909 with this pear-shape purse, but Cordova offered this model by 1913. Its round braided leather handle is attached with a 1-1/2" diamond-shaped copper escutcheon and ring, riveted at its corners to the leather. This design of roses was also gilded on blossoms and foliage and the thorny stems subtly ring the hand-laced perimeter edges. The inside opens wide like a birds-mouth for easy access in spite of the narrow appearance of its top. The foliage at the bottom carries over to the back. 6-1/4"w at bottom by 10"h. *Courtesy of Faire Lees.*

Hidden inside the hand-laced flap is a large Jemco gun metal steel frame that says "genuine gun." It separates the interior into three roomy compartments with pockets for mirror and a flap-snap coin purse. A versatile bellows design permits its user to really cram it full and still keep it secured by the top flap. Fully laced edges, this style continued its popularity into the Cordova Leather catalog of 1927. 6"w x 8"h, but can easily expand to two inch thickness. *Courtesy of Faire Lees.*

Petite Cordova handbag with telescoping stitched leather handle with snap-lock positioning. Built-in large kiss-lock coin and currency purse. 7"w x 5"h. *Courtesy of Faire Lees.*

Cordova's finest and most self-contained clutch or envelope purse first appeared in the 1912 catalog and was still in demand as late as 1927. The lined interior has a hidden gun metal framed pocket, plus a large mirror under the laced, modeled leather flap with leather covered snap. Also has pockets for address book with pencil, coin purse, card case and a large back pocket for gloves or papers. 11"w x 6"h. *Courtesy of Faire Lees.*

An early (because of its round braided leather, lariat style handle) Cordova "Buffalo Nouveau" design of World War I. Its plated steel frame has "pat. apld for" stamp (before the use of Jemco) and it uses a ball kiss-lock closure combined with a turnloc locking mechanism. A roomy purse, suede lined, with a glove pocket on the backside. 8"w x 8"h. *Courtesy of Faire Lees.*

Curiously, while the Roycrofters pumped their rally cry; "Head, Hand and Heart" (1926) the Cordova Shops countered with "As you know, Cordova is hand wrought, hand tooled, hand laced—a product of the hand, the heart, the mind…" (Cordova catalog to retailers, 1927).

Genuine Cordova

Hand wrought   Hand tooled   Hand laced

A product of the hand, the heart and the mind as well as the tools of the craft.

YOU who buy and sell Cordova are dealing in exclusive merchandise indeed!

As you know, Cordova is hand wrought, hand tooled, hand laced— a product of the hand, the heart, the mind as well as the tools of the craft. True there are many of each number made—but each bears the unmistakable individuality of the craftsman who fashioned it. Though all of a number are alike—yet each is different—as different as one personality from another.

If you were to look over the shoulder of a Cordova craftsman as he models his design into leather you would wonder how it is possible that you can buy and sell such painstaking workmanship, such devotion to beauty, such unmistakable quality at such modest prices. There is such a little difference, after all, between the price of these genuine hand made creations and those that are stamped out with monotonous accuracy by machines.

There is always something new in Cordova. Yet no number is placed on the market until we are certain that its style and design will be as thoroughly in good taste in the years to come as the day you buy

Cordova Shops was still going strong in 1927 when this catalog was published. *Courtesy of Jessica Greenway.*

No. 1037. *Swagger Bag.* Geranium design. Flat bottom. Leather-lined. Edges hand-laced. Fitted with Coin-purse and Mirror.
Size, 7 x 6 inches

No. 4. *Swagger Bag.* Arabian design. Inside frame. Round bottom. Leather-lined. Edges hand-laced. Fitted with Coin-purse and Mirror.
Size, 7 x 6½ inches

No. 47. *Hand Bag.* Appleblossom design. Imported gun-metal frame. Round bottom. Leather-lined. Edges hand-laced. Fitted with Coin-purse and Mirror.
Size 1, 6¼ x 6 inches
Size 2, 7¼ x 6¼ inches
Size 3, 8½ x 6¾ inches

No. 108. *Cigarette Case.* Pirate Ship design. Telescope. Hand-sewed. Holds full package of Cigarettes.

No. 307. *Bill Book.* Calf. Pirate Ship design. Three-fold with opening for Pass Card. Calf-lined. Laced or turned edges.
Size, closed, 3 x 4½ inches
Size, open, 4½ x 9 inches

No. 1052. *Envelope Bag.* Conventional design. Gun-metal frame. Broken bottom. Leather-lined. Edges hand-laced. Pocket on back. Fitted with Coin-purse and 3 x 5" Mirror.
Size, 7 x 4½ inches

No. 266. *Purse.* Raeman design. Inside frame. Round bottom. Leather-lined. Edges hand-laced. Fitted with Coin-purse, Mirror and Comb.
Size, 7 x 4½ inches

No. 840. *Book Ends and Mat.* Modeled in Pirate Ship design.
Size 1, Book Ends, 4½ inches high; Mat. 7 x 21 inches.
Size 2, Book Ends, 5½ inches high; Mat. 9 x 24 inches.
Size 3, Book Ends, 6½ inches high; Mat.11 x 27 inches.

CONSULT YOUR PRICE LIST FOR ADDITIONAL DESIGNS IN ANY OF THESE NUMBERS

Cordova has never been over commercialized. Today, as in the past, it reflects the finest of old time traditions of quality, art and craftsmanship. You can buy or you can sell Cordova with a degree of satisfaction that is the uncommon in these days of mass production and quality concessions.

No. 27. *Hand Bag.* Nasturtium design. Leather-lined. Welted edge. Handle and Flap laced. Fitted with Coin-purse and Mirror.
Size, 6 x 5½ inches

No. 50. *Hand Bag.* Sweet Pea design. Broken bottom. Leather-lined. Edges hand-laced. Fitted with Coin-purse and Mirror.
Size, 7 x 5½ inches

No. 61. *Hand Bag.* Rose design. Round bottom. Leather-lined. Edges hand-laced with Coin-purse and Mirror.
Size, 6 x 7½ inches

No. 272. *Purse.* Iceland Poppy design. Broken bottom. Leather-lined. Edges hand-laced. Fitted with Coin-purse, Mirror and Comb.
Size, 8 x 5½ inches

No. 273. *Purse.* Heron design. Inside frame. Broken bottom. Leather-lined. Edges hand-laced. Pocket on back. Fitted with Coin-purse and Mirror.
Size, 8 x 5½ inches

CONSULT YOUR PRICE LIST FOR ADDITIONAL DESIGNS IN ANY OF THESE NUMBERS

A side-by-side examination of Cordova and Roycroft 1915 catalogs show some similarities in styles and some uniqueness of articles. Cordova offered a fire screen (no dimensions furnished) with two designs: "The Salamander untouched by the fire's flames"; and "Cupids building a fire." Roycroft offered an 8-1/2" diameter modeled leather, velvet-lined sewing tray with four buttressed feet, its famous moth design leather mat of 22" diameter, and two styles of leather clad clocks.

This desk-sized, 9-1/2"w x 5-3/4"h, rectangle mat was embellished with the popular oak leaf and acorn design. Other desk items, such as the modeled leather covered inkwell or bookends were also decorated with matching designs to complement the ensemble. *Courtesy Roycroft Arts Museum.*

Round mats in the interpretative square rose design were offered in a wide variety of sizes. This is a 14" diameter, considered to be in good condition since mats suffered the vagaries of stains and regular abuse. *Courtesy Roycroft Arts Museum.*

Cordova document case unfolds to 18-1/2" height x 15" width. Normal closure shown is 15"w x 6-1/2"h. Nicely executed artistic interpretation of a carnation and other handwork shown in the close-up image. Hand-laced edges and double-stitched, sliding handle. *Courtesy of Faire Lees.*

Close up of document case showing the nicely executed artistic interpretation of a carnation and other handwork. *Courtesy of Faire Lees.*

A necklace of art leather jewels decorates these bookends from Cordova. *Courtesy of Jessica Greenway.*

Another large bookend set, 7-1/2"w x 6-3/8"h. These were often design-mated to rectangle mats for an impressive table display. The same style was made in a 4" x 4" size. *Courtesy Roycroft Arts Museum.*

The classic acorn and oak leaf design appears on all four sides of this 3-1/2"w x 3"h Cordova inkwell. *Courtesy Roycroft Arts Museum.*

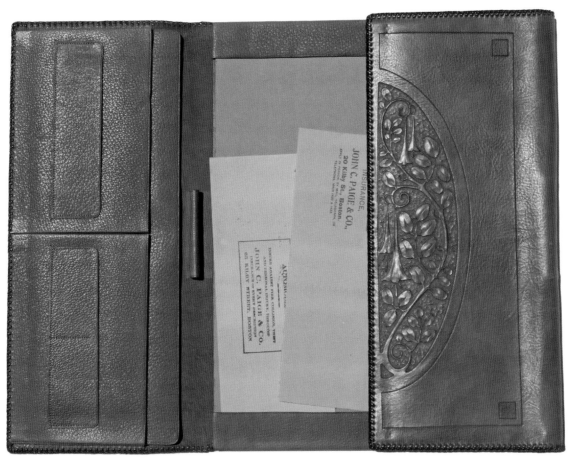

An elegant writing portfolio with stylized fuchsia design. Figure 71 closed is 12-3/4"w x 15-1/4"h; figure 72 is a close-up of the modeling design of the foliage and reminiscent of the early purse with a mirror image of peacocks. Figure 73 is the left hand side opened to show the integral pockets to hold writing paper, envelopes, etc. Total overall dimensions with both flaps open are 38.5"w x 15-1/4"h. *Courtesy Roycroft Arts Museum.*

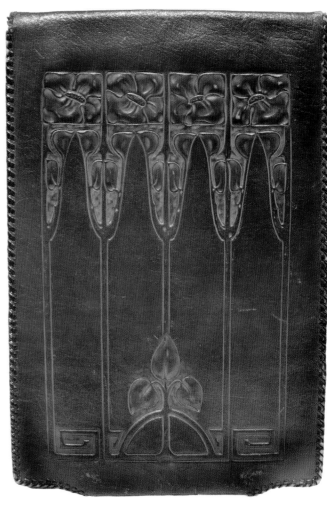

Writing/traveling portfolio, 6'-1/2"w x 10"h. An exceptional example of modeling the rose flower and foliage in a Cordova signature design. Opened, the portfolio neatly retains stationery, stamps and a few documents. The close-up reveals the rose stem with thorns above the two leaves leading upward to the repousse flower. This element is often reproduced as a solo design on other Cordova articles. *Courtesy Roycroft Arts Museum.*

Cordova also offered a group of hand bags unique among modeled leather manufacturers. The crushed calf leather was dyed lavender or purple iridescent. Frames in three sizes were silver plated and encrusted with stones. Edges were laced in a contrasting color. Some styles included a branded coin purse, card case and mirror. A separate group of unmodeled (plain) bags was offered in black only, made from "genuine" seal and sea lion. Cordova also broke the ice into luggage with a "Gladstone grip" modeled leather traveling bag of either 14 or 20 inches in length.

A ScheideMantel forte was the skillful reproduction of the model's features, be it a grasshopper or a woman's head and facial characteristics. This 5-1/2"w x 8-1/4"h handbag with dyed cameo repousse feature has a hand braided round handle, steel Jemco frame and "turnloc" closure, and laced edges. A nearly identical purse is in the collection of Jessica Greenway of Kirkland, Washington, except that the woman is facing right, instead of to the left as this example. *Courtesy Roycroft Arts Museum.*

Close-up of cameo, thought to possibly be profile of Gladys Scheide-Mantel. *Courtesy of Jessica Greenway.*

ScheideMantel artistry for Kaser Art Leather. *Courtesy of Faire Lees.*

Cordova dyed black purse with "G" initial centered in Poppy floral design, contains original mirror. 6 1/2"w x 6"h. *Courtesy of Jessica Greenway.*

Close-up of Cordova Shops impressed mark. *Courtesy of Jessica Greenway.*

A ScheideMantel billfold with a Picasso influence. *Courtesy of Roycroft Arts Museum.*

It is unclear who was the prime designer at Cordova until 1912 or so, when most authorities attribute the marvelous work to Frederick C. Kranz. His involvement with both Roycroft and Cordova is discussed in some detail in the section of Roycroft Modeled Leather.

At the time of his death, January 19, 1919, Frederick C. Kranz, was an officer of the Cordova Shops of Buffalo. This photo was taken around 1913 with his wife, Henrietta, and children. *Courtesy Roycroft Arts Museum.*

An early Buffalo Nouveau design of iris blossoms on an early, c. 1912 Cordova Shops strap handle handbag with concealed steel frame. Closure is by a tab and kiss-lock, without the turnloc mechanism. Interlacing handle of six inches length keeps it securely closed. 7"w x 8"h with 6" hand-laced handle. *Courtesy of Faire Lees.*

An unmarked Cordova Shops wannabe! This shape, early frame and quality of the execution of the sinuous modeled design are faithful replicas of touches Cordova used in its early work. 6-1/4"w x 8"h. *Courtesy of Faire Lees.*

While Roycroft leather articles began to diminish around 1926, it appeared Cordova was in full stride. An enthusiastic outlook was presented in their 20 page *Leatherware—Hand Wrought* retail catalog of 1927. It still offered one of their earliest "Empire" design hand bags, characterized with prominent bat ear loops on the frame for attaching the handle, yet it included the fashionable ostrich leather envelope purse. There were dozens of the popular floral modeled designs and even a few items such as a bill book (a large, two fold wallet) and photo album in Gothic design. In addition, there were some imaginative scenic and figural forms presented.

Purse by Cordova, shown in period advertising as signature model, unusually large size, Arrow-head motif design, with large mirror and coin purse, 8"w by 9-1/2"h. *Courtesy of Jessica Greenway.*

Cordova Leather Shops Mistress Mary purse with close-up design of woman in sun hat and long dress holding a bouquet of flowers in the midst of a carpet of flowers. Identified as "Mary, Mary, Quite Contrary" 1927 Cordova Leatherware Catalog. *Courtesy of Jessica Greenway.*

Close-up of the quartet of stylized grape cluster and leaf design of Cordova purse. *Courtesy of Jessica Greenway.*

Cordova purse with quartet of stylized grape cluster and leaf design on unusual concave top frame, includes original round mirror and eyeglass prescription dated 11/7/24, 8"w x 6"h. *Courtesy of Jessica Greenway.*

Cordova Shops portfolio cover, 9"w x 11"h, with intricate, careful modeling of stylized moth and another great moth at the bottom. This imaginative design is attributed to the influence of Frederick Kranz who worked first at the Roycrofters and then at Cordova Shops. *Courtesy Roycroft Arts Museum.*

Cordova Shops of Buffalo key case (for six keys) of the late 1920s offered sewn instead of laced edges. Shield design provided an option for a monogram. 4-1/4"w x 2-1/4"h. *Courtesy of Faire Lees.*

Cordova Shops three-panel wallet, with deeply modeled trillium design, held ID and business cards and folding currency. A nice example of artistic modeling on a small space. 3"w x 4-1/2"h, 8-3/4" fully opened. *Courtesy of Faire Lees.*

Another Cordova Shops men's wallet of the three panel design permitted separation of paper and coins and held ID or other cards. This early version had fully-laced edges while later ones were sewn. 3"w x 4-1/2"h; opens to 8-3/4". *Courtesy of Faire Lees.*

One hand bag, 8"width x 6" height, portrayed a Japanese tea house with Mount Fujiyama in the distance. Another purse, 8" width x 5-1/2" height showed a Heron prominently in the foreground at the edge of a pond, and another hand bag presented a petite fairy dancing across a meadow and a jewel case, 4-1/2" width x 5-1/2" length x 2-1/4" height, lined with silk velour with either a squirrel or pinecone design. There was also a 10-3/4" height x 16" length x 6" depth woman's overnight case, silk-lined and equipped with a seven-piece set of toilet fittings. Other travel offerings included a suitcase with modeled orange blossom design ranging in sizes from 16 to 20 inches—all fully equipped with toilet fittings, viz. mirror, brushes, combs, and manicure set for the woman.

Tea House & Mount Fujiyama view purse. One of the few landscapes offered by Cordova. This Japanese-styled motif is described in the 1927 catalog as the Fujiyama design. 5-1/2"w x 6-1/2"h. *Courtesy of Jessica Greenway.*

A large 7-3/4"w x 6"d x 3"h Cordova jewel casket with laced seams, key lock and complex modeled top design of two magpies on a bough. *Courtesy Faire Lees.*

This squirrel box is another ScheideMantel-inspired work at Cordova Shops. *Courtesy Faire Lees.*

A simple modeled repousse blossom serves as the lid's lift on this 4-1/2" diameter x 2" deep jewel box signed by George ScheideMantel. *Courtesy Roycroft Arts Museum.*

Another jewel box of 4-1/2"w x 5-1/2"d x 3"h with stylized Cordova pine cone and needle cluster. The same box is often seen with the symbolic squirrel design on top. *Courtesy Roycroft Arts Museum.*

Signed ScheideMantel artistic leather of rose blossom stem design as a gift to a neighbor. 11"w x 4 ½"h . Courtesy of Jessica Greenway.

A wood-lined humidor of 7-3/4"w x 4-3/4"d x 3"h. Cordova artisans decorated many different sizes of boxes for many applications. The impressed shop mark is normally on the bottom. *Courtesy Faire Lees*

The company couldn't shrug off the debilitating effects of the 1929 economic collapse. In 1930 it prepared to move from its downtown Buffalo retail showroom to a less prestigious location at 1399 West Avenue. General Manager J. C. Hoffman was replaced by C. Guy Bevington in late 1931. A new President, Frank B. Brown attempted to revitalize the slumping sales in 1933 with an infusion of his own capital and a new handle "Designers and Makers of Cordova Leather Goods." He, along with Libbie G. Brown as Vice President, managed the limited output through the years 1934 through 1940 at the same 1399 West Avenue location.

Perhaps the most colorful (is bizarre too tame?) design produced at Cordova. Similar designs were adapted to other styles in the late 1920s. Otherwise, laced handle and bag perimeter, and frame top with Jemco "Turnloc" opening are common elements. This purse measures 6"w x 9"h. *Courtesy Roycroft Arts Museum.*

One of Cordova Leather Shop's most compact handbags, 3-3/4"w x 5"h, has three distinct interior functioning areas. Hand-modeled daffodil scene on the face and full lacing around the edges. Three panels of 3-3/4"w x 5"h. *Courtesy of Faire Lees.*

However, the July 1935 issue of *Luggage & Leather Goods* (p. 51), carried this news story on Cordova Shops:

One of the oldest American firms making small leather goods for men, and handbags, has retained Mr. W.G. Publow, formerly with the International Paper Company at Niagara Falls, as general manager. The Cordova Shops, Inc. of Buffalo, NY are to be considerably reorganized under the new set-up, and will again actively participate in the manufacture and distribution of modern types of small leather articles. This firm holds several patents on unusual bill folds and letter cases of very practical design and it is expected that these items will be prominently featured on the Cordova line.

The Cordova Shops offerings of 1918
for men, women and the home.
Courtesy of Jessica Greenway.
(pages 120-127)

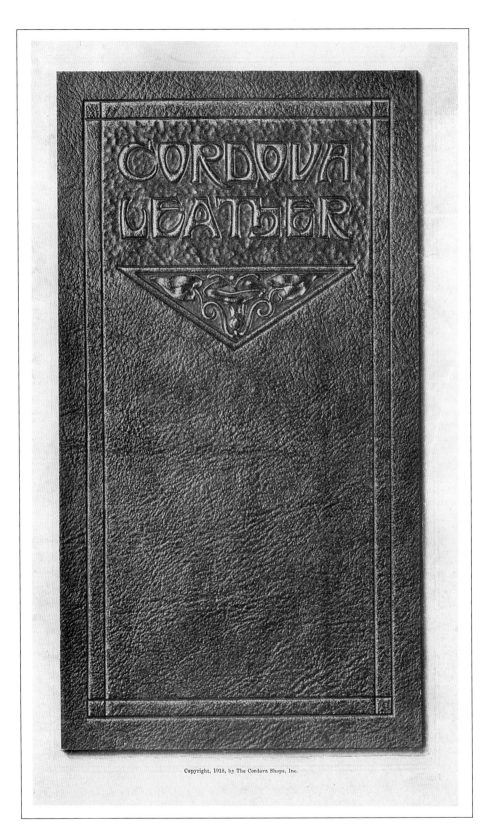

Copyright, 1918, by The Cordova Shops, Inc.

UNIQUE ARTICLES

ALL our products are made regularly in hand-modelled leather. In addition, a great many are produced in genuine seal—available in barley grain, straight grain, cross grain and pin seal. Usually the choice of the grain is left to the discretion of the craftsman, because the size of the article, its shape, and the ultimate use are factors in determining the selection.

That Cordova leather goods cover a wide range is shown by the following list of stock articles:

Albums
  Studio
  Home
  Lodge
Address Books
Bags
Belts
Bill Books
Bill Folds
Blotters
Book Blocks
Book Covers
Book Ends
Card Cases
Cigar Cases
  Telescope
  Folding
Cigarette Cases
  Telescope
  Folding
Collar Boxes
Comb Cases
Cushions
Desk Sets
Document Cases
Engrossing
  Mem'l Resolutions
  Title Pages
Envelope Bags
Fobs
  Men
  Women with Coin Purse
  Fraternity
Glove Cases
Grip Tags
Guest Books
Hand Bags
Handkerchief Cases
Key Ring Cases
Kodak Books

Magazine Covers
Match Cases
Mats
  Desk
  Table
  Piano
  Vase
  Lamp
Memorandum Books
Monograms
  Modeled in Leather
Music Rolls
  Satchels
Music Portfolios
Necktie Cases
Photograph Cases
  Frames
  Albums
  Portfolios
Playing Cards Cases
Pocketbooks
Pillows
Portfolios
Program Covers
Purses
Resolution Covers
Scissor Cases
Screen
  Fire
  Three fold
Shopping Lists
Signature Blotters
Stick Pin Cases
Stogie Cases
Table Covers
Toilet Sets
  Cases
Traveling Bags
Writing Folios
Wallets
Waste Baskets

IT is but a short journey from the ancient Spanish city of Cordova—from whence came the name Cordova leather—famed for its beauty and quality—down to the present home of the same products fashioned by hand at the Cordova Shop of Buffalo. Favorable, indeed, is the comparison by those who know, and proven once more is that old adage of the beaten path to the door of a genius.

In this brochure are illustrated by photography some of the present products of this Shop. We have tried to bring our goods to you for your inspection. Other articles, hand tooled and laced, are listed on page two.

Regarding the manufacture, we have gathered, slowly but surely, the artists of top rank in each profession, so that every article marks the ultimate hope of the brain that conceived it and the hand which made it.

THE CORDOVA SHOPS, INC.
DESIGNERS AND MAKERS OF
CORDOVA LEATHER
237 ELM STREET, BUFFALO, N. Y.

1013

711

1014

93

41

91

CORDOVA products are hand tooled individually, so that each hand bag, for example, carries the distinction of the personal effort of the artist.

Remarkably favorable is the comparison between ancient Cordovan carvings and the products of our present generation exemplified by the Cordova Shops.

You are assured genuine satisfaction with these goods, and the possessor of any Cordova product may well be proud of the mark of good taste implied by his or her possession.

The hand bags, photographically reproduced opposite, are leather lined; carry purse and mirror, harmoniously leathered; the edges are hand-laced; and are made from Spanish steer-hide modeled in designs of various interpretations.

No. 1013. Hand Bag. Modeled in PINE-CONE DESIGN. Leather-lined. Edges hand-laced. Has Coin-purse and Mirror.
Size 6¾ x 5¼ inches

No. 1014. Hand Bag. Modeled in MORNING GLORY DESIGN. Inside frame. Leather-lined. Edges hand-laced. Has Coin-purse and Mirror.
Size 5¼ x 7¾ inches

No. 41. Hand Bag. Modeled in ROSE, LOUIS XIV and BIRD DESIGNS. Lock frame. Leather-lined. Edges hand-laced. Has Coin-Purse and Mirror.
Size 5 x 6¾ inches

No. 711. Hand Bag. Modeled in EMPIRE DESIGN. Leather-lined. Edges hand-laced. Has Coin-Purse and Mirror.
Size 5¾ x 6 inches

No. 93. Hand Bag. Modeled in PINE-CONE and BIRD DESIGNS. Lock frame. Leather-lined. Edges hand-laced. Has Coin-Purse and Mirror.
Size 1, 5 x 5¾ inches
Size 2, 6 x 6½ inches

No. 91. Hand Bag. Modeled in APPLE BLOSSOM and EMPIRE DESIGNS. Leather-lined. Edges hand-laced. Has Coin-Purse and Mirror.
Size 1, 5¾ x 6¾ inches
Size 2, 6¾ x 7¾ inches

67

1011

31

1016

71

89

FASHION'S fancies are pictured here as well as on pages 4, 6, and 10. Intricate designs sometimes are chiseled into the leather with an artistic skill unsurpassed. Beauty is the keynote and richness of appearance the goal. Thus the possessor is assured of individual workmanship in each detail for no machine-made goods are produced.

All lace edges are from African goat skins—hand stained—so that durability is guaranteed.

No. 67. Hand Bag. Modeled in CLEMATIS and EMPIRE DESIGNS. Leather-lined. Edges welted. Has Coin-purse and Mirror.

Size 7½ x 5½ inches

No. 31. Hand Bag. Modeled in POPPY, BLACK BRYONY and HYDRANGEA DESIGNS. Leather-lined. Edges hand-laced. Has Coin-purse and Mirror.

Size 6½ x 7¼ inches

No. 71. Hand Bag. Modeled in EM-PIRE, MORNING GLORY and SOLO-MON'S SEAL DESIGNS. Leather-lined. Edges hand-laced. Has Coin-purse and Mirror.

Size 8 x 8 inches

No. 1011. Hand Bag. Modeled in GOTHIC DESIGN. Leather-lined. Edges hand-laced. Has Coin-purse and Mirror.

Size 7 x 6¾ inches

No. 1016. Hand Bag. Modeled in VASE and FLEUR-DE-LIS DESIGNS. Leather-lined. Edges hand-laced. Pocket on back. Has Coin-purse and Mirror.

Size 7 x 4¾ inches

No. 89. Hand Bag. Modeled in GOTHIC DESIGN. Lock frame. Leather-lined. Edges hand-laced. Has Coin-purse and Mirror.

Size 6 x 7 inches

THE NORTHE

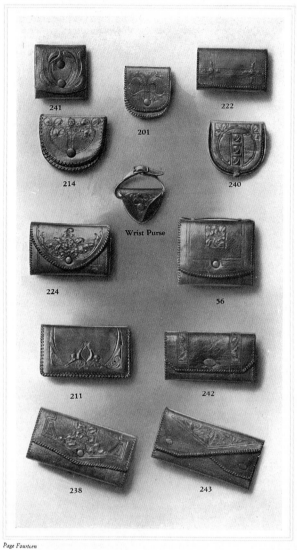

241

222

201

214

240

Wrist Purse

224

56

211

242

238

243

SMALLER purses here are shown grouped to give each its proper value.

Painstaking indeed, must be the artisan on these goods. Their size demands it—and our reputation stands ready to proclaim it.

Should you desire any model not shown—your request for additional information is sought.

"Likely we have it—if not, we will make it."

Numbers 222, 224, 56 and 238 purses are duplicated in genuine seal.

No. 241. Coin Purse. Modeled in CROCUS DESIGN. Leather-lined.
Size 2½ x 2¾ inches

No. 222. Ladies' Purse. Russian Calf modeled in CONVENTIONAL and ROSE DESIGNS. Leather-lined. Lace or turned edge. Strap handle on back.
Size 4⅛ x 2¾ inches

No. 240. Tray Purse. Modeled in ROSE, MARROW and GRAPE DESIGNS. Hand-sewed. Leather-lined.
Size 3⅛ x 2¾ inches

No. 224. Ladies' Purse. Modeled in LOUIS XIV and RENAISSANCE DESIGNS. Leather-lined. Laced or turned edge. Strap handle on back.
Size 4½ x 3¼ inches

No. 211. Ladies' Purse and Card Case. Russian Calf modeled in RENAISSANCE and BAYLEAF DESIGNS. Leather-lined. Edges hand-laced.
Size 4½ x 2½ inches

No. 238. Ladies' Purse. Modeled in CLEMATIS and PHLOX DESIGNS. Leather-lined. Edges hand-laced. Strap handle on back.
Size 6 x 3½ inches

No. 201. Ladies' Coin Purse. Russian Calf modeled in HONEYSUCKLE DESIGN. Leather-lined. Edges hand-laced. Strap handle on back.
Size 3 x 3¼ inches

No. 214-2. Gentleman's Coin Purse. Modeled in CLOVER, OAK and COLONIAL DESIGNS. Leather-lined. Edges hand-laced.
Size 3⅜ x 2¾ inches

Wrist Purse. Russian Calf, embossed. Leather-lined.
Size 2 x 2 inches

No. 56. Ladies' Purse. Modeled in APPLEBLOSSOM, TULIP and RENAISSANCE DESIGNS. Leather-lined. Edges hand-laced. Has Mirror.
Size 4½ x 4¼ inches

No. 242. Ladies' Purse. Modeled in PINECONE and FLEUR-DE-LIS DESIGNS. Leather-lined. Edges hand-laced. Strap handle on back.
Size 2, 5½ x 3 inches
Size 3, 6½ x 3¼ inches

No. 243. Ladies' Purse. Modeled in PINECONE and FLEUR-DE-LIS DESIGNS. Leather-lined. Edges hand-laced. Strap handle on back.
Size 2, 5½ x 3 inches
Size 3, 6½ x 3½ inches

406

Music Bag

520-1

850-2

850-1

Glove Case

THIS page of articles should solve the gift problem for many in distress. A reference to page 2 will list for you other articles of a similar nature. When appropriate, monograms may be added, if desired. Music Satchel No. 406 is so built as to lie flat when opened, holding a full sheet of music. It closes as a satchel but does not crease the sheets. The music bag takes full sheets of music without folding.

No. 406. Music Satchel. Modeled in BARBERRY DESIGN.
    Size, closed, 15 x 9 inches

No. 520-1. Clock. Modeled in EMPIRE DESIGN. Edges hand-laced.
    Size 8 x 5 inches

No. 850-1. Handkerchief Case. Modeled in ROSE DESIGN. Laced or turned edge.
    Size, closed, 5 x 5 inches

Music Bag. Modeled in EMPIRE DESIGN. Gusset sides and top handle. Laced or stitched edge. Will take full sheets of music or music-books without folding.
    Size 15 x 12 inches

No. 850-2. Handkerchief Case. Modeled in PINECONE and GRAPE DESIGNS. Laced or turned edge.
    Size, closed, 6 x 6 inches

Glove Case. Modeled in ROSE DESIGN. Laced or turned edge.
    Size, closed, 4½ x 14¼ inches

THE NORTHE

HOME embellishments are always cherished. Added beauty can never be amiss. These articles furnish increased pleasure each time they are used.

No. 463. Photo Album. Modeled in EMPIRE DESIGN. Loose-Leaf.
    Size 1, 10 x 6½ inches
    Size 2, 12 x 8½ inches

Hand Mirror. Modeled in LILY DESIGN.
    Size 6¼ x 11¾ inches

No 840. Book Ends and Mats. Modeled in PINECONE, DOGWOOD, PHLOX, CALIFORNIA PEPPER, GOTHIC and COLONIAL DESIGNS.
Size 1, Book Ends, 4⅛ inches high, Mat, 7 x 21 inches
Size 2, Book Ends, 5⅛ inches high, Mat, 9 x 24 inches
Size 3, Book Ends, 6¾ inches high, Mat, 11 x 27 inches.

No. 537. Writing Folio. Modeled in HERALDIC and ROSE DESIGNS. Leather-lined. Edges hand-laced. Has writing-tablet, and pockets for stationery, also calendar and loops for fountain-pen and pencil.
    Size 1, Tablet 5   x 8 inches
    Size 2, Tablet 5¾ x 9 inches
    Size 3, Tablet 8   x 10 inches

No. 467. Guest Book. Modeled in BAY-LEAF DESIGN. Leather-lined. Edges hand-laced. Inside print in three colors on Japan Vellum. Ivy border. Title page handsomely illuminated.
    Size 1, 11½ x 9   inches
    Size 2, 15¾ x 11½ inches

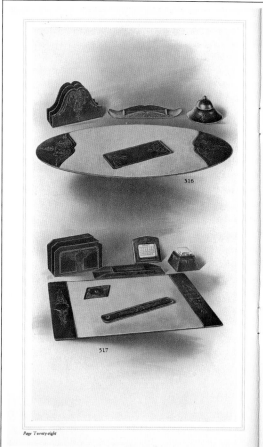

PARTICULARLY beautiful are the desk sets. The final touch toward completeness may be obtained by the use of them. We have chosen purposely two distinct sets —masculine and feminine. The designs are in harmony with period furniture, thus adding a feature relished by refined taste. After a careful choice, it will be gratifying to see how acceptable they are to boudoir or gentleman's den.

No. 516. Desk Set. Modeled in RENAISSANCE DESIGN.
    Pad, 12 x 23 inches

No. 517. Desk Set. Modeled in PINECONE DESIGN.
    Pad, 14 x 20 inches

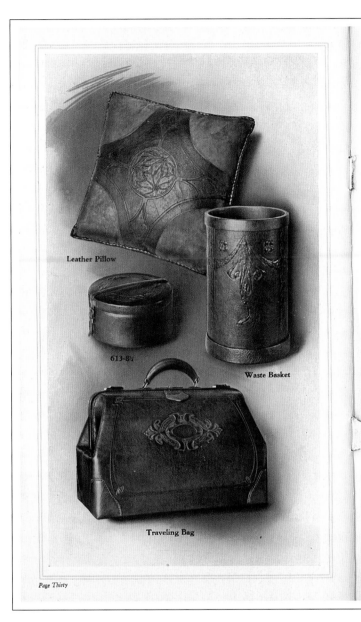

Leather Pillow

613-8¾

Waste Basket

Traveling Bag

ALL of our goods are produced regularly in three shades —bronze, patina and autumn. Frequently we are called upon to deviate from these colors in order to match exactly some existing tone. Our laboratory has been successful in doing this, so that we have made harmonious browns, blacks, blues, greens and grays in exact value to the samples submitted to us.

We have needed public demand to warrant the variety of our goods—and these photographs show only a small proportion of the articles which we make. Our artists are ready to translate into practical production your desires.

Leather Pillow. Modeled in AMARILLIS DESIGN. Edges laced.
Size 20 x 20 inches

Waste Basket. Modeled in COLONIAL and FUCHSIA DESIGNS.
Height 14 inches

No. 613-8¾. Collar Box. Modeled in ROSE DESIGN. Hand-sewed. Copper Buckle.

Traveling Bag. Modeled in EMPIRE and GOTHIC DESIGNS.
Made in sizes 14, 16, 18 and 20 inches

Gun-metal steel frame and this shape is so reminiscent of Cordova Shops, even if unmarked. 6-1/2"w x 8-1/2"h with deep relief design. *Courtesy of Faire Lees*

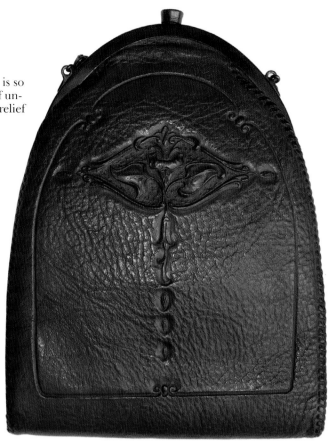

Cordova Leather Shop jewelry box with symbolic squirrel as center cartouche. Design is further embellished with pine boughs and cones. Size: 5-1/2" depth x 4-1/2" width x 3" height. Offered in the 1918 catalog. *Courtesy of Faire Lees.*

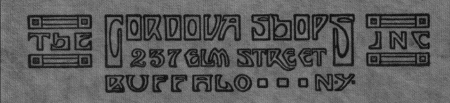

1914
Cordova Hand Bags

❧ ❧ ❧

Home of Cordova Leather in

Waterbury, Conn.

DAVIS & NYE, :: 114 Bank Street

CORDOVA 1914 HAND BAGS

CORDOVA HAND BAGS

Created by designers whose virility of thought and expression is internationally recognized, each season's shapes and designs of Cordova Hand Bags command immediate interest.

The Bags illustrated herewith are but a few of the 1914 offerings. They are moderate priced, practical and especially suited for Spring and Summer use. Photographs of the entire line, including the very De luxe Fall and Winter styles on request.

For 1914, the plans of The Cordova Shops, Inc., provide for a broader, finer and more interesting range of articles than heretofore, and to produce even a higher grade of workmanship and artistic finish.

The Cordova Shops, Inc., call attention to the fact that all designs employed in their work are originated by the artists of these shops and are copyrighted. Permission to reproduce cannot, in any case, be granted, and the copyright protection will be rigidly upheld.

Special booklets of other Cordova articles will be mailed upon application.

THE CORDOVA SHOPS, INC.,
237 ELM STREET,
BUFFALO, :: N. Y.

Leather artistry of the Cordova Shops. *Courtesy of Jessica Greenway.*

Kaser Art Leather Shop, 1913-1940s
Buffalo, New York

The virtues of German family values of self-reliance and hard work helped a Buffalo teenager start this business on a bench in the family home. In less than a decade he had built it into a thriving enterprise. Herbert E. Kaser, son of German born parents Charles and Mary Kaser (home at 545 Madison) served as an apprentice at the Cordova Shops (circa 1909-1914) while attending Buffalo public schools.

"While only 17, Mr. Kaser established a business (1913) under his own name, following similar lines of production at Cordova Shops, but using ideas and designs of his own development." (*Municipality of Buffalo: A History*, Vol. 4, p. 272, 1923)

Exceptional example of hand modeling of the human form; likely done by Georg ScheideMantel as freelance work, c. 1918 for the Kaser Art Leather Studios of Buffalo, NY. 6"w x 6-3/4"h. *Courtesy of Faire Lees.*

THE NORTHEAST

Deep tooling and repousse work on the blossom and foliage with hand-stamped sheep foot pattern around it gives meaning to the style known as "Buffalo Nouveau." This is a Kaser Art Leather Studio handbag, c.1919, with an elaborate Jemco arched steel frame with a gold wash. 7"w x 8"h. *Courtesy of Faire Lees.*

122   THE JEWELER

Moorish Leather

All
Hand-Tooled
Hand-bags
Purses
Bill-folds

Send for illustrated catalogue.

Kaser's Art Leather Shop

45 Brown St.
Buffalo, N. Y.

Kaser Art Leather Company advertisement of its artistic hand-wrought leather offering to upscale retailers in the *Jeweler's Circular* of February, 1922. *Courtesy of Faire Lees.*

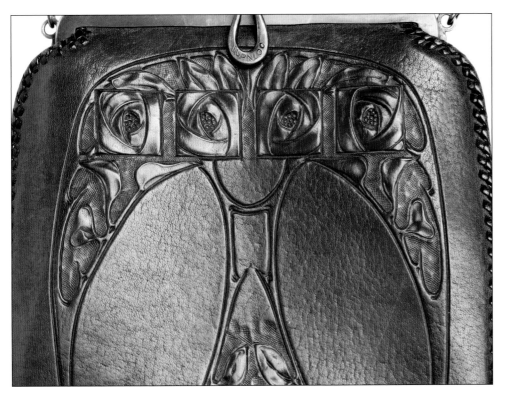

Kaser purse with Dard Hunter style Rose and leaves design, 6"w by 7"h. *Courtesy of Jessica Greenway.*

THE NORTHEAST

In 1915 the growth of the business allowed him to include his younger brother, Fred C. Kaser, as a partner and the firm name became Kaser's Art Leather Shop. (It operated under this name in 1923, the date of the published historical reference quoted above.)

Kaser luggage tag, writable backing.1-7/8" dia. *Courtesy of Jessica Greenway.*

Kaser single flower and leaf design purse, 5-1/2"w by 7-1/2"h. *Courtesy of Jessica Greenway.*

Kaser concentrated on "Hand made, laced Moorish Art Leather purses and hand bags" and marketed the 20-style line to major retail department stores, much as Cordova Shops was doing. In 1923 the shop employed 30 to 40 workers and required 7,500 square feet of space at 1870-72 Genesee Street-(at cross streets of Bailey, about 3 miles Northeast of downtown Buffalo).

Kaser Art Leather Company combined hand pleats with modeled flap design and full hand-lacing. Likely from the late 1920s. Marked K over the steer on the back. 6-1/2"w x 6-1/2"h. *Courtesy of Mary Tanner.*

Kaser quality of workmanship was on a par with both Roycroft and Cordova. Regularly, one will see a Kaser modeled leather purse on eBay® or other internet auctions. There have been some published purse collector's guide books and magazine articles that often attribute anything with the letter K on it to the design of Frederick Kranz. According to Boice Lydell, however, Kranz only used his conjoined initials on a few rare books. In a few instances he marked his work with the profile of a fish. The earliest Kaser identifying mark to be found is a capital K inside a diamond, usually applied to the backside of the hand bag just below the metal frame. Sometimes, it is impressed under a flap.

Kaser purse with cherry and leaf design, contains original mirror and coin purse, 6-1/4"w by 6-1/2"h. *Courtesy of Jessica Greenway.*

After 1915, it may be one of the most recognizable brands on any leather purse. If you see the profile of a steer (cow to you city folks) facing to the left and a large capital K superimposed over the side of it, then you are holding a H. E. Kaser Creation that is fully guaranteed to be hand-made, hand-laced, and tooled! (The Kaser brochure says tooled, not modeled). The K on the cow, or steer, is a registered Kaser trademark. It has absolutely nothing to do with Frederick Kranz.

A contemporary competitor with Cordova Shops and Roycroft, the Kaser Art Leather Company of Buffalo produced this mail order piece in 1924. *Courtesy of Roycroft Arts Museum, Boice Lydell.*

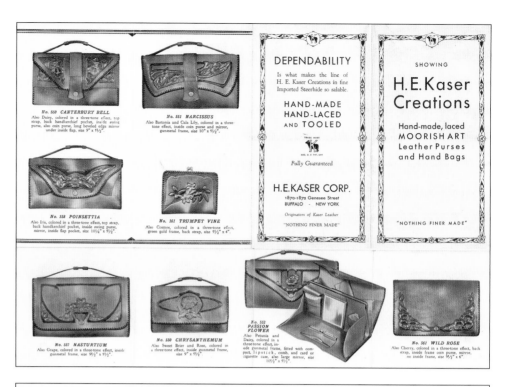

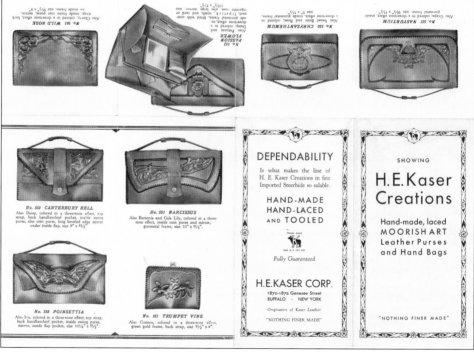

Far left:
Close-up of Kaser Shop mark. *Courtesy of Faire Lees.*

Left:
Alternate Kaser Shop mark on back of purse. *Courtesy of Faire Lees.*

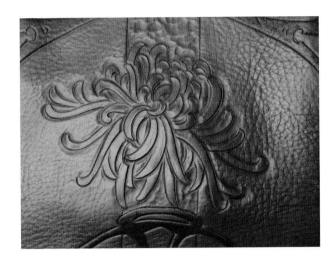

Kaser hand bag floral designs were strong, not wispy, but then so were their bags. They were often large, 8" x 8", and regularly used Jemco frames. Kaser's first leather articles were hand bags and the component mirrors, card cases, and accessories. It took them until 1922 to produce a limited number of billfolds for men. One especially fancy underarm purse, #552 Passion Flower, size 10-1/2" x 5-1/2", broken flap with an inside gunmetal frame, was fitted with a compact, lipstick, comb and card or cigarette case and a large mirror! The design was also available in Petunia or Daisy.

Stylized chrysanthemum design from the early 1920s.
Courtesy of Faire Lees.

Kaser Art Leather Company produced many modeled leather articles for a male that were easily embraced by a woman. This elegantly simple wallet was downsized to hold the new smaller paper currency of 1929. 3-3/4"w x 3-1/4"h, opens to 7-1/2"w.
Courtesy of Faire Lees.

Kaser continued in business, as did the Cordova Shops, through the 1930s and into the beginning of World War II. The founder, Herbert E., had two sons, Herbert E., Jr., and William F. Both were involved in the family business. The Buffalo City Directories consistently listed the firm with the founder as President until 1941 when the brother Fred Kaser was the principal name and was listed simply as "leather worker."

Kaser's mark of Quality

KASER'S MODELED LEATHER
AN ACHIEVEMENT ATTAINED THROUGH QUALITY

KASER'S ART LEATHER SHOP. BUFFALO. N.Y.

H. E. Kaser Company's promotional poster was designed and executed by George ScheideMantel with a stylized self-portrait of him at work. *Courtesy Elbert Hubbard Roycroft Museum.*

A. L. Reed Company,
Richmond Hill, New York City
    Maker of Reedcraft Leather Goods, 1897-1928 merger with Charles K. Cook Company

Charles K. Cook Company,
Camden, New Jersey
    Maker of Cook's Guaranteed Leather Goods, 1898-1928 merger with A. L. Reed Company

There are gaps in their evolutionary chronology, but data from the early 1900s show that both companies began around the same period and produced similar lines of rather plain pocketbooks, coin purses, card cases, etc. City business directories from 1910 onward list both companies under "fancy leather manufacturers." New articles then included hand-tooled or modeled designs on calf leather with ooze or suede leather linings and hand-laced edges and handles. Both used plain to fancy Jemco frames.

The Reed Company was branding its leather articles with "Reedcraft" around 1912 and it continued doing so even after its 1928 merger. Buyers were reassured by the interior label: "Reedcraft—will outlast all other leather in existence." This appeared on a simulated gold foil rectangle firmly attached to the interior of a handbag. Retailers were directed to examine the company's product line at 373 5th Avenue, New York City.

Aside from this location, Reed manufactured its handbags and other leather articles at its Richmond Hill location. Founder Arthur L. Reed was born in England in 1868, migrated to Canada, and was 29 when he began his New York City business.

The Reedcraft logo\mark that served the A.L. Reed Company of New York City and remained after the 1928 merger with the Charles K. Cook company. *Courtesy of Faire Lees.*

There's a fair bit of hand-stippling on this Reedcraft iris design. The gold-washed steel frame with the long turnloc tab bears the date 10-5-15. A small unit at 5-3/4" square. *Courtesy of Faire Lees.*

THE NORTHEAST

When Roycroft leather artisan George ScheideM-antel designed their self-promoting leather blotter, the Charles K. Cook Company operated at N. Fourth Street in Philadelphia, Pennsylvania. In the 1913 Camden Busi-ness Directory it had moved across the Delaware River and was located at 211 South Second St. It still operated at that location at the time of its 1928 merger with the A. L. Reed Company.

The company logo was represented by the word Cook's above longhorn steer horns stamped into the ooze leather interior of a woman's purse. Its motto was "Cook's Guaranteed Leather Goods". The more stylish of the purses of the early years presented a peacock (quite similar to the Roycroft design) on a tree branch; or a long-tailed bird (similar to the Cordova Shops magpie design).

The Cook's Leather Goods Company of Camden, New York, used the longhorn steer head as its in-bag embossed emblem. *Courtesy of Jim Wear.*

A Cook's handbag embellished with a mockingbird in the wisteria. Hand-laced all around, 7-1/8"w x 7-1/8"h. Lime-green sueded interior with two pockets. *Courtesy of Jim Wear.*

Roycroft did it, so Cook's designer featured a bird in the bush. Here, a peacock or two finds a prominent bough as a perch. No design on back. Grey interior with Cook's longhorn steer head logo above two small pockets. Jemco brass frame on this 7"w x 8"h handbag. *Courtesy of Jim Wear.*

Cook's was well-known for its line of women's handbags and this wallet could have served as an accessory to the line. It has three panels featuring strong art nouveau design across each. 2-3/4"w x 5"h, opens to 9" overall. *Courtesy of Faire Lees.*

As the 1928 merger approached, the two firms were building an enormous new factory of over 44-thousand square feet at the Camden location to produce their leather goods.

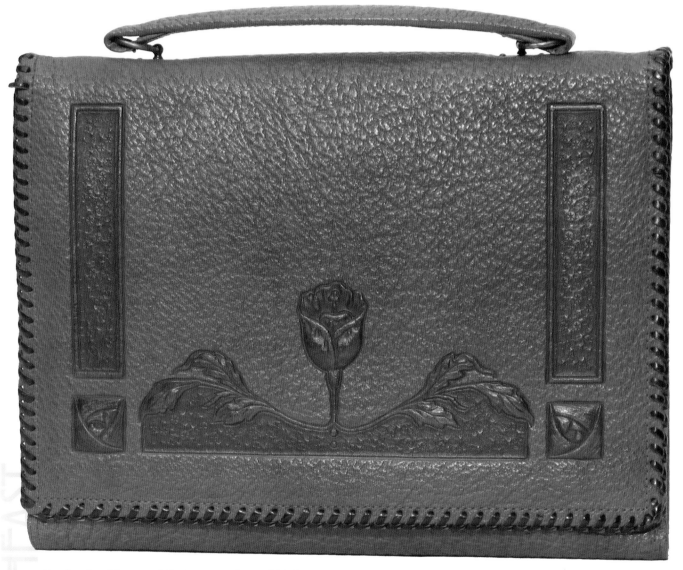

Reedcraft writing portfolio in textured steer hide houses an interior blotter and pocket for 5"w x 8"h writing tablet. Dard Hunter styled roses on face. Two hidden snaps under hand-laced flap. 8-1/2"w x 6-1/2"h. *Courtesy of Faire Lees.*

Reedcraft's fall line for 1927 was shown to the trade in the August issue of Trunk's Leather Goods and Umbrellas. *Courtesy Bag Lady Emporium.*

New York City maker A.L. Reed branded its early 1920s modeled handbags and clutch or envelope models with the name Reedcraft. 11"w x 5-1/2"h. *Courtesy of Faire Lees.*

When the two companies merged, the new major brand became Reed-Cook. Although the new, on-paper firm still offered some hand-tooled and hand-laced articles, it had dramatically expanded its product mix. In its 60-page 1929 catalog aimed at retailers, there were gift ensembles, traveling cases, and toilet kits, even leather covered and patterned cigarette lighters coordinated with billfolds and cigarette cases. Some very Florentine designed and colored leather articles were acquired from Italy along with leather travelers' items from England and dozens of non-leather items. An announcement explained: "You will find many unusual new pieces, some made in our own plant, others are exclusive patterns made for us in the studios of the Old World."

There were still concessions made for the waning Arts and Crafts styles that built their separate reputations. The 1929-1930 sales catalog still carried a few of these. Mostly, the book offered new fashion designs with celluloid trimmed frames and alternative to steer hide leathers such as genuine ostrich, English calf, seal, and the wildly colorful hand decorated Florentine Art flap with patent leather lacing. The firm survived the Depression years and even produced a few leather articles for the U.S. military during World War II.

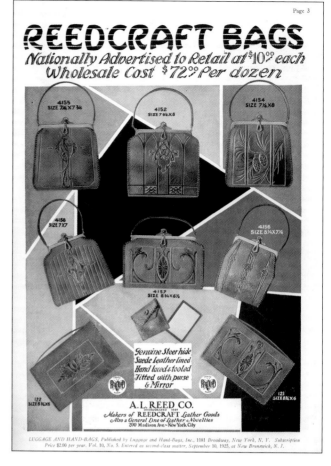

ReedCraft ad dating to before its merger with Charles K. Cook of Camden, May, 1928. *Luggage and Handbags* magazine. *Courtesy Bag Lady Emporium.*

Roycrofter ScheideMantel also produced specialty modeled leather items for many companies. Here's an example for Cook's Leather of Camden, New Jersey. *Courtesy Elbert Hubbard Roycroft Museum.*

This is the marriage certificate between the A.L. Reed and Charles K. Cook companies in September, 1928 in *Trunks and Leather Goods* magazine. *Courtesy Bag Lady Emporium.*

Two Time-Honored Institutions

A. L. REED COMPANY New York City
CHARLES K. COOK COMPANY, Inc., Camden, N. J.

Manufacturers of Quality Leather Goods

have joined hands *for your greater service and profit* under the style

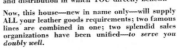

Reed-Cook
INCORPORATED

CHARLES K. COOK   ARTHUR L. REED

THIS merger brings together two prominent houses each of which has enjoyed increasing success for more than thirty years. It enlarges purchasing power, effects economies in manufacture and distribution in which YOU directly benefit.

Now, this house—new in name only—will supply ALL your leather goods requirements; two famous lines are combined in one; two splendid sales organizations have been unified—*to serve you doubly well.*

Large additions to the present Cook factory in Camden, N. J., are under construction and until their completion, broadening demand will necessitate the operation of the two factories—in Camden, N. J., and Richmond Hill, N. Y.

The handsomely-equipped display room at 200 Madison Avenue, New York City will remain as buyers' headquarters; you are invited to make use of its facilities when in New York.

Imported
Novelties

Dollar Gifts

Reedcraft Line

Cook's

Guaranteed

Leather Goods

Main Office and Factory: *Showroom:*
205-215 S. Second St., Camden, N. J.   200 Madison Avenue, New York City

Branch Offices: Philadelphia, Pa. and Chicago, Ill.

Architects' drawing showing entire Camden plant as it will appear when completed

When writing to Advertisers, please mention "Trunks and Leather Goods"

HANDBAGS of the Mode!

Renowned for Originality and Charm.

30-427   31-330   31-062
30-015   31-166   31-062   32-072

Description of Numbers Illustrated

30-427—$27.00 List. Black Beaded Steerhide Underarm with genuine hand decorated Florentine Art Flap. Patent leather lacing; inside frame purse. Size: 7" x 10½"

30-015—$35.00 List. Fine quality Steerhide Underarm. Hand tooled flap. Water Lily motif. Fitted with pencil, address book, purse and mirror. Inside frame purse. Size: 8" x 11"

31-166—$17.00 List. Apple Blossom motif. Back Strap bag. Fancy silver frame. Size: 6" x 9"

31-330—$21.00 List. Genuine Ostrich Pouch Bag. Rose Gold "turnloc" frame. Beige celluloid handle. Size: 6½" x 9"

31-062—$24.00 List. Rococo motif. Swagger style. Gun metal frame. Size: 10" x 7"

31-062—$22.00 List. Hand tooled Steerhide; Bell Flower motif. Genuine gun metal "turnloc" frame with gold and silver inlay. Purse and vanity. Size: 8" x 8"

32-072—$19.00 List. Dogwood motif. Fancy green gold Polychrome frame with green celluloid handle. Size: 7½" x 7½"

From the master hand of true artistry come these splendid creations . . . sounding the modern note in style and craftsmanship. Exquisitely fashioned of *Reedcraft* Steerhide, they are luxuriously appointed . . . with leather-lined interiors, change purse and mirror. Their distinguished charm is further enhanced by the individualistic touch of hand decoration, patent leather lacing, tooled finish, the superb treatment of "turnloc" frame design, the colorful effect of Florentine handicraft. A diversified presentation of originality and distinctive beauty for inclusion in all hand bag lines that attempt modern showings.

TO DEALERS: 50% off all list prices.

Send for New 1929-30 Catalog!

Reed-Cook
INCORPORATED
General Offices and Factory: 205-15 S. 2nd St., Camden, N. J.
Showrooms: 200 Madison Ave., New York City

Handbag of the Mode! A fancy promo by Reed-Cook for November, 1929 in *Luggage and Handbags* magazine. *Courtesy Bag Lady Emporium.*

THE NORTHEAST

Reedcraft showcased this fully-laced body with a Jemco honey-colored Bakelite style frame as its "El Dorado" hand-tooled design. It is on the front only. 9-1/4"w x 6"h. *Courtesy of Faire Lees.*

Unaware of the coming nationwide financial disaster, Reed-Cook presented its 1929 catalog in full color.
Courtesy Faire Lees.

Annah C. Ripley
New York, New York

The San Francisco Business Directory of 1900 lists Ripley as a pyrography artist at 727 Sutton in the Colonial Apt. Anecdotal pass-along information reports she had other sisters and that all moved to New York City after the 1906 earthquake and fire, and opened a studio. In October, 1903, she published, "Leather as a medium for artistic expression" in the journal, *Handicraft*, Vol 11, No. V11, Society of Arts & Crafts, Boston. The November, 1908 edition of *Ladies Home Journal* carried her full page story (p 31) titled "Leather Work as a Handicraft." It featured a variety of cutwork, tooled patterns, rather professionally appearing and decorated in gold and black. Her raison d'etre in the story: "However fair your technique, remember that the process is the means, not the end; that it is the thought—the conception—back of the expression which stamps your work as either vital or lifeless."

A contemporary leather artisan with Elizabeth Burton across the nation, and Mary Ware Dennett of Boston, Annah C. Ripley of New York City was a strong advocate of artistic leather. *Ladies' Home Journal*, p. 31, Nov., 1908. *Courtesy of New York Public Library Express.*

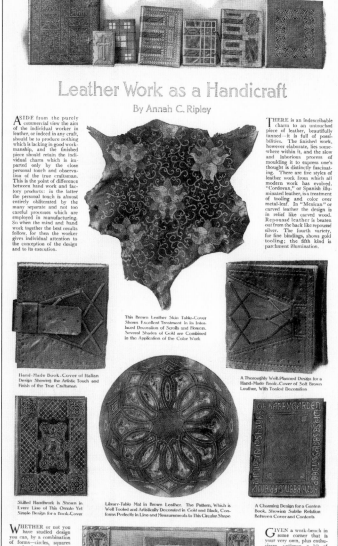

C.F. Rumpp & Sons, 1851-1968
Fifth & Cherry Building
Philadelphia, Pennsylvania

Most renowned for its wide variety of fine and quality leather articles, this firm likely has the distinction of being the first commercial "fancy" leather goods producer in the U.S. It also has some importance to the scholars and collectors of artistic leather of the Arts and Crafts era. Rumpp was the first employer of Otto Hilt—a founder of the Cordova Shops of Buffalo in 1908; and Frederick C. Kranz, the master leather designer and craftsman recruited by Elbert Hubbard for the Roycroft bindery in 1903. Both were already trained leather artisans when they immigrated to America from their German homeland.

The founder, Carl Frederick Rumpp, a native of Nuertingen, Germany, arrived in Philadelphia in 1848 at age 20. He, too, was a journeyman leather worker possessed with an entrepreneurial spirit. A lengthy corporate centennial brochure "C.F. Rumpp & Sons, Inc., 100 years—1850 to 1950" traces the dynamic success of the founder as he designed new products. He supplied the Army of the North during the US civil war with leather cartridge boxes, belts, and other personal leather items. The company was also awarded a Gold Medal at the 1876 Philadelphia Centennial Exposition for "Superlative quality of leather goods."

Rumpp did break ground with leather items popular among leather artisans of 1900. A copyrighted 1897, 16-page brochure *Mexican Hand Carved Leather Goods* is chock-a-block loaded with ladies' combination pocket books (no dimensions or type of leather supplied), kiss-lock framed purses, gent's letter, bill, and card cases, ladies' chatelaine bags with metal framed top openings, ladies' belts, and hand bags with Doctor's-style wide mouth. There were photo frames, traveling clocks, perpetual calendars, and writing cases, all in modeled designs. These were incised onto the surface, and stamped by hand with the typical assortment of patterns. It was likely that Otto Hilt and Frederick Kranz would have been hired to work with this product group.

In a separate 10-page trade catalog of 1904, the company prepared dozens of leather articles of all sizes and purpose "especially adapted to pyrographic decoration." It's *Fancy Leather Goods* 33-page catalog of 1912 presents dozens of items not seen in the other catalogs. These include desk accessories, ladies' and men's' toilet kits, cigarette and cigar cases, writing cases and portfolios, playing card cases, poker chip cases, bridge, whist cases, and straight-edge razor cases with saving paper holder. There were also bags to hold collars, jewelry cases, collapsing cups, and pocket flasks. Virtually all of these leather articles were plain; that is, there was no surface modeling. The firm made quality products, had a strong trademark of a large capital *R* inside an outline of an architectural keystone (the same outline used by the State of Pennsylvania as its motto "The Keystone State"). Leather collectors should note that Rumpp insists that "All articles are stamped with our registered trade-mark."

4) Cover of the 1904 Rumpp catalog with "blank" leather articles prepared for designing and hand-modeling by home leather artisans. *Courtesy of Bag Lady Emporium.*

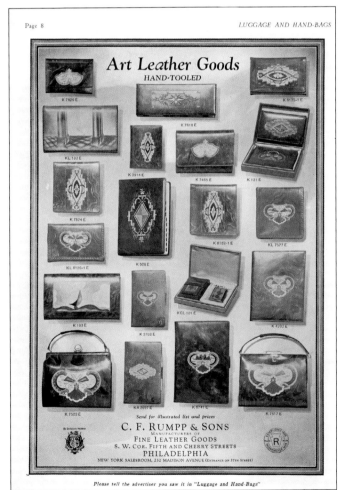

C.F. Rumpp made with the Christmas offerings in its November, 1929 ad in *Luggage and Handbags* magazine. *Courtesy of Bag Lady Emporium.*

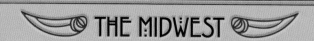
ILLINOIS

Chicago—A Natural Garden for the New Arts & Crafts Movement

That Chicago became a major player of the Arts and Crafts Movement in the nation was mostly due to a unique coalescing of circumstances and personalities. Two women with an urgent mission, Jane Addams and Ellen Gates Starr formed the settlement Hull House in 1889. Its purpose was to mitigate the wretched social and living conditions that the mostly illiterate and poor immigrants (and new to Chicago) endured in order to make a new life in America.

One should recall that the Chicago of 1889 was only 18 years removed from the great fire of 1871. The architect giants we know today—Daniel Burnham, John Root, Louis Sullivan, and Frank Lloyd Wright were fledglings then trying their wings on mansions for the likes of Field, Armour, Pullman, Sherman, and Glessner far out on Prairie Avenue, and planning the skyscrapers of the loop. Yet there was an insatiable need for workers—male and female—young, eager, and willing to hoe the fields of commerce.

> A thousand trains a day entered or left Chicago. Many of these trains brought young women who had never even seen a city but now hoped to make one of the biggest and toughest their home. Jane Addams, founder of Hull House wrote: "Never before in civilization have such numbers of young girls been suddenly released from the protection of the home and permitted to walk unattended upon the city streets and to work under alien roofs." The women sought work as typewriters, stenographers, seamstresses and weavers.
>
> —Larson, Erik, *The Devil in the White City*, Vintage Books, 2004, p. 11.

A few years earlier Addams had visited Charles R. Ashbee's Guild and School of Handicraft at Toynbee Hall in London. It was founded amidst the city's worst slum in an effort to foster handicraft as a way of restoring a worker's dignity and of raising the quality of what they made. Inspired by Ashbee's work and filled with a vision for Chicago, she returned and founded Hull House on Halsted Street.

Perhaps one of the more important reasons the Arts and Crafts Movement flourished in Chicago was the number of influential supporters who were drawn together by their adherence to the principals of Ashbee and Morris. These tenets proclaimed that manual work, when nourished by a reasonable environment, was capable of improving the worker's morality and character.

Gustav Stickley drummed this concept in each issue of *The Craftsman*. In the March, 1908, issue (vol. 13, #6) he wrote: "I believed then, as I believe now, in the immense influence for good in the development of character which is exerted merely by using the hands. To me, this development is the chief end to be attained by fostering the growth of handicrafts."

Not remotely recovered from the great fire, Chicago's housing, streets, sanitation, transportation, public safety, and social opportunities for the working class were still primitive at best in the 1890s. Jacob Riis, the New York journalist who had devoted his career to revealing the squalid housing of America's poor, pronounced much of the city to be worse than anything he had seen in New York.

As the city got bigger, taller, and richer it also grew dirtier, darker, and more dangerous. Erik Larson (*The Devil in the White City*, p. 28) portrayed the typical poor neighborhoods a few years before the 1893 World's Columbian Exposition brought 27 million visitors to Chicago.

> A miasma of cinder-flicked smoke blackened its streets and at times reduced visibility to the distance of a city block, especially in winter, when coal furnaces were

in full roar. In poor neighborhoods garbage mounded in alleys and overflowed giant trash boxes that became banquet halls for rats and bluebottle flies. Billions of flies. Chicago awed visitors and terrified them.

It was these and even more challenging conditions that strengthened the resolve of Hull House supporters and the Chicago Arts and Crafts Society (CACS). One of the most vocal members of CACS was a University of Chicago English instructor, Oscar Lovell Triggs. He is best known for organizing the Industrial Arts League (IAL) of 1899. His principal sympathies were with the workers, the workplace, and the connection between art and life. His goal for the IAL was to dignify labor and inspire and educate the worker. Triggs attracted the support of a prestigious board of Chicago political, business, educational, and creative elite, including architects Louis Sullivan and Frank Lloyd Wright. By 1902, the League had amassed a membership of over 400. It also sponsored hands-on manual training classes. Its first craft workshop and retail show room was the University Guild housed in a two-story building at 5001 Lake Avenue. In 1900 it was equipped with potter's wheels and kilns, tile furnaces, ironworker's forges, power equipment needed for furniture production, and an array of woodworking and metal craft hand tools. It was under the direction of George L. Schreiber who helped design a similarly equipped work shop for apprentice training and a showroom at 264 Michigan Avenue. It was known as the Bohemia Guild.

The British Arts and Crafts Movement and the work of William Morris, the chased silver, and the finely printed and bound books were familiar to the Chicago elite, educators, and collectors. Morris fabrics, wallpapers, and furniture were available at Marshall Field and Company and the Tobey Furniture Company. The leading British design periodical, *The Studio* and the U.S. *International Studio* were available. The unique John and Frances Glessner home (1800 S. Prairie Avenue) designed by H.H. Richardson in 1885, was a showcase for the Arts and Crafts-inspired new Prairie School of architecture. Its proponent architects among a few dozen included Frank Lloyd Wright, Howard Van Doren Shaw, George W. Maher, Walter Burley Griffin, George Grant Elmslie, and Dwight Perkins.

Chicago's publishing industry was awakening to the different shapes, textures, and colors of architecture and home furnishings. Now on the scene, the home and design and fine arts magazines *House Beautiful* (1896), *Fine Arts Journal* (1899), *Brush & Pencil* (1897), *Popular Mechanics* (1902), and *Bohemia Guild* (1892) sprouted and thrived with the movement. These were soon joined by publications that were devoted to the movement. These included Elbert Hubbard's *The Philistine*, *The Fra*, and Roycroft catalogs and advertising, Adelaide Robineau's *Keramic Studio* (1899), Gustav Stickley's *The Craftsman* (1901), and many others that propagated the craft ideals.

A who's who of distinguished English Arts and Crafts Movement leaders made a pilgrimage to the new Chicago colony. Walter Crane lectured at the Art Institute and helped organize an exhibition of his work there in 1892. Charles R. Ashbee, architect and designer visited Chicago twice (1900 and 1908) and later wrote the foreword to Frank Lloyd Wright's work published in Germany in 1911. In 1900 he stayed with his new friend, Jane Addams, and delivered numerous lectures at Hull House and the Art Institute of Chicago, including talks that highlighted his new Guild of Handicraft venture in Chipping-Camden. Joseph Twyman came and stayed and championed the cause of William Morris (who died in 1896) in lectures and articles. Joined by Oscar Lovell Triggs and Richard G. McDougall, they founded the Chicago colony of the Morris Society in 1903. Its broad purpose was aimed at continuing artistic craftsmanship through publications, lectures, and exhibitions and by founding studios, workshops, schools of design, and factories that incorporated the craft ideals. Twyman even guided the development of the Morris Memorial Room collection of fabrics and other articles at the Tobey Furniture Company where he served as chief designer. Later (1907) T. J. Cobden-Sanderson visited and the daughter of William Morris, May, was a featured speaker during her 1909 American tour.

About the time of Crane's 1892 visit, the Art Institute's Louis J. Millet developed a decorative design course curriculum (with night classes too) modeled after the British Movement. Within a decade hundreds of graduates of the hands-on course were espousing, teaching, or practicing the training they'd received under Millet.

The Chicago Arts and Crafts Society, with Addams and Starr leading the way at Hull House was formed October 22, 1897, patterned after London's Arts and Crafts Exhibition Society.

In *Chicago Metalsmiths*, (Chicago Historical Society, 1977, p. 37), author Sharon S. Darling noted:

> The 126 charter members of the new Chicago Arts and Crafts Society included metalworkers, designers, potters, artists and writers as well as reform-minded architects. One of its members, Frank Lloyd Wright, was on the verge of unveiling his first prairie house, which, in its creative use of natural materials and simplification of line and ornament, would incorporate many principles of the Arts and Crafts Movement. From the size and diversity of its charter membership, it would seem that the formation of the Society in 1897 represented a coming together of men and women whose commitment to the Arts and Crafts Movement had been developing simultaneously within various sympathetic contexts throughout the city.

The CACS arranged monthly lectures at Hull House and annual exhibitions of hand-wrought articles. Its first exhibition of 1898, held in conjunction with the Chicago Architectural Club at the Art Institute of Chicago, drew 17,000 visitors.

There was also a groundswell movement among educators to augment the three Rs with coursework in design and what was then known as manual or allied arts—as distinct from the fine arts of painting, sculpture, etc. Students filled classes at the newly-formed Armour Institute of Technology (it became the Illinois Institute of Technology in 1940), the Chicago Manual Training School, and Chicago Vocational High School. William F. Rainey, President of the University of Chicago, and other educators helped develop the manual arts curriculum of the new Bradley Polytechnic Institute of Peoria in 1896. A spin-off formed the Manual Arts Press which developed instruction guides in leather work, jewelry making, needle work, metal crafts, pottery, china painting, and textile design for Allied Arts teachers, schools, and the general public.

From all walks of life, adult men and women enrolled in private classes taught either by decorative design graduates or allied arts teachers who moonlighted during evenings and weekends. This new and readily available form of relaxation or creative self-expression with one's hands was especially appealing. Hull House and dozens of other classrooms thrived as night schools for large numbers of middle-class women who saw this new craft work as a way to augment their, or the family's earnings.

In a *Chicago Tribune*, January 13, 1901 article, the reporter offered an explanation for the development of artistic things of common use.

> It has been discovered that people of wealth and taste are as willing to pay for beautiful and exclusive designs in chairs and tables, in lamps, pottery, carpets, hangings and wall decorations, as for Old Dutch masters and landscapes of the Barbizon School. The demand for "art in things" has stimulated craft work in Chicago and the artist who works out his ideas in wood, metal, textiles, leather or clay is taking rank alongside the one who expresses himself in paint. Many men and women of deft fingers and creative minds are directing their efforts in the line of arts and crafts to the production of artistic things.

According to Darcy L. Evon, artistic leatherwork became popular in Chicago following the World's Columbian Exposition of 1893. From 1895, Louise C. Anderson and her sister Emma A. Kittredge popularized fine burnt and modeled leather in their studio and through exhibitions. Other noted artisans and shops that featured leather objects as part of their craft work included Amelia Hyde Center and Christia M. Reade from the Krayle Company; Mary E. Ludlow, Katherine L. Mills, and Bessie Bennett from the Swastica Shop; and Clara P. Barck, Grace D. Gerow, Marie L. Woodson, Mabel Conde Dickson, and Ruth Raymond from the Kalo Shop. Other influential artisans or instructors in modeled and decorated leatherwork included Leonide C. Lavaron, T. Vernette Morse, Jessie M. Preston, Florence L. Ward, and many others.

That an unusual majority of leathercrafters and teachers (and other artistic art forms too) were young women shouldn't be a surprise. Women were quick to learn, were capable teachers and, most generally, they were endowed with an aesthetic sensitivity. By age 12, most girls of this era were already proficient seamstresses. Certainly, with such numbers of women diligently pursuing a creative art form, even as a hobbyist, those with exceptional talent and determination would grow to professional status.

By the late 1890s large numbers of women attended the School of the Art Institute and little seemed to stop the more ambitious ones from renting their own studios. As Sharon S. Darling wrote:

> Since the Arts and Crafts Movement concerned itself with items for the home, commonly recognized as "woman's proper sphere" it seemed quite natural for women to seek advancement through careers associated with the creation of home furnishings. In Chicago, the first small shops devoted exclusively to the production, exhibition and sale of artistic articles made according to the new philosophy were established by women.
> —*Chicago Metalsmiths*, Chicago Historical Society, 1977, p. 45.

The crafts societies of Chicago began maintaining show and sales rooms by 1898 in the Fine Arts Building. The March, 1902, issue of *The Sketch Book*, published by the Art Institute of Chicago, furnished the following information:

> The Swastica, or gift makers, were the originators of the really artistic possibilities of art leather in Chicago. In the sales room in the Marshall Field Building, may be seen handsome articles for gifts or house decoration, such as table covers, screens, portieres, lamp shades, book case curtains, pillows, etc., all leathers in a great variety of colors, including a six foot table cover of peacock motif."
>
> The "Kalo Shop" in the Commercial Bank Building is a modest looking studio, from which comes the finest of workmanship in burnt leather, and great beauty of coloring card cases, bags, table covers, book covers and belts with hand-wrought clasps."
>
> The "Krayle Company" in the Marshall Field Building, creates metal articles of beaten brass, silver and copper, also tooled leather for chair backs and seats, and hanging screens and pillows.
>
> The Wilro Shop makes a specialty of rich, dark, low-toned leather bags and mats, Chinese in character."

The Kalo Shop, 1900-1970
Chicago & Park Ridge, Illinois

As Elbert Hubbard was preparing to establish a modeled leather department in East Aurora, New York, a group of young Chicago women were already exhibiting their leather artistry to a national audience and at a worldly gathering at the 1904 Louisiana Purchase Exposition in St. Louis.

The Kalo Shop mark usually brings a mental picture of a quality design and execution in hammered sterling silver. Rarely is it ever mentioned that Clara P. Barck (she married George Welles in 1905) and the other young women known as the "Kalo girls" were among the first Chicago designers and modelers of artistic leather. The Kalo Shop was founded in September, 1900, by Miss Barck, Bertha Hall, Rose Dolese, Grace Gerow, Bessie McNeal, and Ruth Raymond. Its studio/sales room was in the Bank of Commerce building at 175 Dearborn, Chicago.

Initially, the output was wall decoration (textiles), pyrography (burnt wood), hammered copper, and decorated and modeled leather. They called the venture The Kalo Shop—Kalo derived from the Greek for "to make beautiful." They were recent graduates of Louis J. Millet's decorative design course at the Chicago Art Institute. With a few other alumni they became the organizers of the Art Institute's annual exhibitions first begun in 1902.

Chicago historian/journalist Darcy L. Evon has studied Millet's work and the lack of recognition he has received, particularly for his extraordinary sense of design, embraced even by Frank Lloyd Wright. He founded the Chicago School of Architecture in 1893 and was its first dean. When he was eased out of the post in 1901 he found a new mission.

In a *Chicago Sun Times*, essay Evon remarked:

> As early as 1894 he had established a practical and popular degree course in decorative designing at the Art Institute where he served as professor from 1891-1918. Courses were taught in the French atelier system with hands-on studio experience in a workshop setting. More than 85 percent of students were women who were eager to learn a meaningful vocation outside of the home. Many excelled as teachers while others became leaders and artisans in the Arts and Crafts Movement just taking hold across the country.

If there was a spiritual and practical mentor of the Chicago Arts and Crafts legacy, it was Millet. He saw a need in 1902 to reunite and gather 500 former students of his decorative-design course, by now scattered across the nation, and establish the first of a prestigious annual Arts & Crafts exhibit. These annual shows attracted displays from leading A&C artisans from Midwest Guilds, as well as established commercial giants. Even Frederick C. Eaton and Elizabeth E. Burton of Santa Barbara, CA exhibited their renowned leather work and shell and metal lighting.

So it was in 1902 that the modeled and pyrographic leather work produced by the Kalo girls achieved some measure of the visibility afforded to work of Louis C. Tiffany, Gustav Stickley, Grueby, Newcomb College, and the mature silver work from the Society of Arts and Crafts of Boston.

Their novel designs and execution on leather were worthy enough to be juried and recommended by Professor Halsey C. Ives for the Applied Arts exhibit at the 1904 Louisiana Purchase Exposition in St. Louis. Ives took part in assembling works of fine art for the earlier 1893 World's Columbia Exposition in Chicago. He knew Millet's work; his dramatic color scheme devised for Louis Sullivan's Transportation Building at this event and the stunning interiors of the Auditorium and the Stock Exchange. If Professor Millet had nominated candidates to show their artistic creations at the Louisiana Purchase Exposition, Ives would have at least been receptive. In fact, a special category of Applied Arts (meaning artistic but utilitarian) was created to augment the Fine Arts of painting, sculpture, etchings, and engravings.

Clara Barck, founded the Kalo Shop and guided the Chicago firm into a premier house noted for its uniquely designed hammered sterling silver articles. *Courtesy of Sharon Darling.*

It was here, under Applied Arts, that artistic leather in the style of Arts and Crafts and Art Nouveau that the Kalo girls' work was first shown to an international audience. C.T.D. Fox, Superintendent, Exhibitor's Bureau of Sales, sent a lengthy closing report to Professor Halsey Ives, Chief of the Department of Art. In it Fox accounts for the artwork sold and records its value.

It is not known if the leather articles designed and sold by the Kalo girls bore The Kalo Shop mark, (all Kalo leatherwork owned by Clara Welles' descendants is unmarked). What they produced was described thusly:

Barck, Clara P.—card case, $5.00, magazine cover $8.00; Dolese, Rose and Minnie, Peacock cushion, $30.00, magazine cover, $10.00, leather case $15.00, leather bag $15.00, leather pouch, $5.00, coin purse, $3.00, card case, $5.00, card case, $5.00, card case, $4.00, portfolio, $12.00, portfolio, $15.00; Gerow, Grace D., two leather card cases, leather bag, $16.50; Raymond, Ruth, decorated leather, three pieces, $12.50. The other Chicago artisans to exhibit and sell leather work were Christia M. Reade (of the Krayle Company) a copper and leather watch fob, $25.00; Florence Ward of The Swastica Shop, six pieces of decorated leather, $33.50.

From Santa Barbara, California, the father/daughter leather and metal artisans of Charles Frederick Eaton and Elizabeth E. Burton were the only other leather artisans presented. Eaton sold a jewelry cabinet, $75.00, a guest book, $40.00, and an illuminated, leather-bound presentation of the 23rd Psalm, $60.00. Burton sold a leather table mat, $20.00, and another leather table mat for $13.00.

St. Louis exhibitors who later became Arts and Crafts icons included: W.D. Gates (Teco); William H. Grueby; Henry Mercer; Newcomb Pottery—Octavia Bailey, Amelia Romain, Hattie Joor, Leona Nicholson and Sabina E. Wells; Dedham Pottery; H.C. Robertson; Adelaide A. Robineau; Rookwood Pottery—Edward Diers, Harriet E. Wilcox, Rose Fecheimer, Laura E. Lindeman, O. Pinney, and Sallie Toohey; Handicraft Guild of Boston—Mary C. Knight, Arthur Stone, Karl F. Leinonen; Louis Tiffany; Van Briggle Pottery—Artus Van Briggle, Willis Borden, Anne Gregory, and George Bowyer Young.

Clara Barck Welles—the inspiration for the Kalo Shop

After early successes, Clara P. Barck incorporated the Kalo Shop in 1905 with capital raised from women investors. She married George Welles in 1905, but he did not own shares in the Kalo corporation, and they moved to nearby Park Ridge. She founded the Kalo Arts Crafts Community there and it became a "school within a workshop" where many accomplished and aspiring artisans taught and trained at the facility. The Kalo Shop expanded its silver work and jewelry production in 1908 (when a cadre of professionally trained immigrant silversmiths joined the organization) but continued making other crafts, including basketry, leatherwork, pottery, weaving, and other metalwork. The shift to focusing almost exclusively on silver and jewelry (there were nearly 25 silversmiths at work) happened in 1914 when Clara consolidated retail and production facilities back in Chicago. A retail showroom was opened in New York City in 1912 and closed in 1916, as the Welles' were separated (1912) and divorced (1916). When the workshops and retail salon moved to 152 E. Ontario Street in 1923, Kalo had become the most successful studio for hand-wrought silver and jewelry in the nation. Clara Welles continued her inspired designs into her 1939 retirement and relocation to San Diego, California. She gave the business to long-time colleague artisans in 1959 and died at age 97 in 1965 in San Diego. The Kalo Shop finally ceased operating in 1970.

The Kalo girls went separate ways and achieved some success. Ruth Raymond taught design and art composition in the Chicago area. In 1914 she became a principal art instructor at the Handicraft Guild of Minneapolis and later served as its last administrator. In 1917 when it was merged into the University of Minnesota's art education department, Raymond headed the new department until her retirement in 1947. Rose and Minnie Dolese continued with what they knew best, designing and producing artistic leather.

One of very few surviving modeled leather articles produced by Clara Barck. It was given by Barck to Helen Riggs on her marriage to Carl William Joehnke. The case is 4-1/4"w x 2-7/8"h, likely before 1902. *Courtesy of Sharon Darling.*

The Wilro Shop, 1902-1909
Fine Arts Building, Chicago, & Evanston, Illinois

Rose Dolese (1866-1932) was one of the original founders of the Kalo Shop. Her sister Minnie (1864-1939) joined the partnership following graduation from Louis Millet's design course in 1901. In 1902, the Kalo Shop moved into the Fine Arts Building, Chicago's most noteworthy facility for the arts, literature and music.

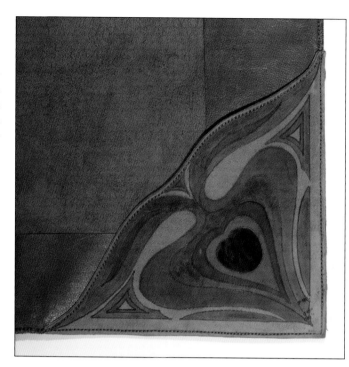

Desk calendar corner modeled after the eye of a peacock tail feather. *Courtesy of Darcy Evon.*

Desk calendar mat; unsigned, but estimated to have been produced in 1902. Rather fine examples of color integrated with design. *Courtesy of Darcy Evon.*

Shortly after the move, the Dolese sisters founded the Wilro Shop as a specialty design studio and operated in the Fine Arts Building from 1902-1909. Afterwards, the sisters maintained a studio from their Evanston home from 1910 until their retirement.

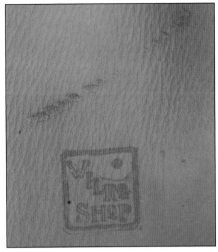

The various shop marks used by Rose and Minnie Dolese. *Courtesy Paul Somerson, Chicagosilver.com.*

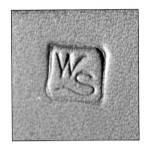

Typical shop signature, WS, applied with a leather press. *Courtesy of Darcy Evon.*

A small Wilro Shop item pricing card, c. 1905. *Courtesy of Paul Somerson, Chicagosilver.com.*

Their artistic leather creations—hand bags, card cases, writing portfolios, address books, blotters, and coin purses, were frequently exhibited at venues such as The Art Institute of Chicago's annual exhibition, the Society of Arts and Crafts of Minneapolis, Minnesota, the Arts and Crafts Society of Portland, Oregon, and the Alaska-Yukon-Pacific Exhibition of 1909 in Seattle, Washington.

Note the peacock eye design in this corner close-up. *Courtesy Paul Somerson, Chicagosilver.com*

Inspired by the peacock, the Dolese sisters placed its tail feather fan's eye at the corners of this suede exterior and blue kid lined card case. Like the other shown it is 6"w when opened by 4-3/8"h. Two interior pockets for cards. *Courtesy Paul Somerson, Chicagosilver.com.*

Leather lined and suede exterior document case has a full-width flap that has the Dolese geometric colored magic. It is 13-13/16"w x 5-1/8"h and secured with the two snaps on the flap. Note the subtle gold colored stitching around all edges. *Courtesy Paul Somerson, Chicagosilver.com.*

A dazzle of intricate patterns and color make up this suede book cover's edges and surround the central dark blue and green field on three sides. It was designed for a small book, for it measures 11"w when opened by 6-34"h. The inside is plain, carrying the Wilro Shop shopmark on the spine/gutter. Note the delicate blue stitching around all edges. *Courtesy Paul Somerson, Chicagosilver.com*

1904 stationery portfolio. Closed it is 7"w x 11-7/8"h. Signed WS with a leather press and priced at $15.00. *Courtesy of Darcy Evon.*

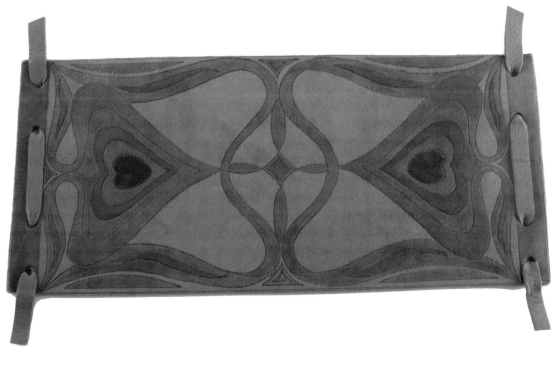

A peacock inspired rectangular suede blotter of 8-7/8"w x 4"h. Blotting side material is replaced by unthreading the short leather strips at each end. *Courtesy Paul Somerson, Chicagosilver.com*

A variation on the typical desk blotter is this approximately 4" square suede piece with four kaleidoscopic patterns in green and blue. The heavy blotting paper on reverse side is held in place by the brass fastener in the center. *Courtesy of Paul Somerson, Chicagosilver.com.*

THE MIDWEST

An imaginative flap and snap coin purse in sueded leather with a subtle colored design snaking along the top. The long tongue on one end of the flap extends around the bottom and fastens to the triangular flap mate at the other end with a brass snap. Approximately 4"w x 3-1/4"h. Gold stitching around all edges. *Courtesy of Paul Somerson, Chicagosilver.com*

Another dazzler in colored suede with the intricate pattern of an Oriental rug. Here, the geometric and floral decoration frames a central navy blue center. This is a card case that opens to 6"w x 4-1/2"h. The inside has two pockets for cards and note the blue and gold stitching against the plain tan interior. Here's a close-up of their artistic work signed Wilro Shop. *Courtesy Paul Somerson, Chicagosilver. com*

The Swastica Shop
Marshall Field Building, Chicago, Illinois

 The Krayle Company
Marshall Field Building, Chicago, Illinois

Art Institute colleagues Bessie Bennett and Florence Ward offered their leather artistry at the nearby Swastica Shop.

An unusual opportunity that boosted awareness of artistic things was afforded by the Marshall Field and Company on State Street. A group of artisan/producers, calling themselves The Krayle Company, produced their specialty articles in their own studios and workshops and offered them for sale at the Marshall Field Annex. Their work comprised a wide range of sterling buckles, clasps, cast brass and bronze candlesticks, decorative sculpture, leather work, etchings, and monotypes, furniture, crests and monograms and illuminated books. By 1901, the Krayle Company membership included Julia M. Bracken, Carl Linden, Robert Jarvie, Ida Burgess, Amelia Hyde Center, Bertha Jaques, Elizabeth Krysher, Henning Ryden, and Christia M. Reade.

Other Art Leather Artisans in Chicago
There was other artistic leather being produced by members of the Chicago Arts and Crafts Society at Hull House as early as 1897. The Industrial Art League founded in 1900 and the University Guild, also founded in 1900 contained other leather artisans, both self-trained and graduates of the decorative designing curriculum at the Art Institute.

Notes:
I am indebted to the earlier research and writings of Chicagoans Sharon S. Darling and Darcy L. Evon, writers and researchers; and Paul Somerson, whose scholarly research and collected images of Arts and Crafts silver, metals and artistic leather are maintained through his website, Chicagosilver.com. Their published work (and photo images) are major contributions to this Chicago section.

Sharon S. Darling is a historian, researcher, writer for the Chicago Historical Society and author of numerous works of the Arts & Crafts Movement, such as: *Chicago Metalsmiths*, Chicago Historical Society, Chicago, IL, 1977.

Darcy L. Evon, former technology columnist for the *Chicago Sun-Times* newspaper is a Chicago Arts and Crafts historian and a freelance author.

The Devil in the White City, Larson, Erik, Vintage Books, 2004, p 11.

Chicago Daily Tribune, Jan. 13, 1901; ProQuest Historical Newspapers, p 54.

"A profitable partnership" by Evans, R. Tripp, *Chicago History*, summer, 1995, p.5-21, Chicago Historical Society

Chicago Directory Co., 1910.

Chicago Sun Times, April 12, 2004; "Millet empowered a generation of female designers", Evon, Darcy L.

Chicago Sun Times, June 20, 2005; "Clara Welles' workshop slated for demolition", Evon, Darcy L.

House Beautiful, vol. 15, #3, Feb. 1904; "Arts and Crafts—some recent work," Emory, Elizabeth, p.132-138

On a much larger scale, modeled and impressed leather articles were commercially produced in the Chicago suburb of Cicero by the P.F. Volland Leathercraft and in Joliet at the Gerlach-Barklow Leather Company. Both produced contemporary women's purses, men's personal accessories, and desktop items for the home or office, such as produced by Meeker or Amity.

Both companies were established in 1907 for the business of publishing. Gerlach-Barklow made its initial mark with illustrated calendars. Volland originally concentrated on beautifully illustrated gift cards and mottoes to compete with the high quality color items that were produced in Germany. It soon added children's books. Among the classics were the profusely illustrated 1915 edition of *Mother Goose* with the magnificent full-color paintings by Frederick Richardson and the timeless 1918 favorite *Raggedy Ann & Andy* series by Johnny Gruelle.

We'd be doing you, the reader, disservice by not mentioning the highly collected Arts & Crafts novelties produced by P.F. Volland. Some mottoes were produced on etched copper plaques decorated with enamel. Others were much more than mere postcards. Many were intended to be framed and were hand-tinted. A unique set of six postcard-sized views of New York City were printed from hand-cut linoleum blocks by artist Rachel Robinson Elmer (some were lithographed too) and these are among the most sought after of the Volland legacy. Both Volland and Gerlach-Barklow had access to a talented pool of Chicago's women artists, many of whom were new graduates of the Art Institute.

While much is in print regarding the publishing empire of German-born Paul F. Volland (and his homicide in 1919) a worthy view of the company was presented by Anne Stewart O'Donnell, Senior Editor, in *Style 1900*, Fall/Winter, 2005-06, vol. 18, #4, p. 58.

P.F. Volland Company/Volland Leathercraft,
1907-1924
Chicago and Cicero, Illinois

Dating the artistic hand-modeled and embossed leather handbags bearing the words *Volland Leathercraft*® and the distinctive corporate emblem has been thwarted by the fact that no sales catalogs, advertisements, or trade journal stories of the day have been located. Even seasoned Volland card and motto collectors are, for the most part, unaware that the company produced such rather high-quality leather handbags. Appropriate historic societies, libraries, and local newspaper reference sources have been queried and these searches were fruitless in turning up worthy data.

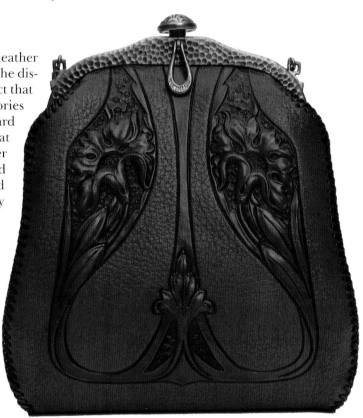

Close-up of the typical Volland Leathercraft branded handbag, produced by the P.F. Volland Company of Chicago about 1928. *Courtesy of Faire Lees.*

THE MIDWEST

Volland Ad of November, 1929.
Courtesy of Bag Lady Emporium.

Volland Leathercraft of Joliet, Illinois, produced many handsome women's purses. This design touts the acorn and oak leaf around 1925. 6-12"w x 6-1/4"h.
Courtesy of Faire Lees.

Even though there are early examples with frame dates prior to World War I, it is our best estimate that Volland Leathercraft handbags, mostly embossed designs with some handwork evident, were made in conjunction with those produced by Gerlach-Barklow and imprinted with the brand *Paragon®*. This was probably around 1925 when Volland was acquired by Gerlach-Barklow and relocated to Joliet. There is just too much similarity about the hand bag design, the grain and color of the leather, the frames of brass coated steel with certain adornments, and the identical accessories of mirror and coin purse. It is as though one leather shop produced both with separate shop marks as the Arts & Crafts era drew to a close.

Volland Leathercraft's large offering, 10"w x 8"h, of the late 1920s. Wide brass frame is decorated with roses and all leather edges are hand-laced. *Courtesy of Faire Lees.*

Chicago area company P.F. Volland and Gerlach-Barklow of Joliet, Illinois, produced remarkable handbags of nearly identical proportions and design. The Volland Leathercraft at left is 7"w x 7-1/2"h; while the Paragon branded bag is 8"w x 7"h. *Courtesy of Faire Lees.*

A rare departure, a Volland handbag finished in midnight blue color. Typically, the finish on Volland and Paragon is a light tan color. 7-1/4"w x 6-1/2"h., 1928. *Courtesy of Faire Lees*

A rare black Volland envelope or clutch handbag with a permanent 4" wide coin purse built-in. Strap on back can accommodate dress gloves. 8"w x 4-3/4"h. *Courtesy of Faire Lees.*

Volland leather-grip on a 9" celluloid letter opener. 1-1/4"w x 4" on the leather portion. *Courtesy of Mary Tanner.*

Customary identifying brand imprinted inside of purse. *Courtesy of Faire Lees.*

Gerlach-Barklow Company/Paragon, 1907-1936
Joliet, Illinois

The artistic leather articles produced by this giant publishing firm are stamped Paragon® and it is found on a broad line of unisex toilet articles, clothes brushes, desk-top accessories, and both men's and women's billfolds and wallets. The rather generously sized women's handbags featured well-delineated and interpretative foliage designs of the classic oak and poppy family. The brass-plated steel handbag frames are furnished by the J. E. Mergott Company (Jemco®) of Newark, New Jersey, and many bear the patent date series ending in July 29, 1918.

A card included in the handbag reads: "Paragon Leather–The Model of Excellence" above a line art drawing of the huge Joliet factory. On the reverse side, the new possessor is reassured with the thought: "This specimen of Paragon Leather is hand-stained and executed from an original hand-tooled design in the Gerlach-Barklow shops at Joliet, U.S.A. and Toronto, Canada." A handbag catalog of this period, 1918-1920, was not available, but it is a reasonable assumption that these handbags were produced and marketed in this time frame, rather than five years later.

The founders of this printing empire were fellow employees at the Thomas D. Murphy Calendar Company of Red Oak, Iowa. Theodore R. Gerlach was the driving force to build a new company in his home town, Joliet, and he enlisted his brother King H. Gerlach and Edward J. Barklow to join him in the new calendar company, chartered June 25, 1907. (Robert E. Sterling, *Joliet: Transportation & Industry*, Volume 1, G. Bradley Publishing, Inc., St. Louis, MO 63131, 1997.)

Paragon of Gerlach-Barklow combined interesting modeling on this smooth calf men's wallet with sewn edges. 4-1/4"w x 4"h. *Courtesy of Faire Lees.*

A typical, Paragon-branded bag, likely 1928. 8"w x 7"h. *Courtesy of Faire Lees.*

THE MIDWEST

Its success was assured from the very first calendar. In the history of Will County, Illinois, it was reported: "That within a decade, the G-B Company had expanded from a small beginning into the largest organization of its kind in existence, employing 800 persons and devoted to the manufacture and sale of art calendars, greeting cards, postcards, direct-by-mail advertising, business greetings, blotters, fans, mottoes, and leather goods. Its factory occupies nearly nine acres of floor space." (August Maue, *History of Will County, Illinois*, Volume Two, p. 1074-75, Historical Publishing Company, Topeka-Indianapolis.)

Calendar and advertising art collectors of the Arts & Crafts era may recognize two prolific women artists, Zula Kenyon and Adelaide Hiebel. They were mainstay producers (Kenyon from 1900 to her 1918 death, and Hiebel's 35 years of art beginning in 1919) at Gerlach-Barklow.

It was the intention of these German-American founders to outdo their German competitors and they succeeded, likely due to the prevailing U.S. hostile attitudes preceding World War I.

On the backside: the card reads: "This specimen of Paragon leather is hand-stained and executed from an original hand-tooled design in the Gerlach-Barklow shops at Joliet, U.S.A. and Toronto, Canada. *Courtesy of Faire Lees.*

A promotional blotter of 1928 by the Gerlach-Barklow Company of Joliet, Illinois, showing off its new factory where Paragon leather products were produced. *Courtesy of Faire Lees.*

In 1924, Gerlach-Barklow acquired control of P.F. Volland, combined it with the Joliet operation and named T. R. Gerlach as its president. Combined, the output of the P. F. Volland Company and Gerlach-Barklow easily made it the largest specialty printing business in the world.

Women's handbags branded Volland Leathercraft now carried a small promotional tag inside each that portrays the Gerlach-Barklow Joliet factory complex. Besides women's handbags, the leather advertising specialties business dramatically expanded right after World War I. Banks, insurance companies, investment brokers, and even brewers were major buyers of billfolds, wallets, coin purses, key cases; savings pass books, and numerous other personal and everyday use items of leather.

Commercial leather companies such as Gerlach-Barklow would offer middle distributors large quantities of these items that could be imprinted with a local firm's business identity, as well as personalized with a customer's name in gold foil.

Gerlach-Barklow was on its way to becoming a major business conglomerate operating as a holding company, the United Printers and Publishers, Inc. Besides the P. F. Volland acquisition, it included the Artographic Company of Joliet that produced calendars in quantities by the millions for distribution by major companies. These were resold to dealer networks for advertising purposes. The Rust Craft Publishers of Boston produced greeting cards for small town America's drug and stationery stores.

By mid-year 1930, United Printers and Publishers had also roped in the Springfield Leather Products Company of Springfield, Ohio, and the Bosca-Reed-McKinnon Company, also of Springfield. (*The New York Times*, June 7, 1930).

Springfield Leather Company, a long-time artistic leather producer, strengthened the market for leather specialties (meaning attractive and still quality handbags, billfolds, wallets, portfolios, key cases, cigarette cases, etc.) sold through stationery and jewelry stores. The acquisition of Bosca-Reed-McKinnon was a move to improve the sales of leather handbags distributed through large department stores. The parent company of Bosca Leather Goods operated separately from this entity and is still in business.

Remember the date, June of 1930, and the beginning of our great depression. Had Theodore R. Gerlach lived, he may have pulled the company through the crisis for he was the quintessential entrepreneur and businessman. He died at age 66 on August 5, 1933.

The Paragon boss's personal letter opener with a blotter beneath the sheath. Overall: 1-3/4"w x 10" l. *Courtesy of Faire Lees.*

THE GERLACH-BARKLOW CO.
JOLIET, U.S.A.   TORONTO, CAN.
No. 515

T. R. GERLACH

WISCONSIN

Chances are if you're sorting through a long-departed relative's personal effects and find an almost pristine billfold, it likely was made in West Bend, Wisconsin. The hundreds of leather workers of Enger-Kress, Amity, and Rolfs probably put more coin purses, wallets, and billfolds in the handbags and hip pockets of America than all the other leather producers combined.

According to a news story in the *West Bend Pilot,* "In 1925, West Bend had the distinction of having a manufacturing output of more than three million men's billfolds and many thousands of beautifully designed and richly embossed handbags and purses for ladies." (*West Bend Pilot,* Jan. 4, 1932.)

The leather articles won't likely be mistaken for Roycroft or Cordova Shops articles. Although the designs are pleasant, it is obvious these are embossed/stamped in the leather rather than hand-modeled. The steer hide is often machine-patterned, the stitching is strong rather than subtle, and the edge-lacing almost bullet proof.

Purchasing agents bought their memo pad covers, card cases, and billfolds by the wagon load. When America embraced the automobile (and there was a need to carry numerous keys) their flap-snapped, laced-edge key cases joined the wallet as a favored gift. But those crafty German leather merchants soon offered a matching-design key case and wallet gift set, and the receiver's initials could even be monogrammed in gold!

Be mindful that the Milwaukee/West Bend region of pre-World War I was very German. At least a third of Wisconsin's population in 1900 was either German-born or had at least one parent who was born in Germany. It was no wonder that Milwaukee was thought of as the Mecklenburg capital of the United States. The language and customs were reinforced in the schools and maintained throughout the business community.

As the *West Bend Pilot* newspaper reminisced in a 1950 story: "Mr. Enger and Mr. Kress and the workers were primarily of German descent and their methods of working were continued. Twice a day during working hours two boys would come into the shop carrying buckets of beer. Then everyone stopped for lunch. When old time German bands came around in spring, Mr. Kress invited them into the shop. All work stopped while the band played a few tunes." (*West Bend Pilot,* April 6, 1950.) Yet Enger-Kress, Amity, and Rolfs were quick to embrace modern production efficiencies and adapted work techniques rivaling an auto assembly line.

Are Enger-Kress or Amity articles as much "Arts & Crafts" as a Roycroft or Cordova Shops article? Not quite. The designs were selected from a die-company's stock catalog instead of originating from a trained designer's mind. The stock design was embossed on the skin side (back) of the leather in multiples; that is, the die patterns for a key case and wallet would be embossed several at a time on a large piece of leather and then the individual pieces were cut apart. However, articles received almost the same number of hand-worked steps. Skillful workers trimmed and fit the leather parts, lined the compartments, attached pockets, turned the ends, crimped frames, creased the borders, applied buttons, laced the edges, inserted loops, and cleaned and polished the article for the next steps—final eyeball inspection and shipment to retailers.

Keep in mind these weren't intended to compete with a totally head, heart, and hand-made article. It is likely that as the user became more fashion conscious and appreciated a sophisticated design and style, these Wisconsin leather articles helped "trade-up" to the best that Roycroft or Cordova Shops offered.

Even today leather is generally the preferred material to hold our cash and business instruments and announce who we are. One can buy a very serviceable wallet or billfold for fifty bucks or make a show with a mega-bucks crocodile or other rare lizard skin article. Roycroft leather or Tiffany lizard was also a choice in 1916.

Enger-Kress, Established 1885-Absorbed 2006

West Bend, Wisconsin

The senior of the Wisconsin manufacturing trio, the Enger-Kress Pocket Book Company, was founded in Milwaukee in 1885 by German-born George Enger and August Kress. George Enger, 27, was already a seasoned merchant when he arrived in America in 1878 from Altenburg, Germany. His initial output of leather articles focused on utilitarian and sturdy coin purses, bill books, and ledger cases. On nearly a parallel course, August C. Kress left Obernburg, Germany, for New York City in 1879 and continued his trade as a leather worker. He too made his way to Milwaukee around 1882 and set up a leather business.

In 1885 Kress joined Enger in their Milwaukee partnership that became immensely successful but short-lived. Neither would live to open the door on their modern fireproof factory still standing today in West Bend, or endure the humiliation caused by the German government's aggression of World War I. Kress was but 50 when he died suddenly May 14, 1911. Enger, at age 62, died the following year, September 23, 1912, in West Bend.

They flourished in Milwaukee for 8 years until a fire destroyed the facility and forced a decision. A group of West Bend community leaders offered them a signing bonus if they would relocate in West Bend, 30 miles to the north in 1894. That signing bonus amounted to 58 local residents becoming stockholders in the company, and Enger-Kress brought a company of loyal workers and setup shop in a deserted school house.

The Enger-Kress product line had such immediate and widespread acceptance from retailers across America that in 1902 the demand caused the relocation into a large wooden structure known as the Schlitz Pavilion and Amusement Park, built in 1879 by John Schlitz of Milwaukee. It served the immediate need, but the founders were planning new manufacturing methods that required more space.

In February, 1911, a lightning strike and fire destroyed the pavilion. Again, the partners swiftly reacted to get a new, fireproof factory built and still honor the stream of orders from retailers. Much of the heavy hide cutting and production work took place in the West Bend Plating Works building while a sales office was established in the store of Henry Rolfs. An inventive plan allowed over 150 workers to perform their special production tasks at their West Bend homes. Leather components and other materials were delivered by horse and wagon (and later gas powered vehicles) to each worker. Completed work was moved to other assembly workers and finished articles picked up for packaging and shipment to retailers.

Enger-Kress was a prolific producer of both men's and women's hand-worked as well as embossed leather goods, beginning in the early 1900s. The full size of this handbag is 7"w x 6"h. The next photo is a close-up of its brand of the Enger-Kress mark. *Courtesy of Faire Lees.*

"When the new fire proof factory came on line in 1912, it was staffed by 400 employees and was the largest and oldest billfold company in the United States." (*The History of Washington County Wisconsin—Past & Present*, Vol. 1, Chapter XXVII, S. J. Clarke Publishing Company, Chicago, IL, 1912). Note: The former E-K Company building at 151 Wisconsin Avenue is home to the River Bend Senior Village, consisting of 52 luxury apartments. The company left this location in 1999 and moved its 50 employees to the Aurora Corporate Center in nearby Addison. At the time of the move the company was manufacturing leather articles for Wal-Mart, Harley-Davidson, and others.

With a modern factory and new management, the company expanded its product line. In 1913 its 80 page catalog carried hundreds of leather articles, primarily for men, produced at West Bend. A popular tri-fold sewn-edged wallet carried a trademark, "*Up to date*" brand. The secretary was Robert H. Rolfs, 25, who in two years would found the Amity Leather Products Company in West Bend.

Catalog print piece of 1914 from Enger-Kress, West Bend, Wisconsin. *Courtesy of Faire Lees.*

Enger-Kress was one of may to adapt a dragonfly design to its leather offerings. This three-panel wallet carried out the motif on all panels. Hand-laced edges. 3"w x 4-1/2"h, opens to 8-3/4" w. *Courtesy of Faire Lees.*

THE MIDW

Although slow to move into the women's hand bags product line, there are numerous hand bags bearing Jemco metal frames with a patent date of 1911. An early maker's mark shows the company name in Old English/Gothic type face and another presents the initials E-K in a circle. The corporate mark of the 1920s resembles a kite outline with E-K inside.

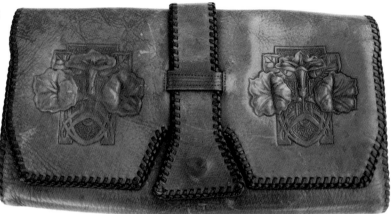

Enger-Kress envelope with hand-worked design and hand-lacing. Inside metal frame dated 8-8-28. 10-1/2"w x 6"h. *Courtesy of Mary Tanner.*

The catalogs of the 1920s carry the kite shape trademark and the hand bag promotional line as: "E-K Bags are made of steer hide, all with suede leather lining. The hand-lacing is of imported goatskin, toughest of all leather. All lacing on bags or handles is done by hand. The staining is applied by hand by skilled artists."

There is a curiosity in a 1924 brochure. It is alongside an artist's drawing of a two-story building that is signed at the top: "The GuildLeather Division of Enger-Kress Co." The caption says: "The building at the left is the Springfield, Ohio, Division of the Enger-Kress Company. The hand bags shown in this catalog are made here."

Now, Springfield, Ohio, was the manufacturing home of several companies that made leather ladies' hand bags of Arts & Crafts era vintage. Springfield City Directories show the Hugo Bosca Company (founded in 1911); the Springfield Leather Company—featuring the Cameo leather products brand (founded in 1904); the Bosca-Reed Company (1922); the Imperial Leather Company (1926); and the GuildLeather Company (1920). Especially curious is that in 1922, the GuildLeather Company Vice President is Otto Hilt. In 1908 he had served as the first technical director for the Cordova Leather Shops of Buffalo, New York.

Enger-Kress favored rather dramatic interpretations of plant material, and pretty much stuck to the steer hide leather in a medium brown color. 6-3/4"w x 6-1/2"h. *Courtesy of Faire Lees.*

Not only that, the GuildLeather Company produced Ladies' hand bags using a shop-mark of a Crusader's Shield with the name Guild-Leather running diagonally across the face of the shield. The ladies' steer hide hand bags carried strong design elements both tooled and embossed, and hand colored. The majority of the early (1914 catalog offerings) billfolds, wallets, card cases, change purses and other unisex articles were quite plain. Widespread use of design elements embossed into the surface didn't occur for these articles until the early 1920s.

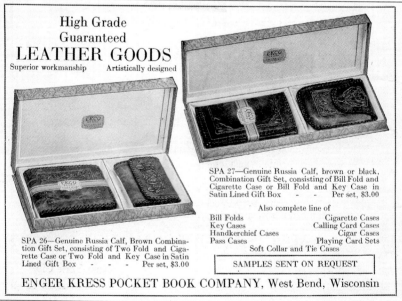
Enger-Kress wallets, key cases and cigarette cases in gift boxes for Christmas from the October, 1926 issue of *Trunks Leather Goods and Umbrellas* magazine. *Courtesy Bag Lady Emporium.*

THE MIDWEST

Amity Leather Products Company, 1915-1950s
West Bend, Wisconsin

Although begun in 1915, at the twilight of the Arts & Crafts era, founder Robert H. Rolfs had cut his teeth in the leather business since 1905. He even served as corporate secretary to the dynamic Enger-Kress Leather Company and quickly grasped the needs of the nation's retailers and their customers. So even though Rolfs had only a one-room factory in West Bend in 1915 he had that "great notion" that mundane leather articles could be turned into fashion accessories.

He quickly convinced his brother Baltus to join him and that he could establish a broad line of leather goods with flair and customer appeal. That, and compelling marketing to retailers, quickly established a buyer's preference for Amity leather goods. Rolfs chose the name Amity for its meaning: Harmony and friendship, and incorporated the company in February, 1916. A year later they opened a New York City showroom. He instilled a measure of pride in the workers to produce a quality product and that, along with smart design and pricing, caught on with major retailers such as Marshall Field, the May Company, Bullocks, etc., as well as rural drug and jewelry stores. The business grew and, since Rolfs had already been instrumental in the development of the efficient Enger-Kress factory, within two years the company had 15 workers.

Amity two-color purse with snap closure, hanging fuchsia design, and "over/under" strap handle. 6-1/4"w by 6-1/2"h. *Courtesy of Jessica Greenway*

Close-up of Amity Fuchsia blossoms & foliage on rare two-color dyed purse. *Courtesy of Jessica Greenway*

Contrasting colored leather strap bisects this fully-laced Amity envelope with flap style handbag from the 1920s. Glove pocket on the backside and telescoping handle adds to its versatility. 10-1/2"w x 6"h. *Courtesy of Faire Lees.*

By 1918 the workforce tripled and Amity was making leather jerkins (vests) lined with wool for the U.S. Army. New designs and products were added and Amity was one of the few that continued to prosper through the depression. A contributing factor was that Amity had designed its modern factory in 1924 and could efficiently produce and offer quality leather goods at prices the consumer considered affordable. Like Elbert Hubbard, Rolfs saw the need to involve the employees in fitness and social activities while at work. The new factory had a recreational room and ball field. Employees were encouraged to join a team or share in the picnics and dances. When the U.S. Government down-sized paper currency (an 18% reduction) Amity was ready with a smaller wallet design known as the "Little Bill," still offered with full-laced edges. Another innovation was the "Findex" billfold of 1928 that had a unique pull-out "drawer" to hold cards and snapshots.

Two colors flank a prominent center daisy pattern with an elaborate gold-washed Jemco steel frame. Marked July 23, 1918. 5-1/2"w x 7"h. *Courtesy of Faire Lees.*

"Exquisitely Design and Tinted by Amity Craftsmen." Amity brochure. Subtly colored with black alongside the laced edge, and a dark olive green on the center panel, the handcrafted design is that of a Dard Hunter or Mackintosh rose at the top. The border/margin is a bending rose stem with thorns pointing inward, and this motif carries over to the two-tone back side. c. 1922. 6"w x 6-3/4"h. *Courtesy of Faire Lees.*

A ROYAL GIFT
AMITY
HANDBAGS

"The Artistry of tooled and hand-laced steer hide bags." Amity brochure. Here's the identical design and sized bag as the "sister" shown in black and dark olive, only with a gun metal frame and smaller turnloc tab, c. 1922. 6"w x 6-3/4"h. *Courtesy of Faire Lees.*

Top of the line Amity hand-worked and hand-laced steer hide bag with a frame of the art deco sunbursts. Subtle two-tone brown on the leather. A large handbag for 1920 at 9"w x 8-1/2"h. *Courtesy of Faire Lees.*

Amity made a dramatic contribution to the West Bend skyline as it again modernized and expanded its factory. In 1929 a seven-story tower of a stepped or zigzag Art Deco appearance was added. It wasn't just for show. The sixth floor of the tower enclosed a huge water tank that supplied the building's fire protection sprinkler system.

Amity was a heavy hitter in trade advertising. Here's its October, 1929 special in *Trunks and Leather Goods* magazine. *Courtesy Bay Lady Emporium.*

Rolfs continued to present new leather designs and was the first to create a billfold for women. Basically, it was a man's wallet that incorporated a tab and snap closure and a coin purse. Such adaptations, backed by national advertising in major home and business magazines, clearly established Amity as the leading billfold manufacturer of the nation.

This Amity three-panel wallet had a wrap-around border design across the full outside with a stylized floral design on the center panel. Goat skin was a smooth and durable material. 3"w x 5"h, opens to 8-1/2" w. *Courtesy of Faire Lees.*

Men's smoking items included non-filter embossed leather cases such as these from Amity, Meeker, and Bosca along with a Brown & Bigelow humidor of 3" dia. X 4"h. Most cigarette cases were 2-1/2"w x 3-1/2"h. The lady's Arden Forest matchbook cover with a daffodil design is 2" x 2". *Courtesy of Faire Lees*

Amity wooden in-store display sign, "If Stamped AMITY It's Leather" and Amity Logo, "Continuation Card Pass and Bill Holder", 12" w. by 5-3/4"h. *Courtesy of Jessica Greenway*

Close-up of Amity logo.
Courtesy of Jessica Greenway

The Rolfs brand of a line of innovative personal leather goods for men and women included unique toiletry sets and was introduced in 1932. In 1934 Amity acquired the LaGarde Handbag Company to create the Rolfs handbag division.

Some credit for Amity's production success was that Rolfs embraced the notion of the "cottage or home-based" business. Much of the production work, especially the lacing, was done in homes around West Bend. An experienced worker, mostly adult women homemakers, but young girls too, could complete the lacing on up to three or four wallets an hour. Their piece work wage was 10-cents per wallet; or 40 cents an hour. Amity trucks would deliver and pickup components to the home. During peak pre-Christmas weeks as many as 400 nearby homes were involved.

Early in World War II, Amity served the U.S. Armed Forces as it produced leather handbags for the women who served as WACS, WAVES, and Nursing Corps. Enger-Kress produced hip and shoulder holsters for the U.S. Navy and U.S. Marine Corps.

We're a long ways from the Arts & Crafts era, but it should be obvious that a company with vision, well-made products, and a caring for its employees could succeed and endure. Robert Rolfs had brothers and sons that learned this in the firm and the Rolfs' family leather business prospered until a leveraged buyout in 1992. The founder Robert Rolfs died unexpectedly in West Bend in 1965 at age 77.

Traveling clothes brushes were popular articles of the era. This assortment includes Amity, Cameo, Cook's and Paragon. Sizes from 2-1/4"w x 5"h; to suitcase model 3"w x 7-1/2"h.
Courtesy of Faire Lees.

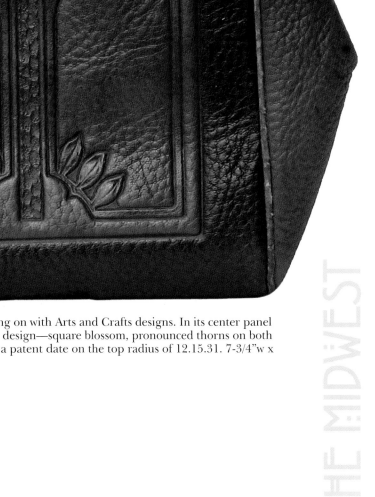

Amity was one of the few companies carrying on with Arts and Crafts designs. In its center panel is the stylized Macintosh\Dard Hunter rose design—square blossom, pronounced thorns on both sides. The copper-plated steel frame bears a patent date on the top radius of 12.15.31. 7-3/4"w x 6-1/2"h. *Courtesy of Faire Lees.*

Mastercraft Leather Goods Company, 1916-1930s
Waukesha, Wisconsin

Another leather company of note in Wisconsin was the Mastercraft Leather Goods Company of Waukesha. This firm continued to produce women's handbags with Arts and Crafts and Art Nouveau designs and hand-produced features into the early 1930s. The March, 1930 trade advertisement in *Luggage and Hand-Bags* magazine reminded retailers: "The assortment of MASTERCRAFT creations come in imported English Steerhide, with edges hand laced with genuine Goatskin. Individually hand colored and tooled design. Fitted with leather coin purse and mirror."

Mastercraft of Waukesha, Wisconsin, combined some hand-enhancing tooling to its embossing, but used hand-lacing to bind the edges. This bears the July 23, 1918 date. 7-1/4"w x 6-1/2"h. *Courtesy of Faire Lees.*

Strong dark color lines seem to confuse, rather than enhance, the central repousse and stippled foliage design of this Mastercraft item, c. 1920. No date on the specialized shaped gold-washed steel frame. 7-3/4"w x 7"h. *Courtesy of Faire Lees.*

Mastercraft creations meet summer's demands. Leather goods that catch the favor of outdoor people—buying for themselves or buying for others. Accessories with individuality in craftsmanship that gives Mastercraft preference. Now's the time to order these *little items that produce big profits*—during the months when you need sales most.

Military Brush Set - $4.00 each
Comb & File Case - $1.25 each

MASTERCRAFT

LEATHER GOODS CO.
WAUKESHA, WIS.

Mastercraft's ad for brush and comb sets with cases in the June, 1929 *Trunks and Leather Goods* magazine. *Courtesy Bag Lady Emporium.*

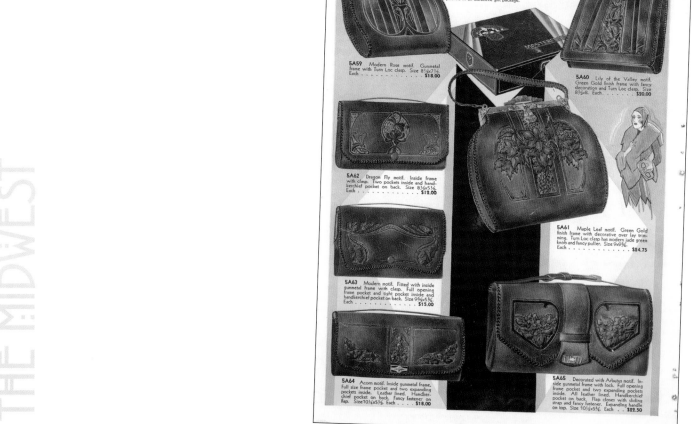

Handbags brochure of
1928-1929. *Courtesy of
Sue Conrad.*

The Handicraft Guild of Minneapolis

These rare photo images of the work of Minneapolis\St. Paul area leather artisans were supplied by the Minnesota Historical Society and the Minnesota Institute of Arts. To learn more about the founding and progress of the Arts & Crafts movement in Minnesota, visit the major work by Marcia G. Anderson, Senior Curator, Minnesota Historical Society. Her essay, *"Art for Life's Sake: The Handicraft Guild of Minneapolis"* shows how the movement was interpreted and led by diversely talented and highly motivated Minnesota women. Her contribution is generously endowed with images of metalwork, pottery and ceramics, jewelry and silversmithing, leatherwork, and textiles that convey a distinctive local inflection. It is part of a major book on Minnesota, *"Art and Life on the Upper Mississippi-1890-1915";* Minnesota 1900, Michael Conforti, Editor; University of Delaware Press, 1994.

As early as the third public exhibition of The Society of Arts and Crafts of Minneapolis, (Jan. 20-24, 1903) the public was rather dazzled by the imaginative leather work assembled. Writing in *The Craftsman* of March, 1903, reporter Katherine Louise Smith marveled at the wide variety of articles presented:

Leatherwork, which is always fascinating to the lover of good craftsmanship, was presented in a number of ways. The warm rich tones of the leather were never better displayed than in the large array of table and piano covers, desk sets, card cases, bags, magazine covers, etc. Work in this material which attracted much attention was that of Charles Frederick Eaton and his associates of Santa Barbara, California whose creations have been exhibited on only one other occasion east of the Mississippi. Mr. Eaton sent chests, boxes and cases, which were marvels of unique construction as well as of beauty. His colors are subdued and all his leather work shows delicacy of treatment and good taste.

Noted Minneapolis leather artisan, Harriet Carmichael, was but 20 when she posed for this image. Photo by Copelin of Chicago. *Courtesy Minnesota Historical Society.*

Carmichael was likely one of the Handicraft Guild's premier leather artisans. The mediums she is reported to have worked in include leather, design, printmaking, and jewelry. This photo, likely c. 1900, shows her at age 35. *Courtesy Minnesota Historical Society.*

Leather and jewelry items made and\or sold at Mary Moulton Cheney's Artcraft Shop; Sign of the Bay Tree, Minneapolis, early 1900s. The versatile Harriet Carmichael likely produced the leather card case and photo album, leather and pierced copper watch fob, as well as the dark green photo album. This measures 8-7/8"w x 5-3/8"h and features the pine cone\spray design typical of the Bay Tree shop. The binding cord is braided leather. The silver and turquoise necklace (possibly by Jessie Preston) was owned by Carmichael who was a partner in the shop with Cheney from 1908 until she moved to Colorado Springs in 1912. *Courtesy Minneapolis Institute of Arts, photographed by Gary Mortensen and Robert Fogt.*

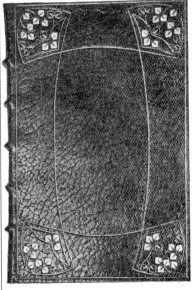

TOOLED LEATHER BOOK BINDING
Designed and executed by Miss Edith Griffith.

Typical book cover artistic leather produced at Handicraft Guild. *Courtesy of the Minnesota Historical Society.*

Although the artistry of Minneapolis and St. Paul is recalled in the pierced, hammered, and acid-etched copper and other metals, pottery and ceramics, there were more than 42 artisans who listed leather work as a prime medium.

Smith described many other fine examples of impressive leatherwork exhibited by artisans outside the Twin Cities area:

> Another notable collection of leatherwork was that of Mrs. Amelia Hyde Center of Chicago. A former member of the Minneapolis society, she still retains an active interest in its welfare. Among the articles sent by this expert crafts woman were two beautiful six-foot tall leather screens; one decorated with an elaborate frieze of carved and embossed leather. Another distinct piece from the same source was a unique leather reredos (a screen or partition) for use behind a mantel. This was embossed in rich peacock blue-green hues in tones as rich as jewels. All Mrs. Center's work shows rare dignity of design, coupled with much sentiment and good execution. Nearly everything that can be made of leather was shown, the exhibitors being members of the Wilro Shop, Kalo Shop, Swastica Shop of Chicago; the Society of Arts and Crafts, Dayton, Ohio, and private individuals."

In only its third public exhibition, the Twin Cities artisans had achieved some remarkable success. Much of it was due to the dedication of a baker's dozen of energetic women who banded together to form the Chalk and Chisel Club on January 5, 1895. It was organized primarily to study design and wood carving and this date established the Twin Cities group as the oldest Arts and Crafts organization in the nation. Surprisingly, the widespread interest by dozens of talented Minnesota women was in art handicraft and this soon led the group to include other crafts mediums.

In 1898, the Chalk and Chisel Club organized Minnesota's first exhibition of Arts and Crafts, Nov. 16-19, in the studio on Hennepin Avenue in Minneapolis. Of the 82 exhibitors, 30 were Minnesota artisans and many presented their leatherwork. "Among the others were the respected talents of Otto Zahn of Memphis (bookbinding and leatherwork); Samuel Bridge Dean, Rookwood Pottery Co., Charles Volkmar, Dedham Pottery, Grueby Faience Co., The Deerfield Society of Blue and White needlework, and Eleanor Klapp, Chicago jeweler." (See Marcia G. Anderson's essay "Art for Life's Sake: The Handicraft Guild of Minneapolis," from *Art and Life on the Upper Mississippi-1890-1915*, University of Delaware Press, 1994.)

The growing community interest in the successes of the Applied Arts led the Chalk and Chisel Club members to reorganize under the name of the Arts and Crafts Society of Minneapolis in November, 1899. The new organization broadened its objectives and admitted associate members who were neither designers nor artisans. As Marcia G. Anderson points out: "This is the first evidence of the pragmatic, populist principles that would shape the Arts and Crafts movement's development in Minnesota, distinguishing it from others in the United States."

The exhibition of 1898 encouraged the core group of society artisans to prepare another public showing of handwork. This second exhibition was held February 5-9, 1901 at the Hennepin Avenue studio and featured work in leather and other traditional disciplines; including for the first time, electric lamps.

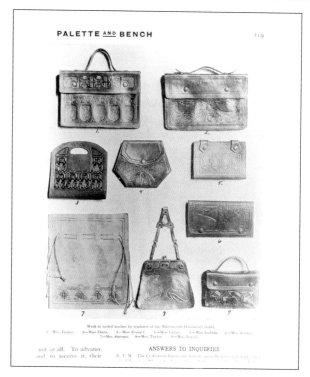

A wide variety of artistic and modeled (some call it tooled) leather articles were produced by young women of the Minneapolis Handicraft Guild. These items were portrayed in the February, 1909 art magazine, *Palette and Bench. Courtesy Minneapolis Institute of Arts.*

One of Chicago's premier jewelry makers, Jessie M. Preston, taught at the Minneapolis School of Fine Arts in 1907 and the Arts and Crafts Guild of St. Paul in 1908. She was known for hammered and pierced metals often combined with semi-precious stones. This showing is from the Minneapolis Society of Fine Arts Bulletin of February, 1907. *Courtesy Minneapolis Institute of Arts.*

The event was covered by Frances R. Sterrett of *House Beautiful* magazine in its April, 1901, issue. Of the limited leather presented she wrote:

> The book-binding and leatherwork were especially attractive. Among the books were several examples from famous old presses and binders, an Elziver, an Aldus, and a Kelmscott, while the modern presses represented by good pieces of work were the Mosher, Philosopher, Roycroft, Vale, Hahn, and Harmon, with bindings by Zoehnsdorf, Tout, Zahn, Riviere, Seymour, and Miss Starr. The leatherwork of Mrs. Amelia Hyde Center was delightful in color and design. A grill of green and brown leather was put together with copper rivets and the curtain of green velour was appliquéd with a conventionalized pattern of leather and copper rivets. Mrs. Center also sent wall coverings, desk fittings, cushions, and magazine covers. Miss Heal had a dictionary cover and Miss Hammer a sermon cover, showing how the rivets may be used to accentuate and enrich a pattern. Other leather-work, all of it strongly modeled in floral patterns was by the Nordhoff bindery, Miss Bulkley, Miss Fenn and Miss Reade.

In late 1904, eleven Minneapolis women founded the Handicraft Guild of Minneapolis and elected Grace Margaret Kiess, a leather artisan, as president. Its mission statement was described in *The Craftsman* of May, 1905:

> The Handicraft Guild came into existence last fall to meet a pressing need for craft classes especially suited to requirements for training teachers of the public schools in handicrafts. There was also a recognized want of such training by others and there was neither salesroom for artistic craft projects nor any means of bringing the work of the local craftsmen to the notice of the buying public. The project of a salesroom in which a stock of articles could be kept and orders taken was heartily approved and furthered by the local Arts and Crafts Society.

Its courses of study in 1905 included design (summer school for elementary and advanced courses) directed by Ernest A. Batchelder of Throop Polytechnic Institute, Pasadena, California. Already renowned as a designer and artist, he returned to direct and teach applied arts theory and practice at the summer schools of 1906 and 1907, and continued his teaching affiliation with the Guild into late 1909. Classes at the 1907 summer session were under the guidance of well-known instructors and besides leatherwork included metalwork, jewelry, pottery, book-binding, woodworking, wood-carving, wood-block printing, and a special course in watercolor painting.

The Handicraft Guild of Minneapolis show room of 1914, loaded with the member's hand-wrought items. *Courtesy of the Minnesota Historical Society.*

In St. Paul there were parallel organizations that evolved to promote the disciplines of fine and applied arts. The St. Paul Institute managed both an Academy/School of Fine Art and a School of Applied Arts. Here, leatherwork remained as an equal discipline alongside metal work, book binding, and jewelry making. The members regularly presented their work at exhibits in major cities across the nation.

Yet, as Marcia G. Anderson lamented: "Few examples remain of guild jewelry, leatherwork, weaving, basket making, wood-block printing and graphic design." (*Art for Life's Sake*, p. 141.) The examples supplied were from the collections of articles and early photographic evidence in the Minnesota Historical Society and include leather work from the St. Paul Institute School of Art, circa 1910.

Some of the illustrious women associates were: Ida Pell Conklin, Jessie Preston, jewelry; Bertha Lum, woodblock design/printing; Nelbert Murphy, Margaret Sheardown, leatherwork; Mary Moulton Cheney, designer, Margaret Cable, pottery; Hilma Berglund, weaving; Elizabeth Chant, painter. Ruth Raymond, artist and designer, (an original "Kalo girl" of Chicago where she produced leather articles in 1904) was the guild's last director (1918). She became Head of the Art Education Department of the University of Minnesota when it absorbed the Guild and its staff and curriculum in 1919 and directed the department until her retirement in 1947.

The leather artisans of this era are gone, but their designs, tools and actual articles may unknowingly reside in the basements and attics of their descendants. Following is a list of leather workers of the Handicraft Guild and the St. Paul Institute that was assembled for *Art for Life's Sake*, p. 177-213. Those who listed their working medium as leather were:

Madge Bartlett, Hilma Berglund, Louise DuBois Berry, Nettie Bryant, May Whitney Buell, Ada M. Burnside, Clara Byholt, Harriet E. Carmichael, Deborah Carter, Mary Moulton Cheney, Stella Frances Cole, Kathryn H. Ellis, Mrs. H.G. Freeman, Grace D. Gerow, Caroline Gilbert, Mary W. Gregory, Jeannette T. Gunckel, Evelyn Harwood, Mabel G. Kaercher, Grace Margaret Kiess, Belle Knuppe, Agnes I. Lodwick, Nora McEwen, June McKinstry, Elizabeth Miller, Evelyn Morrison, Nelbert Murphy, Bertha Nabersberg, Agnes Nelson, Florence Ober, Mrs. R.E. Olds, Helene D. Peck, Ruth Pelton, Catherine Roberts, Margaret Sheardown, Janet Stevens, Louise Tautges, Mrs. A.L.Vrooman, Ethel C. Wheeler, Katherine Whitney, Helen Willard, Florence D. Willets, Ethel O. Williams.

Miscellaneous hammered metal and eleven artistic modeled leather articles were shown by the St. Paul Institute of Art, May, 1910. The photograph album (lower left) was designed with a rectangular painted landscape image. The leather mat of 22+" diameter (lower right) has intertwined peacocks skillfully tooled into the surface. The peacock was a design associated with Ernest Batchelder who taught summer design and composition courses in Minneapolis from 1905-1909. *Courtesy of the Minnesota Historical Society.*

OHIO

The Springfield, Ohio, region had a heritage for being an important leather goods center. The H.V. Bretney tannery, begun in 1830, was the leading harness, shoe, and belting leather producer in the nation by Civil War days. With a major tannery so close, there were numerous harness and industrial equipment makers that called Springfield home. Some adapted to include items for home and personal use.

Not far from Dayton, Springfield became an important modeled/tooled leather products center at the turn of the century. Springfield Leather Products Company began leather work in 1904 and the Cameo line was introduced in 1910. The Hugo Bosca Company would be founded in 1911, the Bosca-Reed Leather Company in 1913, and within 10 years the Guildleather Company and the Imperial Leather Company were established. All made ladies' hand bags and personal leather items for men.

The Hugo Bosca Company, Inc., 1913-Present
1905 West Jefferson Street, Springfield, Ohio

It is rather understood by discerning collectors that a "Bosca Built" branded article has impressive styling and is as well assembled as those of the Cordova Shops of Buffalo. A woman's handbag typically employs the Jemco/Turnloc® closure and steel frame from plain to fanciful designs in a selection of plated finishes. The company was a prolific producer of women's die-embossed design handbags with hand-laced edges and handles. Surprisingly, an internet auction for a pre-World War I handbag occasionally includes the Bosca packaging carton, while most other makers' packaging has been discarded. It is also one of the few companies that offered handbags and accessories in Model-T black!

BNP (Bosca Nelson Pryor) clutch with interior coin purse & attached mirror, detailed landscape design (trees, & water, surrounded by circle of wheat, flowers & leaves, 7"w by 6"h. *Courtesy of Jessica Greenway*

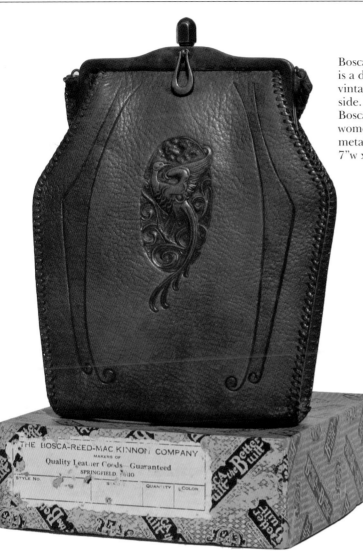

Bosca's hand-tooled version of the Phoenix fowl is a dramatic 3" x 1-3/4" design element on this vintage 1915 handbag. It is repeated on the back side. Located in Springfield, Ohio, the Hugo Bosca Company began production of a line of women's handbags in 1912. Plain Jemco gun metal steel frame with simple turnloc brass tab. 7"w x 8-3/4"h. *Courtesy of Faire Lees.*

Black isn't an ideal color to show off hand-tooling, especially with this nouveau iris design on both sides. Minimally engraved steel and silver plated frame with early ball and socket top closure. Fully laced body and handle. 6-1/2"w x 6"h. *Courtesy of Faire Lees.*

Bosca merged with a number of makers, but always kept the Bosca nameplate going. This purse is branded BNP, for Bosca-Nelson-Pryor, with a dateless frame, saying only "pat. apld for". 6"w x 7"h. *Courtesy of Faire Lees.*

The Williams' Springfield City Directories show that in 1914 and 1915 Columbo Bosca was a foreman in the case making department at the Elwood Myers Company. In 1916 and 1917, Columbo Bosca appeared as foreman in the leather department and Hugo Bosca was a designer. In 1918, Hugo Bosca and George Reed had become the Bosca and Reed Leather Company. Columbo, Hugo's brother, served as a principal, along with Hugo, as partnerships evolved through a series of business transfers. Columbo also served as a production manager and general superintendent of his brother's firm during the Bosca-Reed years. This partnership continued as such until 1923 when it added George MacKinnon and became the Bosca-Reed-MacKinnon Company.

Early in its production, Bosca also favored a flask-shaped unit embracing the Jemco gun metal steel frame. It dates July 23, 1918. Again, Bosca went the extra mile and hand-tooled the design on both sides. 6"w x 7-1/2"h. *Courtesy Faire Lees.*

Here's an especially well-executed job of hand-tooling stylized rose blossoms, foliage and thorny stems in a symmetrically balanced design. The telescoping or sliding handle is needed for this roomy, three compartment model. Beneath the flap is a built-in, 3" x 5" mirror. Fully hand-laced edges and a large pocket on the back. 10-1/4"w x 6-1/4"h. *Courtesy of Faire Lees.*

Both sides of this handbag are profusely hand-cut. The design is contained in a simple steel frame, once plated with gold luster, that bears a 1.25.21 date. 6-3/4"w x 6"h. *Courtesy of Faire Lees*

Bosca Built purse, stunning design of Dragon Fly, surrounded by stylized design with Nasturtium leaves. *Courtesy of Jessica Greenway*

It is notable that Bosca and affiliates was among the few makers that consistently produced women's handbags with strong designs on both sides. These are typically die-embossed mirror images with some hand work, rather than the totally hand-modeled articles produced at Roycroft, Cordova Shops, or H.E. Kaser Art Leather Company of Buffalo.

Touting its quality, Bosca-Reed-Mackinnon made its statement in *Luggage and Handbags* magazine for September, 1925. *Courtesy Bag Lady Emporium.*

"The Line Distinctive"
TAILORED BAGS

VALUE— That is the *Big Word* in merchandise, and it covers all the features that have given "Bosca Built" Bags preferment among shrewd buyers.

Shall we send a Salesman? A Post Card will bring one.

THE BOSCA-REED-MACKINNON COMPANY

Springfield   Ohio

By the late 1920s the firm billed itself as the producer of the largest number of different kinds of leather articles to include all sorts of handbags, purses, pass and card cases, men's billfolds, luggage tags, and key and cigarette cases.

Leather makers regularly embossed club and organization emblems on the backside of cigarette cases. Here's an Elks emblem on a case made by Bosca-Nelson-Pryor. *Courtesy of Faire Lees.*

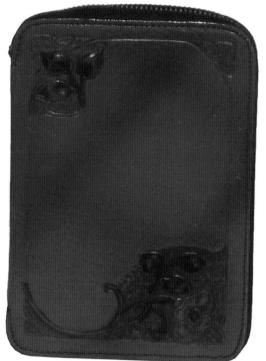

With hand-cut roses at the corners, the steer hide Bosca case contains a well-equipped, traveling personal grooming set of tools. Companion image shows its interior layout. 3-3/4"w x 5-1/4"h. *Courtesy of Faire Lees.*

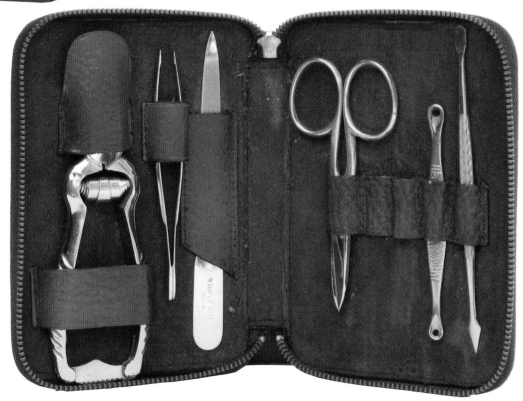

Even the Bosca-Nelson-Pryor petite clutch earned a rose design at its flap corners and a large built-in mirror beneath the flap. Likely from the mid 1920s. 6-1/2"w x 3-3/4"h. *Courtesy of Faire Lees.*

Bosca-Reed-Mackinnon brings the customer into the photo with this November, 1929 ad in *Luggage and Handbags* magazine. *Courtesy Bag Lady Emporium.*

THE MIDWEST

A *Springfield News-Sun* newspaper article of February 16, 1930, listed Hugo Bosca as vice president and general superintendent of the Bosca-Reed-MacKinnon Company. It reported:

> He is a native of Italy and has gathered a number of foreign craftsmen into his organization, including representatives from Switzerland, Germany, Italy and England. The business was founded here in 1913 and first was housed in the old Armory building on W. Main. In 1923 the firm moved to its present quarters at 207 E. Main Street where it occupies two floors. The company employs an average of 135 persons the year round. Present officers are: George Reed, president; Hugo Bosca, vice president and general superintendent and H.W. MacKinnon, secretary-treasurer and general manager.

The firm became the Hugo Bosca Co., Inc., in 1948 and the founder, Hugo, died in 1952 at the age of 65. In 1954, his sons, Mario, president; and Orsino, vice president; built a new factory and headquarters at 1905 W. Jefferson. By this time, Bosca was a nationally known manufacturer of fine leather articles such as billfolds, key cases, pocket secretaries, brief cases, envelopes utility, and sample and catalog cases.

After 90+ years, the firm is still operating and its leather articles are carried by major retailers Lord and Taylor, Nordstrom's, and Macy's.

Close to a harlequin design, the pre-dyed leather received the deep modeling treatment on both sides. The steel gold-washed frame with ball and socket closure sports a date of 1.25.21. Full hand-lacing on all edges. 6"w x 5-1/2"h. *Courtesy of Faire Lees.*

A tight design of rose blossoms and companion foliage is hand-modeled on this Bosca-Nelson-Pryor of Webb City, Missouri, design. 5-3/4"w x 6-3/4"h. *Courtesy of Faire Lees.*

Beneath the irregular edge flap with the unusual presentation of a peacock lies the mark of BNP-Bosca-Nelson-Pryor. Even past the prime of the Arts and Crafts era, the design work on this clutch is skillfully hand-cut and shaded. 8-3/4"w x 5"h. *Courtesy of Faire Lees.*

Springfield Leather Products Company, 1904-1962
226 N. Fountain Avenue, Springfield, Ohio

"It's a CAMEO…"

Inside the purse you may be fortunate enough to recognize the trademark; a cameo head profile of a helmeted Greek warrior and the words "Cameo Quality" beneath the oval. The line of personal leather goods, mostly ladies' hand bags, that was begun in 1904 didn't receive the Cameo trademark until 1910. The firm began production as the leather products division of the Elwood Myers Company of Springfield. Elwood Myers Company made leather advertising specialty items, and was in business around 1900. It made combinations of leather, cloth, paper and metal containers, display cases and signs. It also produced inexpensive "give away" leather advertising specialty, typically presented by banks and insurance companies to their clients. It became the training ground for many leather workers who soon established businesses of their own.

The earliest Cameo image–a floral device–before the classic human profile, facing left. *Courtesy of Faire Lees.*

Close-up of the recognizable Cameo brand, a mark of the Springfield Leather Company, Springfield, Ohio. *Courtesy of Faire Lees.*

When an opportunity arose to acquire the leather goods department, Mr. Robert N. Lupfer, the production manager, and a group of employees bought the operation. They had a good product but they needed an easily remembered name. One evening at dinner, Lupfer noticed the cameo shell pin his wife was wearing. The next morning he presented the idea of the Cameo name to his colleagues. A cameo was a fashion statement of 1910 and would continue to be so into the 1930s.

If bigger is better, this Cameo handbag is terrific. Inside the gun metal steel frame (pat. Oct. 5, 1915) is roomy by today's standards—with two pockets on one side for a mirror and coin purse. Some hand work shows in its embossed fuchsia design and it is fully hand-laced. 10-1/2"w x 6-1/2"h. *Courtesy of Faire Lees.*

Every man's closet needed a tie holder in the 1920s and many commercial leather makers supplied them. Here's a Cameo version with embossed pine cones and needle sprays. The leather is 2"w x 8" l; overall its 5-1/2"w x 9-1/2" l. *Courtesy of Faire Lees.*

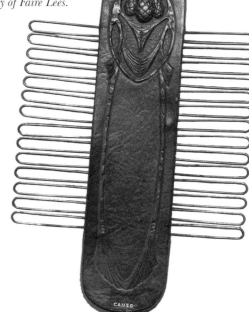

A Cameo petite handbag with deeply modeled tulips and rich brown coloring with suede lining; perfect for Sunday services at 5-3/4"w x 5-3/4"h. *Courtesy of Faire Lees.*

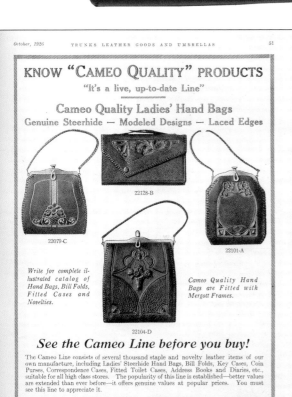
Springfield Leather Company shows the new additions to the Cameo line for the fall, October, 1926 in *Trunks, Leather Goods and Umbrellas. Courtesy of Bag Lady Emporium.*

Although production figures were not available, the Cameo line was broad and articles were produced in large numbers. There were matching ensembles—that is, a hand bag, notebook, key case, diary, etc., with the same design and color. Also, the articles were often produced with a wash of different colored dye over the design giving the appearance of a two-tone leather article. The primary second color was most often a green-mustard or ochre, and the effect was durable. Sometimes a unique design component was dyed black in order to attract attention to the primary design element. For instance, a typical handbag of 7-1/2" height x 7-1/4" width would have a gun metal finish Jemco/Turnloc® frame. The main body was a dark mottled brown. The design element (only on one side) might be a flower vase motif at the bottom with a profusion of foliage extending upward. This area would be given a greenish-yellow dye to enhance the foliage. Often, several 1/4" width design elements would be dyed black in contrast to the dark brown body. The handle was laced and the loop stitch lacing around it and the purse was also dyed black. The lining was dark olive green suede with two pockets to hold a matching mirror and coin purse.

In its early years, Springfield Leather Company marketed leather goods through "dry goods" retailers and department stores. After World War I the Cameo mark began to achieve recognition, for it was fairly heavily advertised in major women's magazines. The line was broadened and became available in luggage, jewelry, and drug stores. Cameo also adapted its styles and "fashion statement" leathers. While the Arts and Crafts era hand bags were available only in Spanish steer or cow hide, beginning in the mid-1920s articles were also made from calf, pigskin, ostrich, alligator, and seal. Articles were also available in fashionable colors other than brown or black.

The company survived the lean years of the great depression and World War II with innovative products. It was the first to make a "stitchless" billfold, a type in which the entire body was made from a single piece of leather. Its French purses incorporated a built-in, snap-lock billfold and it was a leader in producing gift-set combination products—such as a billfold, cigarette case, and leather-wrapped lighter in multiple colors of leather. It regularly added or modified articles in colored leather to keep in step with fashion trends. By 1960 Cameo leather goods were available in 4,000 jewelry, luggage, department, men's wear, and drug stores across the country.

One of the production shortcuts has created an identity problem for today's collectors. The Cameo logo/trademark was loosely imprinted in gold ink on the suede lining. It was not hot stamped as was Cordova Shops, Meeker Made, Justin Leather, Nocona Company, or Volland Leathercraft. As a result, the continued touching of other objects against it caused it to deteriorate. It is rare to find a reasonably clear original mark. Many of these hand bags cannot be positively identified as Cameo and are referred to as a "Meeker type." It appeared that the company later recog-

Cameo Studio Leather promotion of 1927. *Courtesy of Faire Lees*

nized this problem and attempted a quick fix. The hand bag was already assembled so the Cameo gold ink imprint couldn't be re-done in a more permanent manner. It was possible to set up a word in letter press type and many hand bags have the word Cameo stamped into the leather on the underside of the handle.

These moderately priced innovative items allowed the company to continue into the early 1960s when the Cameo line was available in 4,000 jewelry, luggage, men's wear, department, and drug stores.

Cameo Studio Leather promotion of 1927. *Courtesy of Faire Lees.*

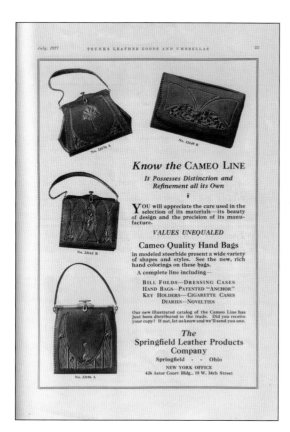

Springfield Leather Company regularly presented its new Cameo designs in the trade magazine, *Trunks, Leather Goods and Umbrellas*, of Philadelphia, PA. This is from July, 1927. *Courtesy Bag Lady Emporium.*

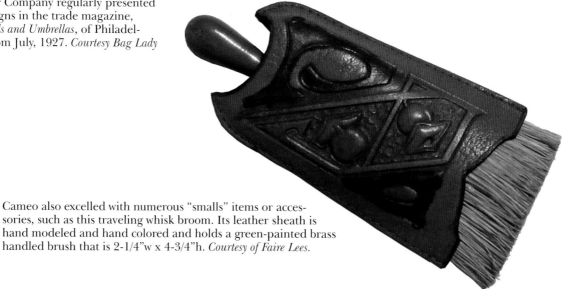

Cameo also excelled with numerous "smalls" items or accessories, such as this traveling whisk broom. Its leather sheath is hand modeled and hand colored and holds a green-painted brass handled brush that is 2-1/4"w x 4-3/4"h. *Courtesy of Faire Lees.*

Guild Leather, 1921 & Imperial Leather Company, 1926
Springfield, Ohio

The GuildLeather Company, makers of "Guild Craft" branded handbags and other personal articles, appeared in 1921 with an Otto Hilt as vice president. This was the same designer who helped found the Cordova Shops of Buffalo in 1908. Another Springfield firm whose handbags and other articles have endured was the Imperial Leather Company. It appeared in 1926.

GuildLeather Company of Springfield, Ohio, branded Imperial handbag from a 1914 design. 8-1/2"w x 8-1/4"h with fuchsia design. *Courtesy of Faire Lees.*

TRUE BEAUTY
AND EXCEPTIONAL VALUE ARE THE FOUNDATIONS UPON WHICH OUR LINE IS BUILT

QUICK SELLING
HAND LACED, TOOLED
LEATHER
GOODS

No. 290

HOLIDAY ITEMS
WRITE FOR
SAMPLES AND
PRICES

No. 291

IMPERIAL LEATHER CRAFTERS

No. 351

The IMPERIAL LEATHER COMPANY
SPRINGFIELD, OHIO
New York Office—Marbridge Bldg., 47 W. 34th Street

Imperial Leather Company draws attention with a small ad in *Luggage and Handbags* magazine in November, 1929. *Courtesy Bag Lady Emporium.*

Forest Craft Guild, 1905-1918
Grand Rapids, Michigan

One of the bright and enduring talents of the Arts and Crafts Movement was Forest Emerson Mann who energized a few talented artisans in Grand Rapids, Michigan, that became the Forest Craft Guild. From 1902 and for the next decade Mann shuttled between Dayton, Ohio, Grand Rapids, and New York City as he taught design fundamentals and produced distinct jewelry.

It is rather amazing that this 22 year-old prolific artisan readily assimilated the theories of Arthur Wesley Dow and other noted designers while at Pratt Institute of Brooklyn. He quickly applied the concepts to his designs for pottery and jewelry. At age 23, in 1902, he had already founded the Miami pottery in Dayton and helped organize the city's Arts and Crafts society. Simultaneously, he was planning a similar school of design organization for Grand Rapids and establishing himself as a leading maker of hand-wrought metal work recognized for its strong kinship to the medieval workshop.

It is not our intent to reassess the dedication of Forest Mann (that kept him active into the 1930s) when this work has already been successfully documented. The work of this entrepreneur has been researched and his, along with other articles of the Forest Craft Guild, beautifully photographed. See it in the originative work: *Grand Rapids Art Metalwork, 1902-1918,* by author Don Marek of Heartwood Antiques in Grand Rapids. A long time scholar of Mann and other similar jewelry makers and metal workers of the early 20th century, Marek also presented a case for the art of Forest Mann in David Rago's early *Arts and Crafts Quarterly Magazine,* November, 1993, Vol VI. No.3, p. 18-21. It has since morphed into *Style 1900.*

We've merely set the table to show you that by 1911, the work of the Forest Craft Guild included some rather distinctive artistic ooze and calf leather hand bags. These were adorned with designs in hammered, acid-etched and pierced metals—copper, brass, German silver—and often set with a semi-precious stone or a unique colored glass cabochon.

Mann was a leading proponent of producing such articles—handbags and pouch purses for women, and watch fobs and other accessories for men. Colored suedes were considered quite fashionable accessories both for purses and cloche head wear for some daring women. Handbag colors were: black, gray, brown, blue, tan, green, purple, lavender, and dark red.

Pierced copper with amber glass embellishment on brown suede strap, and its original branded box! Photo by Don Van Essen, collection of Steve and Mary Ann Voorhees. *Courtesy of Don Marek.*

Ooze leather handbags with silk lining, patinated brass, glass cabochon with braided silk cord. Left: 7-1/4"w x 5"h; Right: 7"w x 4-3/4"h. Photo by Brett Beimers. *Courtesy of Don Marek.*

THE MIDWEST

A 1911 Christmas season advertisement, "Inexpensive Gifts Out of the Ordinary" in the *Grand Rapids Press* (December 15, 1911, p.27), offered three sizeable ooze leather hand bags: velvet calf shopping bags with pierced copper top, set with amethyst or topaz–from $1.25 to $8.00; ooze leather, silk lined shopping and opera bags–from $3.00 to $8.00; and set watch fobs, ooze leather strap–from $1.00 to $2.00.

Although the handbags were not signed, author Marek has documented that it was artisan Jeanette Sears who should be credited with the inspiration to enhance and develop a group of new designs. Raised in Michigan, she began her Forest Craft Guild career in 1909, first doing clerical work and rather quickly advancing into production. The *Grand Rapids City Directory of 1913* lists her as the foreman of the group, now totaling 18 employees. (*Grand Rapids Art Metalwork*, p. 34, 93.) She and Mann were an item for some time, even while he oversaw the retail showroom in New York City. They were married there on Christmas Eve, 1914.

An important Guild explanatory print piece of November, 1913, entitled *A Gift Folio* (courtesy of JMW Gallery, Boston, Massachusetts) reassures the reader that he or she is making a wise buying decision with any item.

The Guild has built up in eight years a splendid following which is now rapidly increasing in every state. The production of the Guild may be found in the better class of art shops, book and stationery stores and craft shops in every city. The ooze leather bags, with special designs in hand-wrought metal ornaments of dull brass, old copper and silver in jeweled effects is an original conception of the Guild workers. All these have met with the enthusiastic approval of all lovers of good things.

The initial page identifies the piece as the "Forest Craft Guild of 333 Fourth Avenue, between 24th and 25th Streets, Formerly Tiffany Studios, New York City." It reminds the reader that: "Here may be seen and examined a great variety of articles, thoughtfully designed and executed to fill the requirements of good taste in jewelry, metalwork, textiles, leather-work, art plaques and pottery." While the main showroom was in New York City, the production of all leather articles, metal work, and items best described as gifts for the home or office took place in Grand Rapids.

Gift folio offerings from November, 1913.
Courtesy of Don Marek.

A gift folio of November, 1913 presented Christmas offerings in jewelry and ooze leather handbags with hammered and pierced top metal designs.
Courtesy of Don Marek.

Gift folio offerings from November, 1913.
Courtesy of Don Marek.

The *Folio* presents a page devoted to "Ooze Leather Hand Bags and Purses, with Metal Fixtures in Copper and Silver." It mentions:

> The Guild Bags are well known. They are executed from our own designs and embellished with hand-wrought ornaments making a combination of metal and leather distinctly characteristic and always in excellent taste.
>
> They may be obtained in the following colors: black, gray, brown, blue tan, green, purple, lavender and dark red. Sample colors sent on request. All bags have silk cords to match the leather.

Of the seven articles presented, one was a palm-sized purse of 4-1/2 x 2-3/4 inches and it sold for one dollar. The largest and most expensive at ten dollars was a 9-3/8w x 9-1/2h inches, of ooze calf with pierced German silver ornaments with a long cord to match the leather, and silk-lined.

However, consumer interest in the articles faded rapidly at the close of World War I, 1918. The Mann's, then in their early 30s, remained in New York City after the dissolution of the Guild in this year. They returned to Grand Rapids in the early 1950s and Mann continued his metal work and taught others the craft.

As Marek notes:

> His creative abilities in jewelry and metalwork alone have earned him a place in the history of the Arts and Crafts Movement. He had a genuine gift for composition, a finely-tuned sense of color, and an energetic, playful spirit. There is a timeless quality to his work that makes it seem fresh and contemporary nearly a century later. Collectors who have encountered this work have invariably derived pleasure from it."

(*Grand Rapids Art Metalwork*, p. 87.)

Ooze leather handbag with a Forest Mann pierced brass design to hold the Venetian enamel cabochon. Matching silk cord handle with brass beads at ends. Often referred to as an opera bag. 8-1/2"w x 7-1/2"h. Photo by David Lubbers. *Courtesy of Don Marek.*

Suede purse with repousse brass hardware at top centering an oval purple bezel-set stone on each side. Original twisted cord handle. 7-1/8"w x 4-3/8"h. *Courtesy of Paul Somerson, Chicagosilver.com*

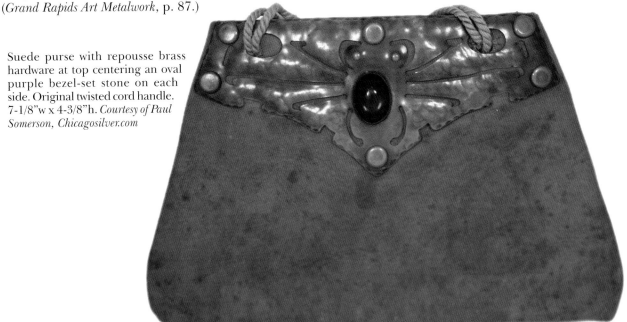

The Meeker Company, 1908-1959
7th & School Streets, Joplin, Missouri

Of all the companies that produced modeled or tooled leather articles in the Arts & Crafts style, Meeker seems to be the most widely known. It is typical for an internet seller who doesn't know leather to refer to an unmarked handbag or bookends as "looks to be like a Meeker." In fact, rarely did an item leave the Meeker factory without the hot stamp brand *"Meeker Made"* on it.

Gunmetal frame with a ball-joint closure dates the production of this Meeker model to 1920-1923. 6-1/2"w x 6"h. *Courtesy of Faire Lees.*

Meeker designed smaller and more compact for the changing fashions of the 1920s. Flap conceals a snap fastener and built in, kiss-lock coin purse. 5"w x 4-1/4"h. *Courtesy of Faire Lees.*

THE MIDWEST

"The company's involvement in personal leather articles dates back to 1908 when the founder, Mr. Cory Meeker, opened his Joplin, Missouri, leather department as a sideline to his regular business of leather specialties advertising," according to Evelyn Haertig's extensive interview in her book, *More Beautiful Purses* (p. 114, Gallery Graphic Press, 1990, Santa Barbara, CA).

Both U.S. and European modeled leather purses and other personal articles were first seen at the St. Louis World's Fair of 1904. Early in 1908, Meeker received an inquiry regarding production of similar leather items from an advertising specialties client, the Stix, Baer and Fuller Department Store of St. Louis. Within a year, Meeker had made contact with the J.E. Mergott Company in New Jersey for a line of metal frames and began to assemble a work force of mostly local women for their first factory at Third and Michigan. The dates of first production of what is thought of as modeled or tooled leather articles vary, but the year 1912 is mentioned by the local newspaper, the *Joplin Globe*, when Meeker shifted into production of purses, billfolds, and other quality leather goods. A typical card included in a purse reassures the owner "Guaranteed Genuine Steerhide—Hand Modeled/Hand Laced—In the Leather Shops of The Meeker Co., Inc., Joplin, Missouri, U.S.A."

Meeker Made purse with exquisitely detailed design of 2 moths feasting on blossoms with etched frame, with original mirror inside, 7 ¼"w by 8"h. *Courtesy of Jessica Greenway*

Meeker letter opener and combination sheath and blotter below it. 2"w x9-1/2"l. Modeled leather handle is 3-3/8" l. *Courtesy of Mary Tanner.*

Meeker half-round modeled coin purse. Fully laced edges on this 3-1/4"w x 2-1/4"h model. *Courtesy of Faire Lees.*

While the modeled leather article production at Roycroft was waning in 1925, and was soon followed by the H.E. Kaser Art Leather Company and the Cordova Shops of Buffalo, Meeker was thriving. It had laid plans for a 33,000 square foot factory in Joplin (it opened in early 1929) and was a consistent advertiser in major consumer magazines of the day, such as *Vogue, Liberty, Harper's Bazaar, Photoplay,* and others, despite the approaching black Friday disaster of 1929. By this time Meeker was turning out a prodigious number of vanities, billfolds, bridge and desk sets, key cases, toilet cases, book covers, bookends, writing sets, and cigarette cases in addition to its mainstay of handbags. Its line was marketed through major department stores.

Meeker featured handbag styling with its July, 1927 trade offering in *Trunks, Leather Goods and Umbrellas* of Philadelphia, PA. *Courtesy Bag Lady Emporium.*

Engraved steel frame carries a "pat. 10-5-15" stamp and no others, and this Meeker sports a silver-plated copper lock-tab, rather than the later brass one. 6-1/4"w x 6-1/2"h. *Courtesy of Faire Lees.*

A Meeker wallet of 1918 was customarily hand-work and laced along its full perimeter. 4-1/4"w x 3-1/2"h, opens to 8-3/4" width. *Courtesy of Faire Lees.*

Meeker reminds the trade of the need for "New and Smaller" currency billfolds since the Federal Reserve shrunk the paper money. *Trunks and Leather Goods* magazine. *Courtesy Bag Lady Emporium.*

A Meeker-made solution for storing a lady's set of handkerchiefs, both at home and when traveling. Silk-lined and internal flaps to secure the items. 6"w x 6-3/4"h. *Courtesy of Faire Lees.*

In spite of the depression year of 1932, Meeker was employing four hundred skilled men and women at their peak seasons. Women outnumbered the men by three to one, especially in the departments of hand coloring, hand lacing, sewing, and assembly. The company even designed and promoted a small leather purse with wrist-strap, known as the "Madge Bellamy" after the moderately popular film actress of the 1920s and into the era of the "talkies." By the way, it is the only producer to warrant the namesake on a handbag.

Still hand-worked, laced and colored, Meeker's wrist-strap mini-handbag made a hit in 1926. A similar bag was advertised in *Trunks and Leather Goods*, October, 1926. Purse *courtesy Faire Lees, advertisement courtesy Bag Lady Emporium.*

The
Most Beautiful Line

from the LARGEST MANUFACTURERS OF STEERHIDE LEATHER GOODS IN THE U. S. A.

Designed and colored to harmonize with every smart shade in the costume mode... appreciated by customers who instinctively select the best.

For the Fall and Holiday Season
New,
hand laced and hand colored genuine steerhide

HAND BAGS   UNDER ARM BAGS
VANITIES   BILL FOLDS
NOVELTIES

We will gladly send samples or representative if requested

MEEKER MADE

to please your trade

The Meeker Company, Inc.
Joplin, Missouri

Largest Manufacturers of Steerhide Leather Goods in the U. S. A.

A Meeker purse that survived with its original colored petunia elements. Its extra-fancy turnloc tab and top of frame opener suggest a date of mid-1920s. 7-3/4"w x 8"h. *Courtesy of Faire Lees.*

A Meeker Made article is far more common than the "big three" (Roycroft, Cordova Shops, or H. E. Kaser Art Leather Company) produced in the Buffalo area. For this reason, it doesn't command the feeding frenzy of collectors willing to chase it into ridiculous high dollars. For instance, on eBay® action, a quality Meeker wallet with a laced edge and in very good condition sells in the $50 range. At nearly the same time a Roycroft wallet of similar style and condition will sell for $300. It is fairly common for a Meeker woman's handbag in fine condition (no broken laces on the body or handle, no missing turnloc tab, and no serious stains on the interior) to sell close to $150. I said "sell" at that range, for many internet dealers have an inflated notion of value and often slap a unrealistic price on a handbag. This may be partly due to information supplied by syndicated antiques/collectibles newspaper columns and guidebooks. Recently, one such response to a writer's question regarding the value of a Meeker leather bag with a pair of hummingbirds on both sides stated, "Meeker bags are very collectible. Yours could sell for $500 or more."

Perhaps there is an underground market for these articles! Our advice is to use eBay® as a sounding board. Go to the category "Men's and Women's Accessories>Handbags, Purses" and keystroke in Meeker, or vintage leather. Watch this category over a few months (or check what has been sold in the past 30 days for either) and see what price Meeker or others, are bringing.

Meeker's custom modeling featured a giant sequoia for the Big Tree Award of the Pacific Mutual Life Insurance Company of California. Two inside flapped compartments, all laced edges. 4-1/4"w x 7"h. *Courtesy of Faire Lees.*

Askew Saddlery Company,
Kansas City, Missouri

By Jim Wear, master leather worker
Laramie, Wyoming

In the days following the Civil War waves of immigrants, many of them farmers, headed for our northern plains states. The federal homestead acts and railroad land promotions set into motion a surge of new settlers moving west of the Mississippi. Some came by train, but the majority was in wagons powered by horses, mules, or oxen. The land and forests were worked with these animals and in the cities they moved goods from place to place. There were close to a million draft horses and mules that required harness; and a few hundred thousand riding horses that needed saddles, bridles and other tack.

That brings us to the early entrepreneurs who recognized this need, including one of the largest leather firms, the Askew Saddlery Company. Harness makers like Askew knew what it took to make a set of harness for draft horses, as well as their lighter cousins, the buggy horses. It would be common for a large wholesale leather goods maker to

employ a hundred or more leather workers. They'd have to, for a set of harness was so complex that it would take a craftsman 12 days to complete an outfit from collar to crupper. The company catalog carried pages of harnesses for horses, mules, and colts, as well as hame strap parts, horse and mule collars, saddles, bridles and tack, and a complete line of saddle leather, trees, and hardware for remote shops that made custom saddles and built harness.

Askew would likely serve end users and remote harness shops in eight bordering states, and their customers would likely extend to the Canadian and Mexican borders and the Rocky Mountains.

It was expected that such an operation would also produce the personal leather articles farmers and shopkeepers needed. Men needed bill books, wallets, collar boxes, belts, and revolver holsters. Women would also use some of these as well as needle and scissor cases, and, as fashion evolved, the sturdy but fashionable leather purses to dress out her "go to meeting" outfit or traveling attire.

The purse page of the Askew Saddlery Company catalog from 1921 with handbag #5565. Among the dozen pages were hand-tooled flap style bags, under arm or clutch styles, referred to as a "hand" purse and "wrist purses" with a sewn leather strap. Askew already had been in business 61 years—since 1860, as a harness maker and saddlery equipment company. *Courtesy of Jim Wear.*

When the Askew catalog #61 was published in 1921, they had been in business for over 80 years. This catalog includes a rather expanded line of leather "novelties," hand-tooled designs on men's bill pockets, check book covers, hip billfolds, coin purses, cigar cases, and music bags. The women's leather purses had designs that matched those of Cordova Shops, Meeker, or Justin in 1921.

The firm makes a point of this to its potential buyers. "Special Notice—Novelties. We are equipped to manufacture for responsible parties, all kinds of leather novelties in quantity orders."

The Kansas City, Missouri, saddle maker, Askew Saddlery Company offered a line of hand-wrought purses from 1918 and into the 1920s. Here's a typical steerhide offering in a Jemco frame, 6"w x 7"h. *Courtesy of Faire Lees.*

THE MIDWEST

The woman's purse #5565 is a hand-tooled floral piece with foliage, 6"w x 7-1/2"h with full laced edges fastened to a Jemco "genuine gun" plain steel frame. Under its snap closure flap was a pocket for a 3"w x 2"h mirror. The suede interior contains a sewn pocket for a card case, change purse, or compact. Another purse showed a rather original hand-tooled design of a pond with cattails done on brown calf. It was 6-1/2"w x 7-1/2"h with two large compartments in the suede interior. It is triple-laced with a fancy snap fastener and listed at $30.45 each—priced about the same as Roycroft and Cordova Shops in 1921, but far above those in the Sears & Roebuck catalog or those of Meeker and Justin.

A popular styled Askew snap-under-flap securing handbag. Hand-tooled oval design, hand-laced edges, brown sueded interior with one pocket. Askew offered a diverse line of hand-tooled leather "novelties" such as bill pocket, bill books, checkbook covers, cigar cases, music bags, hip billfolds, coin purses, card cases, handbags, and women's leather accessories. *Courtesy of Jim Wear.*

J.C. Teitzel, 1875-1916
Fort Riley, Kansas

 Teitzel-Jones, 1916-1950
Wichita, Kansas
Nocona, Texas

Boots & Saddles & Ladies' Purses Too!

Just as modeled leather for fine bookbinding and personal Arts & Crafts era articles were characteristic of German artisans, their shoemaking artistry produced a uniquely American icon—the cowboy boot!

Some authorities credit H.J. Justin of Gainesville, Texas, as the originator of "das boot" (his first boot appeared in 1879). But many German bootmaker "brethren" were cobbling boots for cowboys at the same time. Justin (originally the Prussian spelling was Justan) had a young German competitor up north in Olathe, Kansas, where Charles H. Hyer had a thriving boot business going in 1875. In the same region and decade another young Austrian, Gustav C. Blucher, was credited with making the best custom cowboy boot.

J.C. Teitzel established himself as the premier cavalry officer bootmaker as he positioned his shop in 1875 just outside the main gate of Fort Riley, Kansas, the leading command for the U.S. Army's Cavalry Corps. It makes one wonder if Custer died with Teitzel boots on. Teitzel took on a partner, another cobbler of Ger-

man descent, C.C. Dehner, who made the rounds of the Army forts taking foot measurements and boot orders. Dehner remained at Fort Riley when Teitzel moved to Wichita, Kansas, in 1916. There he paired up with Schuyler Jones, an experienced shoe maker and leather worker. The firm soon expanded into custom cowboy boots and shoes and fancy leather goods—meaning purses and accessories.

Schuyler Jones assumed full ownership of the company in 1930 and continued to make boots for the U.S. military until the horse cavalry was phased out at the close of World War II.

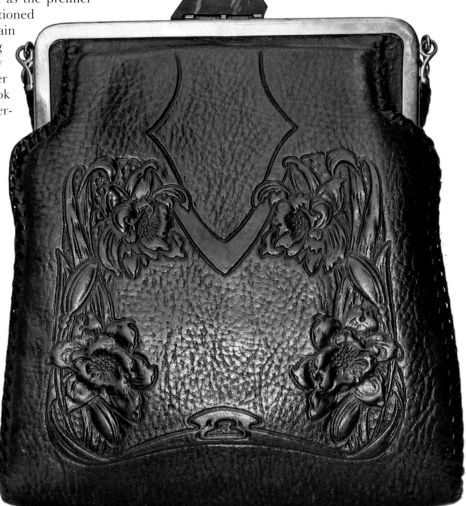

Teitzel-Jones Boot Company of Wichita, Kansas, combined in 1916 and quickly began offering hand-tooled and laced women's purses as an addition to their line of military and cowboy boots. The view with the black tab centered at the frame is the front face, while that without the tab is the back design. The item is branded inside with "Made by Teitzel." 7"w x 7-1/2"h. *Courtesy of Faire Lees.*

Known as the "dancing maiden" by its maker, Teitzel, this was designed to slip over the wrist. The exterior is 3-1/2"width x 6" length, and a 6" handle; and contains a variety of goodies a young woman needs for a quick touch-up in the powder room. *Courtesy of Lori Blaser, co-author of: "A Passion for Purses," published by Schiffer Publishing.*

Here's the same dancing maiden form used on the wrist-strap version, only much embellished and applied to a larger Teitzel handbag of 7"w x 9"h. *Courtesy of Mary Tanner.*

Besides artistic and dirt plain cowboy boots, Teitzel leather workers turned scrap steerhide into hand-tooled handbags. This model has stylized daffodils skillfully modeled across the front. The frame is bronze and plain on this 7"w x 8-1/2"h, pigskin-lined model of 1916. *Courtesy James Davis.*

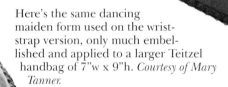

The shop mark brand of the Teitzel Company. *Courtesy of James Davis.*

The handbags, coin purses, and billfolds bear the trademark stamp "Made by Teitzel" and were likely made between 1918 and 1930. Although innovative in style, they don't present the design or craftsmanship of a Roycroft, Cordova, or Meeker branded handbag.

[Note: Much of the information for this story was contributed by James Davis, a collector of vintage cowboy and cowgirl boots; and the publisher of vintagecowboyboots.blogspot.com If you're interested in all things cowboy, give his site a once over to examine his personal collections of boots and maker catalog.]

LOUISIANA

Newcomb College
Founded 1886 as the Sophie Newcomb Memorial College
New Orleans, Louisiana

Long before the Roycrofters, the Cordova Shop and even Gustav's Craftsmen, leather working thrived at Newcomb College in New Orleans. The work also had legs, for it not only outlasted leather production at the respected Arts and Crafts companies of western New York, it extended its artistic stride into the mid-1930s.

As an element of the 1890-91 curriculum of the Newcomb Art School, leather stamping was taught in conjunction with wood carving and clay modeling. Before their own facilities were made available to Newcomb students, any handicraft classes prior to 1895 were offered at 149 Baronne Street. This was known as the Tulane Decorative Art League. Classes were taught by the Woodward brothers and were open to Newcomb College girls and others. Suzanne Ormond and Mary E. Irvine reported in *Louisiana's Art Nouveau, The Crafts of the Newcomb Style* (Pelican Publishing, 1976) that "Newcomb students produced in soft suede desk sets of blotters, inkwells, and covers for cloth penwipers, each of which was hand tooled with the design of the Newcomb style. Leather embroidered silk cases and needle holders were also crafted."

There of course were elaborately modeled and gilded experimental leather articles being produced by Mary Ware Dennett and her sister, Clara, of Boston. The work of master German leather worker, Georg Hulbe of Hamburg, would have been known among allied arts academicians, but the work at Newcomb was ongoing before being embraced by the Art Institute of Chicago or that emerging at SAC Boston exhibitions. It also predated, by a decade, the work of Chicagoan and Art Institute graduate Clara P. Barck and a few of her female colleagues at the turn of the century, as well as the work of Roycroft and Cordova Shops in New York, and even C.F. Eaton and his daughter Elizabeth Eaton Burton, who were producing modeled leather in the late 1890s.

A leading Newcomb College authority, Jean Bragg, The Jean Bragg Gallery, New Orleans, Louisiana, has long collected and sold Newcomb College textiles and pottery. Her 2002 book *The Newcomb Style* (co-authored with Dr. Susan Saward) furnishes a brief insight into leather work and bookbinding along with the other dozen art programs at Newcomb.

As Jean Bragg observed:

> For a regional woman's college to develop and leave such a legacy of marvelous art is a tribute to

the adventurous spirit encouraged by its founding faculty—namely the brothers Woodward, William, the eldest, and Ellsworth.

In its first 10 years, the college only graduated 32 artists, yet over the years many of the graduates return to join the faculty. The Newcomb Art School opened in 1886 with a conventional fine arts curriculum, before the introduction of the applied arts for which it became so famous—china painting and pottery was created in 1895. Both William and Ellsworth Woodward were hired at Newcomb to teach drawing and painting. It was their training as artists, preference of material and style, as well as choice of subject matter, that shaped the students and created the characteristic Newcomb Style.

Hand-tooled and pyrographed pieces. *Left:* green suede needle case with pine cone\needle motif, 3-1/2"w x 6-1/2"h in the manner produced by the Newcomb College women. *Courtesy of Faire Lees. Right:* Silks case designed and executed by Laura West in brown chamois and fastened with leather thong. The Louisiana iris is a classic flower motif used at Newcomb College. 3"w x 9"h. *Courtesy of Lorrie Moore.*

Actual articles or even the visual images of the Newcomb leather legacy are rare, even though much of the work was produced during the 1930s. The work was available at New Orleans department stores, smaller shops, and at annual outdoor fairs. According to Bragg,

> Earlier, around 1917, when the telephone became widespread, a standard wedding gift of the day around New Orleans was a hand tooled cover for the telephone directory. Travel cases for stationery were also a popular gift for the International vacationer. Other popular modeled leather gift sets were travel diaries, luggage tags, watch fobs, desk sets, book marks and book covers. Leather items for the home included bowls and boxes, furniture throws and pillows, screens and wastebaskets. Women's handbags or purses were also popular. As the pottery was marked with a capital N inside a capital C (Newcomb College) so was the leather stamped.

The top view of a woman's petite collapsible, traveling foot rest of five inches height. Handwrought, colored and gilded design of daisies is comparable to the leather work done at Newcomb College in the mid-1920s, even if unsigned. *Courtesy of Faire Lees.*

Two of the best known leather designers and master craftsman designates in multiple disciplines, were Juanita Mauras (1882-1952); and Cynthia Littlejohn, (1884-1959). Mauras was a triple-threat, do-it-all woman, for she excelled in embroidery, leaded glass, silversmithing, jewelry making and metalwork. She signed her work J.M.

Littlejohn also excelled in jewelry making and signed her work with a C. L. or a conjoined version of these initials. Both were graduated in 1906 and Mauras remained on as faculty until 1945. Littlejohn had 15 years of broken service as a faculty member from 1906 to 1920, and as a visiting instructor in the 1930s.

One of their protégés, also known for working leather, but best known for her hammered silver and copper and jewelry, was Rosalie Mildred Roos (1889-1982). She married a New Orleans businessman A.L. Weiner while in her sophomore year and left Newcomb in 1925. She returned as a special student in 1929. Even though she modeled leather, her forte was the production of exceptional hammered silver articles, silver flat wear, and silver and gold with semi-precious stone jewelry. She maintained this award-winning career path at Newcomb into 1935.

While the art form of modeled leather had all but vanished at the well known Arts and Crafts companies (and most allied arts college curriculum too) in the mid-1930s, it was flourishing at Newcomb. According to Bragg, "Both Mauras and Littlejohn were particularly active in this craft. In the 1930s they studied modeled leather work at Columbia University in the summer." At this time, Mauras would have been in her early 50s, while Littlejohn would be approaching 50.

At a Works Progress Administration Arts & Crafts Exhibition, held in 1933-34 at the Isaac Delgado Museum of Art, New Orleans, Mauras and Littlejohn presented leather articles using this new technique of modeling in high relief—or repousse. Mauras made large desk blotters, envelope cases, and purses into the mid-1930s.

Attributed by Jean Bragg to Newcomb College, this dark brown purse has an 18 carat gold cartouche monogram. 7"w x 9"h, moiré silk-lined. *Courtesy of Faire Lees.*

Justin Leather Goods Company, 1919-1955
Nocona & Fort Worth, Texas

It seems that a combination of frugality, ingenuity, and a 10-foot tall pile of scrap leather were enough of a reason to establish a group to make leather articles. It was enough of a reason for Elbert Hubbard and the Roycrofters and they set the standard for quality modeled leather goods in America. A decade later and a thousand miles southwest, a similar dilemma was being faced by H. J. Justin & Sons, the cowboy boot maker of Nocona, Texas.

They were loaded with leather scrap from boot-making and the saving habits encouraged during World War I. Up until the war they just burned the scrap, but an idea was born. Coin purses weren't new, all the mail order catalogs showed them, so the need must have been great. The Justins made up coin purse samples and presented them to banks across Texas. The test venture was surprisingly well-received and orders poured in. The banks distributed them to their customers imprinted with the bank's name. That was in late 1918. Within a year Justin's experienced boot makers, who were accustomed to the precision cutting, tooling, sewing, and lacing of fine leather, were producing handbags.

Their first wholesale catalog of 1919 presented 34 different designed hand bags in pouch, broken flap, and underarm styles. It is likely the designer "went to school" on designs produced by Bosca, Cordova Shops, and even Roycroft. Many offerings used the nicely styled Jemco decorated frames in brass or steel with gun metal, silver, or gold plating. It would have been natural for the Jemco frame sales representative to "sell up" their better styles of frames to Justin. Then too, Jemco was in a position to explain (based on their history with other leather hand bag makers) how their frames would compliment Justin's principally art nouveau modeled designs.

The celebrated Justin cowboy boot had an established reputation with both retailers and loyal cowboy customers. It was continually enhanced by the voluntary testimonials of Justin-booted celebrities Tom Mix, Roy Rogers, Gene Autry, Will Rogers and the head of the Texas Rangers, Tom R. Hickman. Nocona could easily lay claim to the cowboy boot capital of the world for Justin turned out a pair of boots every 10-12 minutes, over nine thousand pair in 1922.

Justin had success with the flask-shaped handbag. Here's a gun metal steel frame system that augments the cascade of blossoms in the design. This hand-laced beauty was still shown in the Justin Leather Goods catalog of 1928. 6-1/4"w x 6-1/4"h. *Courtesy of Faire Lees.*

Deep modeling on the laced pocket, this simple style with a plain steel frame appeared in Justin's 1919 catalog. 6"w x 8"h. *Courtesy of Faire Lees.*

Justin's reputation for quality helped its leather hand bag sales. While Roycroft marketed to the finer department stores and Cordova targeted the quality gift and jewelry stores, Justin promoted its leather goods through dry goods retailers that carried the Justin boot line. There was built-in acceptance by farm and ranch women for a sturdy but stylish and economically priced leather handbag.

In a swirl of foliage, a humming bird approaches a blossom. The clunky turnloc button tab design covers up much of the delicate leatherwork of its wing. A pleasing Justin design and shape nevertheless. 6"w x 7-1/2"h. *Courtesy of Faire Lees.*

Carefully crafted roses surround an oval eye-trap for a monogram on the hand-laced irregular flap. It conceals a pocket for makeup. Rose appliquéd metal pieces across the gold tone frame. 6-1/4"w x 7-1/2"h. *Courtesy of Faire Lees.*

In 1925, the Leather Goods operation moved into the factory vacated by the boot manufacturing company. The boot company had been restructured as a corporation (with the same name) and had relocated to Fort Worth, ninety miles south of Nocona. The Leather Goods organization grew to 80 to 100 workers and now supplied nearly one thousand handbags weekly. It also expanded the product line to include men's billfolds and key cases.

Fancy sunburst and diamond pattern frame give this petite model a touch of class. 5-3/4"w x 5-3/4"h. *Courtesy of Faire Lees.*

By the mid-1930s, the era of Justin's experience with Arts and Crafts styled handbags was over. Even with labor and leather shortages of World War II, the company developed new designs enhanced with smooth, colored leather. In 1955, the leather goods company was sold to the parent H.J. Justin & Sons organization and later closed.

Belying its Jemco July 23, 1918, fancy gold-tone frame and Bakelite tower, this Justin would appear to be from the 1930s. Leather is a two-tone harlequin diamond design. Large fixed inside coin purse. 8"w x 6-1/2"h. *Courtesy of Faire Lees.*

Two-toned leather on this Justin design employs art nouveau design elements. Gold-washed steel frame is embellished with green highlights around the appliquéd blossom devices and turnloc tab. Laced handle is concealed\fastened on the back for cleaner styling. 7-1/4"w x 5-1/2"h. *Courtesy of Faire Lees.*

It's fairly easy to identify a Justin leather handbag of the Arts & Crafts era. They proudly slapped a hot-stamp brand on the sueded interior beginning with a capital J—one-half inch tall. The mark reads: Justin Leather Goods.

Justin's memorable brand with the big J: Justin Leather Goods appears in several sizes. *Courtesy of Faire Lees.*

Nocona Leather Goods Company
Nocona, Texas

It appears that Nocona artistic handbags bearing a July 23, 1918, patent date on the Jemco frame may have been produced several years later. The search to verify pre-1918 production of handbags bearing the Nocona trademark phrase "Nocona Bags—No Better Made" keeps returning to the benchmark date—1926.

The evidence compiled in a 1989 history: *"Stories of Montague County, Texas—Its Past and Present"* shows the Nocona Leather Goods Company was formed August 25, 1926. Capitalized at $30,000, it had a board of directors and a manufacturing location in the old Masonic Lodge on Clay Street in downtown Nocona.

One would think that being the second firm with such an idea in such a small place, in less than a decade, wouldn't necessarily be successful. Only a few years earlier, 1919, the Justin Boot Company of Nocona began a successful new venture to use its left-over scrap leather from producing hand-made cowboy boots. The Nocona investors likely saw that their new leather company could achieve similar success.

In its articles of incorporation, Nocona Leather Goods had purchased the J.C. Teitzel Leather Goods of Wichita, Kansas and moved its equipment and stock to Nocona. The Teitzel Company, like the Justin Boot Company, was renowned as a maker of high-quality cowboy boots. Quite possibly, the handbag frames with the July 23, 1918 date were among the inventory/assets acquired by Nocona and used to assemble its new line of handbags.

Early Nocona handbags featured simple gun metal steel frames—often with the ball-socket locking device. Cut into the steerhide, a swallowtail butterfly flits against a starry background. An early flask-shape of 5-1/2"w x 6-1/2"h. *Courtesy of Faire Lees.*

After 1918 Nocona branded its articles in a script: "Nocona Bags—No Better Made." *Courtesy of Faire Lees.*

Then too, it is possible the J.E. Mergott Company of Newark, New Jersey, the nation's leading handbag frame maker, supplied the newly formed company with frames that carried the 1918 date.

An embossed fuchsia design on steerhide still required hand lacing and hand coloring. This model #9016 carried a note from its young bride: "Tommie bought this bag for me on our wedding trip—1925." It also has the original guarantee of the Nocona Leather Goods Company of Nocona, Texas. 8"w x 8"h with a concealed interior genuine gun steel frame. *Courtesy of Faire Lees.*

The irregular shape allows a wide opening making it easier to reach the bottom. The fancy frame with a hand-cut design suggests a later year and this model turned up in the Nocona 1929 catalog. 7"w x 6-1/2"h in brown steerhide. *Courtesy of Faire Lees.*

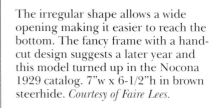

Even when the Justin brothers relocated the Boot Company to Ft. Worth in 1925, their sister, Enid, refused to make the jump. She stayed in Nocona and founded her own venture, the Nocona Boot Company. The point is, there was a lot of steerhide and experienced leather workers at the ready for the Nocona Leather Goods Company. In a surprisingly short time there was a move to a larger factory to handle increased business. The company's 1928-1929 catalog featured 41 different style purses; seven billfolds, brush and comb sets, cigar and cigarette cases, coin purses, key cases and letter cases.

Then came the depression of 1930. Fortunately, the company reorganized along the idea to expand its leather producing capability to athletic equipment; that is baseball, softball, and boxing gloves, football helmets and accessories, and all the inflatable sports balls popular in the nation. The bright idea originated with R. E. "Bob" Storey, a Rice college baseball player and the son-in-law of the firm's banker-president, Cadmus S. McCall. The move to produce quality gloves and be accepted among the leaders of athletic equipment industry such as Wilson, Rawlings and Spaulding saved the company. From that day it has prospered and remained in the Storey family for more than three generations.

The last Nocona billfolds and purses were produced in 1945. The Storey's added "dba" Nocona Athletic Goods Company to its original firm name in 1973. It is the last American firm standing to still hand-make softball and baseball gloves for both amateur and professional players.

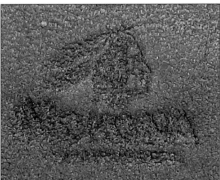

The later Nocona trademark of an Indian profile with the name spelled Nokona, after the north Texas chief of the region. *Courtesy of Faire Lees.*

The irregular hand-laced front pocket is a nice design touch, holding gloves without having to open the handbag. The heavy steel frame has a tab enhanced with a grape & ivy design and was silverplated. 9"w x 7"h. *Courtesy of Faire Lees.*

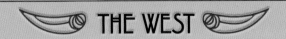
CALIFORNIA

Among the reasons it is difficult to validate if an artist was once a leather artisan is that the major reference sources have ignored this aspect of his or her career. Of the following biographies of artists who were known for leather work early in their careers, the 2002 Edan M. Hughes *Artists in California: 1786-1940* mentions the word "leather" in only two cases. *Davenport's Art Reference of 2004* didn't mention the medium at all. Chris Petty's *Dictionary of Women Artists Born Before 1900*, did refer to Elizabeth Eaton Burton, Santa Barbara, as an "American painter and crafts worker working in leather, appliqué, creating decorative pieces using peacock feathers, shells, etc." (p.10)

At best, when an individual had artistic skills other than the fine arts of painting, etching, sculpture, etc., the description most used is the catch-all work of "craftsman." Regularly, the dramatic and artistic leather legacy of Mary Ware Dennett, of Boston, or Frederick C. Eaton and Elizabeth Eaton Burton, of Santa Barbara, is omitted in art references. It is as though the creation of artistic leather should be considered as a youth camp summer's diversion by these art world authorities. In reality, the creative artistry with the medium of leather was a studied and well-developed passion equal to any trained painter.

Perhaps the reluctance to recognize the modeling of leather—mostly by women—was a carry-over of the discrimination that many female painters, sculptors, other fine artists, and architects long endured from male critics and reviewers.

Even as the 20th century began, the art form was among the favorites of European royalty. Emperors, nobles and bishops (and their royal interior designers) were enthralled over the modeled, gilded, and sometimes jeweled leather that covered their thrones, chests, books and walls. American leather artisans mentioned earlier, as well as Californian partners Charles F. Ingerson and George A. Dennison of Los Gatos, received commissions for contemporary thrones, chests, family crests, coats of arms for the financial kings of America and their imitators.

It would appear, especially for the artistically gifted who caught the California fever, that they recognized the diminishing collectability of their leather artistry. They were designers with the capability to move into the fine arts and other design careers. Quite a number married artists, painters and adapted to a new medium. They were remembered only by the medium they last touched in their final tribute news stories.

The following is a compendium of some of those artisans who achieved prominence as part of the Arts and Crafts movement in California.

D'Arcy Gaw / Dirk Van Erp
Hammered Copper & Tooled Leather

One of the few examples of leather modeling by Darcy Gaw is the paneling on these hammered copper bookends when she was associated with the Dirk Van Erp Shop of San Francisco in 1911. Gaw was a 1900 graduate of the Art Institute of Chicago and maintained a design studio there before moving to San Francisco. *Courtesy Voorhees Craftsman.*

An early champion of things Arts & Crafts, especially those of California artisans, was Paul Elder of San Francisco. Besides being an important Arts & Crafts press and a publisher of social criticism, Elder promoted those he deemed to be important contributors and interpreters of the movement. His retail operation traditionally offered paintings and other decorative items for sale, and this included furniture, hammered metals, pottery, china, art glass, jewelry and artistic leather.

In his catalog of 1906 (not long after the great fire of April, 1905) he offered some strong praise for the leather articles produced by some local women. About the new offerings of Lillian O'Hara and Grace Livermore, who had elected to market their work through his studio he mused: "This work is most unusual and distinctive. Upon soft leather in green and brown tones, oriental brocades are inlaid, thus producing a decidedly effective blending of harmonious colors. Their regular offerings include a variety of useful and beautiful objects, such as desk sets of five pieces, purses, bags, bride books and photograph albums, bag covers, card cases and portfolios."

Artistic leather offerings of 1906 in the Paul Elder Bookshop Catalog. *Courtesy of Bruce Smith.*

Anna C. Crane's forte was in modeled leather bookcovers and desktop accessories. *Courtesy of Bruce Smith.*

Carnation Writing Pad, from Desk Set.

Artistic leather produced by Anna Crane for Paul Elder
Bookstore, 1906. *Courtesy of Bruce Smith*.

Tulip Book Rack. Price, $7.50.

Artistic leather produced by Anna Crane for Paul Elder Bookstore, 1906. *Courtesy of Bruce Smith*.

Original designs in leather work by Mrs. Dixon.

Artistic leather produced by Lillian Tobey-Dixon (not Anna Crane) for Paul Elder bookstore, 1906. *Courtesy of Bruce Smith*.

He especially admired the design and its execution produced by Miss Lillian W. Tobey (who soon became the wife of artist Maynard Dixon). He cites her work in the 1906 catalog: "Now president of the San Francisco Guild of Arts and Crafts, she has been developing her art of embossed leather work, based upon Old German and Viennese influence, attaining results of marked distinction. The designs in all cases are original, and combined with her individual craft of hand-dyeing and polishing, produce original and beautiful effects. Besides the many small pieces represented elsewhere, Miss Tobey's work includes many large pieces—screens, cushions, table covers and impressive desk sets."

Workers in Leather

Original designs in leather work by Mrs. Dixon.

Lillian W. Dixon

To those who know aught of the German or Austrian craftsmanship of the last two centuries it will be no surprise to see the humble calfskin with which we are shod transformed into objects of useful and artistic beauty; nor that we have in San Francisco a craftswoman who has grasped the possibilities of this material as a *texture*, worthy of a high order of design and finish. The originality of design, the skill of execution, the beauty and refinement of coloring, and the fine but durable quality of surface finish which Mrs. Dixon has attained in her work may well surprise many who have not heretofore been familiar with it as the work of Miss Lillian W. Tobey. In following her ambition to make this medium express all it is worthy and capable of, Mrs. Dixon has gained a recognition for her original work in leather that is accorded it by all whose taste and culture enable them to appreciate the true value of being surrounded by objects of use and beauty.

*Chair with leather work	$ 15.00	Desk portfolio, with copper	$ 20.00
*Fire screen	25.00	Desk portfolio, with brass	12.50
*Fire screen, three leaves	150.00	Ink bottles	1.50
*Box	8.00	Ink bottle and tray	3.00
Magazine covers	8.00 to 10.00	Wallet	6.00
Kodak book	10.00	Music rolls	10.00
Scrap book, with copper	20.00	Small blotters	2.00
Clippings book	15.00	Belts	3.00
Memorandum books, large size	3.00	Purses	7.00 to 15.00
Memorandum books, small size	2.00	Shopping bag with old coins	12.50
Note books, indexed	3.00	Cushions — brown, green, red and	
Tablet covers	5.00	green	15.00 to 20.00
Desk set, six pieces, poppy design	15.00	Telephone pad	7.00
Desk set, six pieces, bluebell design	15.00	Book rack	8.00

*Woodwork from the craftsman shop of F. H. Meyer.

[23]

Lillian W. Tobey was an accomplished leather artisan at the time she married renowned painter Maynard Dixon. *Courtesy of Bruce Smith.*

Isabel More Austin
b. Copley, Ohio, Dec. 9, 1863
d. Santa Barbara, California, July 9, 1941,

Lifelong Santa Barbara leather artisan and wife of artist Charles P. Austin. Educated at Mills College, Oakland and later acclaimed for her landscapes and still life in oil and watercolor. (Edan Hughes, *"Artists in California, 1786-1940"*, Santa Barbara News Press, July 11, 1941 p. 18.)

Elizabeth Eaton Burton

b. Paris, France, 1869,
d Santa Barbara, California, Nov. 15, 1937

Quite possibly Elizabeth Eaton Burton was America's renaissance woman—an artisan who mastered every medium she touched. Yet, only a few of the most devout Arts & Crafts scholars and collectors have an understanding of her broad artistic contributions. Perhaps best known for her hand-wrought, repousse and cutout copper and sea shell electric lamps and sconces (early 1900s) she won the admiration of Gustav Stickley and L.C. Tiffany with her imaginative leathercraft.

Here's what Gustav Stickley had to say about her 3-panel leather screen "The Redwood Forest" (*The Craftsman* "Nature and Art in California," Vol. 6, #4, p. 390, July, 1904):

The leather is colored as desired, cut and "applied" by sewing. The materials used were, besides the wood, leathers of various admirable tones and the Philippine window shell, which gives an opalescent effect softer than that of jeweled glass. The wood was carved into the semblance of tree-trunks, burned and stained; so reproducing the appearance of the bark by broad and general suggestions in which there was no touch of the feminine or the trivial, while the soft lights and tints of the sky were rendered in leather and pigments. Before this exquisite work of art I lingered long and in deep thought. It was a small object made by the human hand, and I was fresh from the contemplation of the mighty, overpowering works of nature. Yet for that reason the picture did not condense into insignificance. And the idea of a great forest was here visibly represented to me, without confusing details and in strong, sensuous terms.

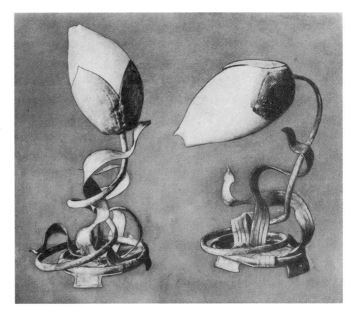

Reminiscent of Sci-Fi flix, these "electroliers" as Burton called them in 1902, were just a few of the fanciful lighting fixtures she created with brass and sea shells off the Santa Barbara beaches. *Courtesy of Craftsman Farms.*

Burton called this the "Redwood Forest," a large compilation of colored, burned and painted leather that awed Gustav Stickley when he saw it in 1904. *Courtesy of Craftsman Farms.*

Stickley had been urged to go and see the new work for himself by his *Craftsman* scribe Arthur Inkersley who wrote in *The Craftsman*, vol. 6, #1, April, 1904:

Mrs. Burton of Santa Barbara, much of whose work has for some years been sold in New York, combines pyrography with tinted and appliqué leather. She uses calf and sheep skins, but does the piercing necessary in large panels and screens so neatly, that it almost defies detection. Several of Mrs. Burton's designs are quite daring, as, for example, a border of purple grapes and pome-granates on a yellow sheepskin. The flowers in her work are applied with fine machine stitching, and are then tinted or etched with the hot iron to heighten the effect.

There were equally as complimentary features about her breakthrough artistic leather in *Vogue Magazine*, titled "Decorative Possibilities of Leatherwork" (January, 1901, Vol. 17, #421, p. 43 & 47), and *House and Garden*, May, 1903. Although her work in these magazines is shown only in black and white photography, the writers have diligently described the intricate patterns and numerous color shades.

Burton's elegantly colorful leather was shown in *Vogue Magazine* titled *Decorative Possibilities of Leatherwork* in January, 1901. *Courtesy New York Public Library.*

HANDSOME DESIGNS IN LEATHER
BY MRS. ELIZABETH BURTON
SEE TEXT—DECORATIVE POSSIBILITIES OF LEATHER WORK

43

One typical image and description of the 10 items shown is presented in order to acquaint you with what was considered the art leather technique of the new century. The *Vogue* reporter presents her impression:

From among the many designs of sofa cushions, all equally beautiful, it is hard to choose two representative pillows; but for beauty of design, the one at the top can hardly be excelled, while for beauty of material and execution the oblong cushion in the middle is unique. The latter is of pale fawn suede, in effect like panne velvet. The tulips are of pale yellow kid, superimposed, that is, dyed leather is cut out and appliquéd. The leaves are in various shades of green over lapping. A shaded background of burnt leather throws the whole design into bold relief while the flowers and leaves are modeled with the "paint" into almost lifelike beauty.

These are hard to find (you can order a photocopy from the New York Public Library Express archives) but there is one lengthy feature within reach. That is a scholarly examination of the artist and her work by Victoria Rodriguez Thiessen in *Antiques, The Magazine*, p. 96-103, April, 2002.

Burton's leather style regularly included colored, modeled, and burned layers of leather. This decorative panel, approx. 12"w x 16"h, was likely destined for a panel in a room screen. It appeared in *Antiques, The Magazine*, p. 99,April, 2002. *Image through the. Courtesy of Cathers and Dembrosky.*

The author begins:

Stickley, Roycroft, Grueby. These are the names typically associated with the arts and crafts movement. Few women are remembered and recognized for their contributions. Yet Elizabeth Eaton Burton typified the Arts and Crafts movement of southern California, using simple and local materials, emphasizing hand-craftsmanship and expounding on local traditions.

Besides Stickley, other artists and critics admired her prolific leather and metalwork. As she matured her career moved into other artistic fields, including painting, photography, block printmaking, as well as writing for the theatre and theatrical criticism.

From early childhood she was imprinted with the "head, heart and hand" influence of her artistic father, Charles Frederick Eaton. Although best known as a Californian, Mrs. Burton was born in Paris while both her father and mother, Helen Justice Mitchell, were young Sorbonne painters. She grew up tutored in the artistic life of Paris, the cote d' Azur of southern France, Germany and England. As her mother's respiratory health worsened, Charles decided that the Santa Barbara climate would encourage a recovery. In 1886 he had already visited the area, and now purchased a large tract of hillside on the edge of a village (it is now covered over by Montecito) where he established a horticultural estate and grand home. He was a skilled arts and crafts designer and produced handmade leather bound books, articles in tooled leather, and metal wares such as lamps and chafing dish screens (used to shield the burner flame from extinguishing drafts). These often incorporated shells as an important design element. Eaton was also a master furniture maker, horticulturist, antiques collector, and proponent of using local materials to create a style often referred to as California regionalism.

Again, colored, burned, and painted-on leather pieces made up dramatic perches for two peacocks. No dimensions given on this tall screen in 1904, but it is likely close to 60"w x 72"h. *Courtesy of Craftsman Farms.*

Burton painted and shaded by burning much of her leather art. From 1904, here is a tall screen with almost pre-Raphaelite depiction titled, "garden, chase and sea". *Courtesy Craftsman Farms.*

Elizabeth Eaton (later Burton) was only 17 when she began handcrafting leather, copper, and brass and combining marine shells into artistic articles. These were notably lamps illuminated by Edison's new invention, the incandescent light bulb. Except for estates of wealthy Easterners, Santa Barbara was still an unsettled community. Remember, it was only 40 years earlier that California had been ceded to the U.S. by the Mexican government. Nearby were large cattle ranches with the need for vaqueros, cowboy tack, saddles, bridles, chaps, and many other leather articles, many of which was artistically tooled. The carved and stamped processes were known as Mexican art leather.

It was an established Mexican industry in California from north of Santa Barbara and the Los Angeles region. Long before Elbert Hubbard developed the Roycroft Leather Department (1905), California-born Mexican leather workers were turning out art portfolios, collar boxes, cuff link boxes, satchels, music roles, purses, cigar cases, and dozens of household objects fashioned from hand-worked leather.

With such a flurry of leather working in Santa Barbara, it is reasonable to imagine that young Elizabeth observed the leather craftsman at work on the cowboy tack, gifts for visitors, and, notably, the tooled leather jewelry caskets and chests. She took up the challenge and began to produce tooled leather chests of a medieval nature decorated with brass nails and enameled designs, very similar to her father's interpretations.

She found a mate in William Waples Burton and they were married in 1893 when she was 24. Not much is written about William W. Burton, only that they had a son Phil-ip,1893-1974; and a daughter Helen, 1897-1986, and that he died in 1930. There is no mention that he too produced any artistic articles. Elizabeth Burton did maintain a diary/journal replete with drawings and photographs. According to the Thiessen article, the original is in the possession of Mary Burton Fussell and a copy of it is in the special collections of the Amon Carter Library in Ft. Worth, Texas.

Even with a daughter to nurse, Ms. Burton's output expanded to include leather cushions, panels, friezes, hangings, and all manner of leather decorations. In 1900 she applied for a patent for a "certain new and useful improvement in Ornamental Leather Work" claiming an improved method of producing shades of color and gradation and combination of shades, as well as for "producing the effect of low relief in ornamental leather work." Although at first her claim was refused, she was granted the patent in 1905, Patent number 788,092, United States Patent Office, Washington, D.C. This is the year she was juried into membership in the "Society of Arts and Crafts of Boston," listed as a metal worker.

Although a bit enthusiastic, a feature interview in the *Santa Barbara Morning Press*, June 30, 1910, describes this new patentable process.

Much of her work is of a style seldom if ever seen. The appliqué work, consisting of designs in leather embellished with shells, appliquéd on the leather or velours or silk of the hanging or panel or screen was evolved from her 'inner consciousness' as it were over 12 years ago. Beginning with flowers, adapted from the tropical vegetation of

Night prowling, large hunter cats were regular subjects portrayed in colored, burned, and built-up or appliquéd leather pieces. Stickley noted this and other images when he visited her Montecito, California, studio in 1904. *Courtesy of Craftsman Farms.*

California, she branched out into bold and original designs with sweeping lines and wonderful color combinations secured by means of texture, shells, metal, semi precious stones, even fish scales, tinted to blend with the color scheme employed. It is doubtful if anyone in this country is doing quite the same work. But in the leather screen this artist is, perhaps, seen at her best. Here the material employed is white ooze, decorated in water color and by burning, for the attainment of a mottled effect of singular beauty. The leather is colored as desired, cut, and "applied" by sewing. Layers of this material are thus couched, one on the other, until they oftentimes reach twelve in number; certain parts of the edges being left exposed, if necessary to the desired effect and other cunning devices used to secure contrast which is the decorator's substitute for perspective.

Praise such as this was commonplace, for Burton's output was prodigious. She and her father Charles both exhibited in the "Allied Arts" class in the 1904 Louisiana Purchase Exposition in Saint Louis. She sent a leather chest decorated with silver leaf and bound with iron (valued for sale at fifty dollars), two leather and shell table mats (one for twenty dollars, the other for thirteen dollars), plus several hammered copper and brass electrolier lamps with shell enhancements. She wasn't awarded any medals, but Charles took home a bronze medal for a patinated tin and shell, three-panel tea screen.

At the 1909 Alaska-Yukon-Pacific Exposition in Seattle (with over 4 million visitors) she brought 13 items of dazzling leather and leather combined with other materials, such as shells or brass, including one of her famed three-panel leather screen landscapes (priced at one hundred seventy-five dollars). Her work included appliquéd or stacked leather cushions, table covers, and a portiere; a leather and Philippine shell screen, leather and mixed material picture frames, and a guest book. She also presented electrolier lamps, chests, desk pads, table covers, and appliquéd leather cushions. She brought home the gold medal for this effort. Afterwards, what wasn't sold was displayed at the Blanchard Music and Art Building in Los Angeles.

Not to be outdone, her father showed 11 items, two which were leather, a photograph album and wedding book illuminated by Robert Hyde, his Montecito workman colleague. He too was a gold medalist. By now, Burton's small home studio had expanded into a downtown Santa Barbara building at 1225 State Street and included eight or more workers skilled in metal and leather working.

The perspective of this book is to present an insight into the decorated and artistic leather of individual artisans as well as those of the commercial modeled leather ventures. It would be an injustice to confine Elizabeth Burton's legacy to only her imaginative leather work. She designed and produced some of the most stupefying hammered metal lighting fixtures ever seen. It is possible the notions of large hammered and patinated rough metal embodied with

cutouts and apertures holding shells of abalone, sea conch, nautilus, or chiton were too avant garde for its time.

Many of the perforated repousse metal shades were quite large, as great as 24 inches in diameter at the bottom. Some sconces were made for candle light, some were readily adaptable to an oil lamp chimney, but most were designed to embrace the new technology of incandescent light bulbs. The luminous output of a 1890s bulb, with its tantalum or carbon coated bamboo filament, was that of a flashlight with a battery about to fail. It was barely a warm yellow glow. Even with the advent of tungsten filament in 1904, bulb technology had not caught up to what one expected of a table lamp. It was, therefore, common for a table lamp to have three or more bulb sockets, and the light output was meant to be enhanced with glass shades. Burton's large metal helmet lampshades make one fantasize of a Jules Verne undersea apparatus or a mesmerizing sea creature. It was more than a table lamp, it was organic sculpture. Nevertheless, she and her workers produced an inventory of the pieces and in 1905 she published a catalog entitled *Handwrought Electric Lamps and Sconces* (see CC B95 in the California Historical Society Library, San Francisco) that showed more than thirty models of lamps, sconces, and electroliers. These were available in patinated or plain copper and brass, and included a variety of shells, most often chiton or small abalone from the Santa Barbara channel.

In his 1904 article (*The Craftsman*, "Nature and Art in California," p. 388), Gustav Stickley paid tribute to her lamps and sconces:

> In these the exquisite choice of the shells, the intelligent use of the patina or iridescent coating of the metal, such as would result from inhumation- as well as the studies of line offered by the design awakens the admiration of one who carefully examines them even to the point of surprise.

She must have possessed boundless energy, for at age 36 (in 1905), with two teenage children, she had organized new venues for her artistic output and was reaching out to broaden her perceived abilities as just a metal or leather worker.

The *"Santa Barbara Morning Press"* story on June 30, 1910, explained:

> A number of notable exhibits of Mrs. Burton's work are ongoing in several eastern cities during the past few years. In Boston her beautiful creations can be seen at the Doll and Richards galleries. She was also induced by many friends and relatives of Providence, RI (her father's native city) to send some of her beautiful things for exhibition at the green galleries of the Tilden Thurber Company.
>
> This versatile artist has also done some excellent work in landscape garden design, thus following in the footsteps of her famous father, Charles Frederick Eaton. The special effects she created for I. G. Waterman's Mira Vista estate have been

praised by *House and Garden* magazine, and stands as evergreen evidence of her genius in this direction.

Now, however, though Mrs. Burton will continue to make and exhibit lovely things from her own hands, and those of her assistants, it is her intention to make a new departure—that of interior decorations. A dining room which Mrs. Burton decorated for Mrs. Herbert Wadsworth of Washington, D.C. had mural panels, leather-screens, etc. done in the amethystine tones of ripe grapes. Another panel was in a peacock feather design, with the feathers in leather appliqué on a blue-green leather, the eyes done with abalone shells and the cluster tied with a silver appliqué. This also embodies the color scheme of a room which Mrs. Burton decorated for Mrs. William Miller Graham of Bellosguardo. The walls of the room are done in feather panels of this design and all the fixtures are in iron and steel and shell to harmonize with the peacock feather color scheme.

Entries for special projects from her "Santa Barbara scrapbook" are for a "who's who" of socially prominent (and wealthy) patrons such as Rockefeller, Morgan, Vanderbilt, Armour, Safe, Hearst, Crocker, and Huntington. Perhaps single-handedly, through her creations in leather and metal and shell, she interpreted and brought the symbolic beauty of the southern California landscape into homes across the country. This should have been accomplishment enough, but Burton's curiosity had only begun to stir. At 51, she returned to a young girl's hobby of painting and developed into a fair enough artist to be shown in a San Francisco gallery. She returned to France in 1924 and over the next three years painted scenes of her childhood in Brittany. During this interlude she was also engaged in a diplomatic mission on behalf of the Alliance Francaise and the Institut Francais aux Etats-Unis—a good will mission with a goal of explaining Americans to the French, and when back home explaining the French point of view to Americans. She briefly served on a lecture tour and one New York publisher (H. Vinal, New York City, 1928) found her point of view worthy to print as *Paris Vignettes* with illustrations by the author.

Back in Santa Barbara, at a still active age of 59, she immersed herself in drama and the arts. Her 1928 listing in *Women of the West* (Max Binheim, editor, Publisher's Press, Los Angeles, 1928) pays homage to her involvement in civic organizations such as: Founder of the Santa Barbara Stroller's Club (a dramatic society); former president of the Drama League; director of the Three Arts Club; Artist, Lecturer, Exhibitor of paintings, writer, and for the 12 years, at the head of the Creative Studio of Decorative Art.

She died at age 68, November 15, 1937, in Los Angeles and was buried at Santa Barbara. Scholars identify Elizabeth Burton as one of the premier Arts and Crafts artisans. The fact her work is so highly collected by institutions suggests it is among the finest produced that is characteristic of her California roots.

Ms. Thiessen closes her *Antiques, The Magazine* tribute to her in this manner:

Diplomat, artist, designer, painter, photographer, landscaper, critic, and writer, Elizabeth Eaton Burton embodied an exhaustive range of artistic abilities. Her many interests might reflect a series of hobbies rather than a career with a direct trajectory, yet her contributions to various fields were recognized. Perhaps her most successful venture was as an arts and crafts artist, for it is this work that has survived the test of time to remain popular and characteristic of its place and era.

 ## Henry Busse
College of Fine Arts, Los Angeles.

A citation shows he exhibited a leather and hammered metal mat and a leather wall panel at the Alaska-Yukon-Pacific Exposition (AYPE) of 1909, Seattle, Washington. He was awarded a gold medal for excellence.

Cathedral Oaks
Alma/Los Gatos

George Austin Dennison
b. New Boston, Illinois,1873
d. Los Gatos, March 26, 1966

Charles Frank Ingerson
b. Victory Mills, New York, 1880
d. Los Gatos, March 15, 1968

This company was established by two lifelong bachelor partners of 65 years, who early in their careers (1909) were leather modelers, but moved on to international acclaim as artists, interior designers, expert gold and silversmiths and nearly all the other art mediums.

In 1904 Dennison served as secretary to the California Commission at the Louisiana Purchase Exposition, St. Louis, and installed the San Francisco room at this venue. He repeated the role in 1909 at the Alaska-Yukon-Pacific Expo in Seattle.

Ingerson attended Pratt Institute in Brooklyn in 1900 and associated early with Dennison. In 1909 Ingerson began teaching decorative design at the California School of Design, San Francisco Institute of Art. He was a new exhibitor at the Alaska-Yukon-Pacific Expo of 1909 in Seattle. His three-panel leather screen with koa wood was priced at $250, or a figure greater than a good horse and buggy! Ingerson exhibited numerous bookend pairs, magazine covers, and letter holders, and received a grand prize for his modeled leather screen and a gold medal for the rest of the display. The catalog showed his address to be 1321 Sutter, San Francisco.

In 1910, Dennison purchased property in Alma and with Ingerson formed the Cathedral Oaks Studio in 1911 on the property. Over the next decades the two receive important decorating commissions; 1917-1918, Casa Dorinda, a 65 room house for William H. Bliss in Montecito; 1920, Samarkand Hotel, Santa Barbara; 1925-1927. They were commissioned to build a 10-foot high model of the biblical Ark of the Covenant in memory of Marcus S. Koshland of San Francisco. The work took 14 months in the London Foundry of A.B. Burton and on February 5, 1927, it was formally dedicated at Temple Emanu-El, San Francisco. (*Los Gatos Weekly Times*, Feb. 19, 1997; *Photos courtesy Forbes Mill Museum of Los Gatos*.)

A painting of the two leather workers and all-around artists, George Dennison (L) and Charles Ingerson were life-long partners in the Cathedral Oaks Studios. *Courtesy Vonda Breed and the museums of Los Gatos, CA.*

The highly modeled, gilded and
silvered leather chair back and seat
was produced by the Cathedral Oaks
Studios of Alma, California, not far
from Los Gatos. *Courtesy of Vonda Breed
and the museums of Los Gatos, CA.*

Companeros Colony
Santa Rosa, early 1900s

Companeros Colony (*Companeros* is Spanish for Comrade) exhibited six leather items at the Alaska-Yukon-Pacific Exhibition in 1909, Seattle: a copper and leather jewel caskets studded with semi-precious cabochons; leather portfolios; change purses; cigar cases; book covers; and handbags. In 1910, the firm appeared in the catalog of the 3rd Annual Exhibition of the Arts & Crafts Society of Portland, Oregon, with several dozen leather and parchment items, such as: 13 table mats; four purses or handbags; four scissor holders; seven pen wipers; and an assortment of blotters, napkin rings, card cases, and book covers.

The thrust behind this band of leather artisans is attributed to three expatriate Roycrofters—a brother and two sisters. The eldest was John Comstock, (b. Evanston, Illinois, 1883), who served at Roycroft Shops, East Aurora, New York, at least until 1903 as a book plate designer and etcher. He later became a physician but still maintained his etching artistry and died in Del Mar, Dec. 26, 1970. Sister Catherine Comstock (b. Evanston, Illinois, 1885), was a leather modeler at Roycroft Shops; as was the youngest sister, Cordelia (b. Evanston, Illinois, 1887), who married James Matthews of Carmel and died there April 13, 1966. Other brothers James H., George F., Hugh, and Hurd, grew up in Sonoma when the family moved there from Evanston in the early 1900s.

A rare printed insight into the group's artistic beginnings in California is excerpted from *The Crafters Magazine*, Vol. 2, No. One, October, 1910, published in Kansas City, Missouri:

> About three years ago (1907) comrade John Comstock and his two sisters, Catherine and Cordelia, determined to organize a band of workers in the Arts and Crafts, and to locate in some progressive western city. They had California in mind, as being best adapted to the work, and most suited to their wishes. They began work in very small quarters with lean purses, a large capital of hopes and ideas, and no visible market for their product, which at that time consisted solely of hand-wrought leather. Comrade John was business manager and chief

designer. Catherine Comstock was master craftsman of leather work, and her training under one of the best German masters now in America, ably fitted her for the task. [Note: This likely refers to the Roycrofter Frederick Kranz, but it could mean the master bookbinder, Louis Kinder.] From the first, their work received recognition and support and after two years of activity they counted some fifty shops and societies that carried their leather products, besides a large special business. They also added to their activities book plate designing, jewelry, metal work and illuminated cards, for all of which they found a ready sale. Last Spring (1909) friend John decided that Santa Barbara offered a better opportunity than Santa Rosa for his own work. Very fortunately he secured an able partner to take over his interest, in the person of Miss Bess Woodward of Santa Rosa. Miss Woodward is one of his pupils in jewelry work and she combines with this knowledge a thorough understanding of business methods. The shop was moved into larger quarters designed by John. A working Guild of Craftsmen was organized under his direction, consisting of talented Santa Rosa girls; most of whom had studied with him. The members of this guild are allowed the use of all tools and equipment and unlimited time in the workroom. Their work is under the artistic guidance of Miss Catherine Comstock and Miss Bess Woodward. The finished product must first pass a fixed standard of artistic merit before being placed in the salesroom or sent to other shops. All sales are subject to a shop commission.

The group of artisans also worked outdoors in nearby Kenwood Hills in the summer weeks and, in the autumn, John Comstock, and occasionally the sisters, worked their craft in Santa Barbara. [Sources: "Artists in California, 1786-1940," Edan Hughes; *Head, Heart and Hand*, University of Rochester Press, 1994, authors, Marie Via and Marjorie B. Searl, Robert C. Rust, 2/R Design, Roycroft Associates.]

The Companeros Colony of Santa Rosa, California, had their leader John Comstock (a Roycroft ex-pat leather worker) to thank for their new studio. *Courtesy Robert Rust, 2/R Design, Roycroft Associates.*

Interior--Gift Shop of the Companeros, Santa Rosa, Cal. Designed by John Comstock. Color Scheme, Dark Redwood, Soft Browns and Orange. Balcony for Guild Workers.

 ### Charles Frederick Eaton
b. Providence, Rhode Island, Dec.12, 1842
d. Montecito, California, Aug. 21, 1930

Like L.C. Tiffany's artistic objects for everyday use, Charles F. Eaton's extraordinary articles were made for an appreciative connoisseur—a person of means for whom the price was incidental. As Leslie Green Bowman noted in her essay "The Arts & Crafts Movement in the Southland," "Eaton's designs are characteristically of multiple simple materials, as seen in his tea screen from about 1904. They relate not to the simple, clean aesthetic of Stickley's democratic art but to a revival of intricate craftsmanship in humble, vernacular materials, but not inexpensive." (*The Arts & Crafts Movement in California*, Leslie Green Bowman, p. 188, The Oakland Museum and Abbeville Press, 1993.)

However, his imaginative mind saw ingenious applications combining such utilitarian and regional materials as leather, ocean shells, beach pebbles along with tin, copper, brass, iron, and wood. Eaton wasn't what we've grown to know as a "starving artist" who had to raid scrap piles and alleys for materials to produce his constructions. He was born into the wealthy household of Levi Curtis Eaton and Sarah Brown in Providence, Rhode Island, on December 12, 1842. In his favor he didn't become a wastrel or dissipate his resources foolishly. He was tutored in life, even

while traveling abroad; attended and graduated from Brown University (1860-62) went on to study art in Bonnat's Paris Studio; attended the Sorbonne and painted his way across the continent; and met and married Helen Justice Mitchell, a Sorbonne compatriot from Philadelphia in 1867. They continued living the good life in Italy and France, until Helen's health forced a change.

Helen Eaton's health had been deteriorating during the mid-1880s while they were in the south of France. Eaton had made a special pilgrimage to scout a home site in California that would be beneficial to her recovery. He selected Santa Barbara for its clear air, warmth, and a vista looking out toward Santa Cruz Island. They (along with their precocious daughter Elizabeth) migrated in 1886, never to leave, and called their new home on Palm Drive the villa estate of Riso Rivo—"Laughing Brook"—about four miles from today's downtown Santa Barbara. Eaton began transforming the landscape of the 200 acre hillside in Montecito with an immense variety of plant materials, built an elaborate water system with streams, reservoir and ponds; and he and his workmen built a picturesque, multi-level house of stone and redwood, with broad overhangs. Helen Eaton lived there until her death in 1892. Charles married Florence Baxter in 1898 in Santa Barbara.

According to many feature stories in major artistic and home magazines, Eaton was an affable host. In the early 1900s a procession of editors visited, took photos (sadly for

Standing center is Charles F. Eaton in his Montecito, CA studio, c. 1904, when interviewed by Gustav Stickley for *The Craftsman*. *Courtesy Craftsman Farms.*

us, only marginal black and white images are available) and reported what they had experienced while with the man and his work. One of the first was Gustav Stickley who was given a tour of Eaton's estate and wrote about it in 1904.

Stickley inquired of Eaton why he'd chosen this site and Eaton observed:

> There is a color quality in a California landscape which occurs nowhere else in the world. At least in no country with which I am familiar. I mean that rich golden bronze. Turn whatever way you will, it presents itself to the eye. In the live oak, it is the predominating tone, and when the tar-weeds fade and die, they give the same character to the entire 'floor' of the valley in which they grow. From this rich, sonorous background the oranges and lemons obtain greater fullness of color, as do also the great yellow masses of mustard, jasmine, sunflower, goldenrod and California poppies, those 'cups of gold' which so delighted the Spaniards. My guide then pointed to the south where lay a scene, beautiful and brilliant, resembling and rivaling the world famous one at Sorrento.

("Nature and Art in California," *The Craftsman*, Vol. 6, #4, July, 1904.)

Here's another impression furnished by Isabel McDougall in *House Beautiful*, Vol. 16, February, 1905, as they, too, walked the ground.

> He is his own engineer, as well as his own architect and landscape gardener. By birth he is an Eastern man, by education cosmopolitan, with seventeen years of life in Europe before settling in California. Of these, three years were spent painting with Bonnat in Paris, as much more in the study of landscape-gardening in Italy and the south of France, in the study of antique furniture and the collection of choice pieces. Many of these now enrich his home.
>
> In the main living room is a sixteenth century wedding chest of sarcophagus form, claw footed and elaborately carved. Here too, is a fine table with six twisted legs and chairs and fauteuils of old French make while the walls are hung with the noblest of coverings, Arras tapestry.

THE WEST

Entirely in accord with his antiquities is the vast fireplace with a carved mantel towering to the ceiling. This is not ancient, but was carved in all the quaint fancies of the Renaissance by Mr. Eaton's own pupils working under his direction in his studio in Nice. The wood used was that of old olive presses, yet it takes its place right genially under a ten-foot beamed ceiling of California redwood.

Reading what was written 100 years ago, it sounds as though almost all the interviewers were somewhat mystified by Eaton and didn't quite know what to make of his artistic endeavors. Stickley was impressed with the magnitude of his landscaping and in the same article summed up Eaton in this manner:

It is seldom that a person artistically gifted, evidences his abilities in a single form. This is especially true of those endowed with the capability to conceive, plan and construct; those in whom the reasoning faculties exceed the emotional power. What is judged to be versatility in such individuals is but the exercise in many forms of one talent. Thus I found my host and guide at Montecito to be equally a landscape gardener, an architect, and a craftsman producing peculiar objects of household decoration."

(Stickley did rave about the leather and metal work of Eaton's daughter, Elizabeth Eaton Burton in the same article.)

The facsimile of a copper tag shop mark used by Charles F. Eaton studios of Montecito, CA, early 1900s, on many items. *Courtesy JMW Gallery.*

Somehow, Eaton had carved out a niche for "peculiar objects" using leather and different metals incorporated with local materials such as abalone and other shells, stones, cedar, and redwood. There was much that was familiar in the manner of tooled leather chests, silver caskets with semi-precious stones, hand made and often oversized guest, friendship and wedding books with medieval feeling illuminations and figural portrayals by Eaton's on-site colleague, Robert Wilson Hyde. These were usually bound in ooze leather with wrought-metal mounts, often inlaid with the pearly abalone shell. Wherever the objects produced by Charles Frederick Eaton & Associates, Craft Workers, Santa Barbara, California, were displayed they seemed to attract the attention of the art loving public.

The first major recorded exhibit east of the Mississippi was when the Art Institute of Chicago (AIC) offered its "First Annual Exhibition of Original Designs for Decorations and Examples of Art Crafts having Distinctive Artistic Merit" (1902-1903). Eaton and Associates made their eyes gloss over with 35 entries. These included a silver or jewel coffer of copper, leather, and stones; a jewel casket of leather, brass, and stones; illuminated wedding, guest and friendship books bound in white and tan leathers, brass and stones with first rate illumination in gold leaf, ink, and paint by Robert Wilson Hyde; iron and copper tea screens with redwood and stones; to more simple leather golf score card cases, writing pads of leather with fine sequoia cone petals and stones; photograph albums, and a variety of less dazzling brass and iron letter racks. Hyde, a Chicagoan and Art Institute graduate, had just joined Eaton at Riso Rivo in 1902, yet wasn't mentioned in Stickley's 1904 story.

The Art Institute had now established a three-week exhibition date, usually in December and running into January for future exhibitions. For the second AIC Exhibition (1903-1904) Eaton brought along illuminator and book designer, Robert Wilson Hyde, and his craft workers, Henry Roland Johnson, Guadaloupe Buelna, and Alonzo Shad. They also displayed, for the first time, the new lamp shades of pierced and repousse brass, with abalone and other shells, a shade of a design of a peacock in pierced and repousse iron and shell, and lantern style sconces in iron and shell. Otherwise, the 58 offerings were pretty much the stunning selections of leather, hammered metal, and shell, Hyde-illuminated 9 x 12, and 12 x 16 inch wedding guest and friendship books; metal and shell tea screens, picture frames in repousse design copper and iron, an assortment of personal leather card cases with copper and stone, and writing cases.

The third (1904-1905) and fourth (1905-1906) AIC exhibits featured fewer (12 in 04-05; 7 in 05-06) but no less dramatic articles. The third exhibit was strong on electroliers, pierced and hammered electric lamp shades of brass, iron, and melon shell. The extraordinary leather bound wedding, guest, and friendship books with hammered metal and shell adornments, were all illuminated by Robert W. Hyde.

It is one thing to examine the black and white photos, read the terse exhibit catalog descriptions and attempt to interpret the reaction to the articles on display 100 years ago. Instead, why not allow you, the reader, to feel the drama of that moment through the eyes of the reporter who saw and touched Eaton's work, and had done so the previous year in Chicago? Here's what Elizabeth Emery reported to readers of the day in *House Beautiful*, February, 1904, (Vol. 15, #3):

Last year this Californian was the sensation of the Institute exhibition. He fairly dazzled with brilliancy. Today, if less of a sensation, he is a truer success, and we now accord him our full admiration. In the niche reserved for the Santa Barbara exhibit are several leather covered and metal and shell studded coffers and caskets; a beautiful metal lamp-shade, and many leather and metal book covers. These covers are among the finest things that have come from the Eaton workshop. In design they are extremely simple and each shows a sympathetic touch. Most attractive are the guest-books and wedding-books, with their boldly simple leather covers and their illuminated initials and borders. The catalog titles are suggestive: "Guest-book-Rose Bower," "Guest Book-Pomegranate," "Guest Book- Ye Ornament," "Guest Book-Auld Lang Syne," "Wedding Book-Orange Flower," "Wedding Book–Aucassin and Nicolete." This contains a cover of white leather with hammered brass strap hinges, while inside on its open page a colored rendering in flat tones of the marriage ceremony. Attendants in doublet and hose and DeMonvel-looking ladies in high pointed caps make a brilliant picture. In old script runs the legend, "Then Aucassin Married Nicolete And Became The Lady Beaucaire." Another parchment page bears the words of the wedding ceremony, illumed by Mr. Hyde with border of a choice design, the whole making a brilliant picture. In these we see the worker's versatility combined with painstaking and fine craftsmanship.

At the end of the first AIC exhibition in January 1903, Eaton continued on to the Arts and Crafts Exhibition at Minneapolis. Beside his tooled leather chests of wood leather and stone studded, he offered medieval-styled suede leather and brass trimmed coffers and caskets to hold silver or jewelry. A trademark novelty was 3-panel tea screens. These were most often in patinated tin, copper, or brass. Some presented a panoramic, repousse hammered landscape scene where the sky was often panes of oyster or abalone shell. Others were of a diamond geometric design and were of several sizes, usually at least 5" height by 15" width. Writing in *The Craftsman*, March, 1903, Katherine Louise Smith reported about the earlier Minneapolis Exhibition: "These metal screens designed to set on a table in order to protect an alcohol flame (of tea kettle or chafing dish) from draughts, were unique affairs that appealed instantly to the connoisseur."

Interspersed with the AIC exhibits, Eaton entered the 1904 Louisiana Purchase Exposition in St. Louis with fourteen articles. He sent a large leather and shell studded jewelry cabinet (sold at $75); a 12 x 16 inch leather and repousse metal guest book (sold at $40); a leather-bound folio with Hyde illuminated parchment of the 23rd Psalm (sold at $60); and won a bronze medal for a patinated and repousse tin and shell adorned 3-panel 8 x 16 inch tea screen. His daughter Elizabeth Burton exhibited separately. She sent several leather articles and two large leather table mats which sold for $20 and $13.

At the 1909 Alaska-Yukon-Pacific Exposition in Seattle, Eaton presented 11 items, most of which included leather as a significant design element; they included a guest book, and jewelry caskets, two of which were leather, a photograph album that sold for $20; and a 12 x 16 inch modeled leather wedding book with hammered brass hinges, inset with aba-

lone. This was profusely illuminated by Hyde. It sold for $85 and won a gold medal. Again, exhibiting separately, daughter Elizabeth Burton presented 13 articles, nine of which were tooled and decorated leather, including her signature 3-panel leather landscape screen priced at $175 (the price of a horse, harness and buggy!). She was awarded a gold medal for this entry.

Since Eaton's work, presented at Minneapolis, Chicago, St. Louis, and Seattle, was seen by at least a thousand potential buyers for his stratospherically priced objects, and the vast readership of numerous favorable national magazine articles as well as those in magazines and newspapers of California, it's likely that there were many new orders for his creations. The San Francisco earthquake and disastrous fire of 1906 may have required replacement of large numbers of Arts and Crafts decorative objects, and Eaton could likely have furnished many of these. They were available at Paul Elder's Arts and Crafts Book Store, a leading retailer of fine modeled leather, hammered copper and other metals (though the original store was lost in the 1906 fire, it temporarily relocated to Van Ess at Bush while Bernard Maybeck was designing a new building destined to open in 1909 at 239 Grant Avenue). Meanwhile, some of Eaton's and Hyde's articles were available at Elder's Arts and Crafts Book Store in Santa Barbara. More and more wealthy Easterners and the celebrity actors were building estates all over Santa Barbara and could have visited Elder's store or Eaton's workshop in downtown Santa Barbara.

One of the last feature articles, before the nation's attention was focused on San Francisco, again presented Eaton's work as akin to fine art. In "A California Craftsman And His Work," Katherine Louise Smith was permitted five pages to extol Eaton's craft, (*Home and Garden*, Vol. 9, January 1906):

The array of leather work is fairly dazzling. All sizes of chests and jewel caskets are sent out from this marvelous workshop. They cost, it is true, a tidy sum, but the happy possessor has something that cannot be duplicated. Silver chests, with innumerable tiny drawers, come in leather covers that are bound in brass and inset with semi-precious stones. Coffers, caskets and metal over leather book covers are of such workmanship that once seen, one can always recognize them as belonging to this California craftsman. These are things not met with in shops. They are examples of handicraft that must be sought to be obtained and are only purchased by those who are educated to a proper appreciation. Visitors to California see the work in the studio; others who are less favored become conversant with it through the various Arts and Crafts exhibitions, or they meet isolated pieces in the homes of the cultivated.

With such a buildup how could you possibly not purchase a monogrammed leather jewelry casket, replete with abalone cut like jewels, and a secret drawer for your diary?

Ruth Stensrud Gordon

Reported to have practiced leather modeling, Gordon worked for the Van Erp studio in 1917 and earned a degree in design in 1925 from Stanford University. She is academically linked with Pedro Lemos while he was director of the Museum of Art at Stanford.

Magazine cover of 8-1/2"w x 11"h dramatically incorporating a fanciful songbird into modeled foliage. Attributed to San Francisco area artist Ruth Stensrud Gordon during her association with designer Pedro Lemos. The piece is also decorated with small modeled insets of foliage and berries on the inside cover retainer flaps. *Courtesy of Faire Lees.*

Ellen A. Kleinschmidt,
b. Washington, Missouri, Sept. 8, 1851
d. Berkeley, California, Aug. 29, 1927

Bertha Kleinschmidt
Berkeley, California

Ellen Kleinschmidt, was the mother of Bertha Kleinschmidt, and both lived at 2946 Claremont Avenue, Berkeley. Exhibit records of the Alaska-Yukon-Pacific Exposition of 1909, Seattle, showed that they submitted two modeled leather shopping bags, bookends, and desk top accessories. At the 3rd Annual Exhibition of the Arts & Crafts Society of Portland, Oregon, 1910, the Kleinschmidts presented 21 articles, seven of jewelry and other metal, and 14 of modeled leather including purses, wallets, card and cigar cases and a book cover.

O'Hara & Livermore Studios

Lillian Ada O'Hara,
b. Bowmansville, Ontario, Canada, April 8, 1864
d. San Anselmo, California, Nov. 28, 1959

Grace G. Livermore,
b. Wisconsin, Aug. 3, 1867
d. San Anselmo, California, July 16, 1927

O'Hara became a U.S. citizen in 1889 and was largely self-educated. She met Livermore in San Francisco in 1892, and with Marea van Vleck they opened an artists' studio and interior decoration shop at Room 70, 120 Sutter St., San Francisco. The firm was selected to design the San Francisco Women's Committee Room in the California Building at the 1893 World's Columbian Exposition, Chicago. In 1904 the Pasadena branch of O'Hare & Livermore opened at 38 South Raymond St. The firm had more than a dozen artisans working in applied arts, burnt leather goods, bronze lamps, etc. Their work was mostly suede or soft leather of green and brown tones, often with inlaid brocades behind cutwork and harmoniously colored leather articles, often with laced edges.

Both O'Hara and Livermore were diminutive and in 1905 they designed and built a small redwood cottage, Klah-ha-ne, in San Anselmo. They opened a Boston branch that year at 2 Arlington St. Before and after the 1906 San Francisco earthquake and fire, their leather work was sold through the Paul Elder & Company Book Shop. The Boston shop closed in 1908. O'Hare & Livermore exhibited six objects, including modeled leather bookends with peacock feathers, letter holders, desk top blotters, and two transparent watercolor screens at the Alaska-Yukon-Pacific Exhibition

A close-up of the cutwork to show how peacock feathers were used in design around 1900. *Courtesy of Faire Lees.*

of 1909. The screens won a silver medal. The shop moves often but in 1915 they displayed at the Panama Pacific International Exposition in San Francisco. Gradually, the firm became known for its interior decorating and, in 1924, Arthur Baken joined as a partner. Livermore died in 1927, but O'Hara continued in business until her 1959 death.

Pre-San Francisco earthquake (1905) cut-out bookends, backed by the Peacock's tail-feather eyes. Easy laced edge and stamped on the bottom, O'Hara and Livermore, Designers and Manufacturers, San Francisco. 8"w x 6"h. *Courtesy of Faire Lees.*

THE WEST

Catherine Comstock Seideneck
b. Evanston, Illinois, Nov.1, 1885,
d. Carmel/Monterey, California, Feb. 13, 1967,

After attending the school of design at the Art Institute of Chicago, Catherine, 16, was drawn to the Roycroft Shops by her brother John, an etcher and bookplate designer. Shortly after, a younger sister, Cordelia, joined Catherine as a leather modeler. In 1903 the Comstocks left East Aurora for Santa Rosa, the new home of their parents and other brothers and sisters. Catherine continued leather modeling and, by 1907, had aligned herself with Frederick H. Meyer at the California School of Arts and Crafts, Berkeley. She was instrumental in guiding brother John and his sister Cordelia to become the core of the Companeros colony of Santa Rosa. This craft guild exhibited modeled leather articles at the 1909 Alaska-Yukon-Pacific Exposition in Seattle, and the 1910 3rd annual Exhibition of the Arts & Crafts Society of Portland, Oregon.

In *A Tribute to Yesterday: The History of Carmel and Surrounding Communities* (Valley Publishers of Santa Cruz, 1980), author Sharon Lee Hale reports: "Catherine was a teacher of leather work at the School of Fine Arts at the University of California at Berkeley, and she was known internationally for her work in tooled leather." That may be a reference to her dramatic over-mantel leather sculpture of a peacock design at the 1915 Panama Pacific Exposition in San Francisco. It won a gold medal.

She married George Seideneck in 1920. He was a Chicago artist of some renown who had come to Carmel on a sketching tour in 1918. Although she "taught leather sculpture at the Caramel Arts and Crafts Summer School" (Edan Hughes, *Artists in California—1786-1940*, p. 1002), she took up the palette and painted alongside husband George in the late 1920s. She was known as a watercolorist and accomplished pastel illustrator. Both were active in the Carmel Art Association where George was its first president. The Comstock name is also synonymous with Carmel. Catherine's younger brothers Hugh and Hurd came to Carmel in 1924, married and stayed. Hugh became the architect/designer of the many quaint cottages that gave Carmel its storybook qualities of the late 1920s and 1930s.

OREGON

Arts and Crafts Society
Portland, Oregon

An Arts & Crafts Society didn't just happen out of civic pride. On the contrary, there was rather widespread resistance by the fine arts culture cops to grudgingly recognize what we today revere of the art pottery, metals, or textiles. In the early 1900s it was difficult to present such handicraft at a public showing of fine art. Even with major recognition at the Louisiana Purchase World's Fair in St. Louis of 1904 such handicraft was resigned to the back of the bus.

Virtually every Arts & Crafts Society owes much to the influence of the movement's parent organization that emerged in 1897 as the Society of Arts and Crafts Boston. On its tenth anniversary celebration (1907), its members proposed a means to facilitate other cities to found a society based on their formula for success. This umbrella organization was the National League of Handicraft Societies, which numbered twenty-four societies with room to grow to thirty five. Julia Christianson Hoffman was at this event and became determined to make Portland a chartered Arts and Crafts society.

Hoffman was a socially recognized artisan, a painter, photographer, metalsmith, and weaver. She was just the sort of leader needed to breathe life into this new art form, possessing the stature and commitment to champion and enlist others to the cause.

In 1907, Hoffman was given the SACBoston Craftsman designation as a silversmith and needle worker. She had been a student and long time friend of Boston master silversmith George Gebelein. In addition to attending the anniversary celebration, she was in Boston to arrange for and become the curator of a collection of quality craftwork (metals, jewelry, needlework, leather) from the Boston society that could be displayed at the Portland Art Museum. This would be augmented with other well-executed handmade objects from Portland families that would serve as a "loan collection."

She also began communications to obtain a silversmith of some renown to teach a summer school of metalwork in Portland. She succeeded on all objectives.

It would seem that the recently concluded Lewis and Clark Exposition of 1905 in Portland (that did have a display of handicraft) inspired Julia Hoffman and her like-minded colleague, Henrietta Failing, curator of the Portland Art Museum. This was likely the first opportunity for the citizenry of Portland and the Pacific Northwest to examine objects of contemporary design, the arts and crafts hand work. The emerging mainstream art and homemaking magazines showed only a scattering of this artisan work. Even Roycroft, in 1905, was in its fledgling production of hammered copper and modeled leather.

Through their devotion and hard work, the first exhibit of applied art would open April 30 to May 18, 1907 at the Portland Art Museum. (*The Oregonian*, May 3, 1907). According to a review in Lawrence Kreisman and Glenn Mason's book, *The Arts and Crafts Movement in the Pacific Northwest*, (Timber Press Inc., 2007, pp. 70-71):

The names included in the Portland Art Museum's catalog for the exhibition were a virtual

"Who's Who" of American Arts and Crafts of the day. Jewelry and metal exhibitors included Elizabeth Copeland, Seth Ek, George C. Gebelein, Karl F. Leinonen, L.H. Martin, Arthur Stone and the Kalo Shop. Leather work and book plates from Amy Sacker, printed materials lent by Bruce Rogers and art pottery by Arthur Eugene Baggs also were on display. The items listed in the loan collection from Portland area families indicated the donors' knowledge of Arts and Crafts work created in other parts of the country. Leather work by the Misses Ripley of New York City and pottery from Rookwood, Volkmar, Newcomb, Van Briggle, Teco, Grueby and Dedham were listed as being owned by local individuals."

The *Spectator* of Portland, in describing the exhibit, said: "The display of the Arts and Crafts includes silver, copper, pewter, and jewelry in charming and unique form; basketry that astonishes with the variety of work; leather, illumed and embossed in fine design and soft tones; volumes showing how beautiful books can be when art works with craft." (*Spectator*, vol. I, no.8, May 4, 1907: 5)

Following the success exhibition, a group of 150 people gathered at the Art Museum on October 9, 1907, to adopt a constitution, elect officers, and enlist member for the Arts and Crafts Society of Portland. Among these was Julia Hoffman, who became one of the original trustees and its second president. Its purpose was to "cultivate an appreciation for craftsmanship and handicrafts." (Robert S. Christen, *Oregon Historical Quarterly*, Vol. 109, no. 4)

Among their efforts was the extension of the 1907 into and annual event at the Portland Art Museum. The First Annual Exhibition of the Arts and Crafts Society of Portland was held May 19-June 9, 1908 and was called the "beginning" one of many to come. The Sunday *Oregonian* of May 17 offered a sneak peak into the venue held at the Portland Museum of Art. "The exhibit includes handsome articles in metal, leather, wood, textile, jewelry and specimens of the handwork of many of the foremost craftsmen of the United States, including Portland. All are original with the artist consigning the article to the exhibition. Portland contributors are sending in many rare specimens in basketry, bookbinding, metal work, leather articles, woodwork, illuminating, etc." (*Oregonian*, May 17, 1908.)

Notable local contributors of leather items included: Miss F.G. Crocker, magazine cover, blotter, five notebooks; Miss Roma J. McKnight, tooled mat, handbag, card case and two fan bags; Miss M.M. DeWert, tooled mat; Miss Lilly Fox, notebook, tooled mat. Lenders included Mrs. W.B. Ayer, leather case executed by Yandell of New York; Mrs. Ralph Wilbur, tooled mat, clipping book, bellows, executed by Miss F. G. Crocker; Mrs. Julia Hoffman, writing pad and traveling mirror executed by Mrs. F.C. Stevens of Portland; Mrs. T.L. Eliot, tooled mat executed by Mrs. Ralph Wilbur; Miss Georgiana Burns, tooled mat

and book cover executed by her; Mrs. M.P. Deady, tooled mat executed by Mrs. Henderson Deady; Mrs. Agnes G. Veasie, two book covers executed by her. (*Catalog, First Annual Exhibition of the Arts and Crafts Society of Portland/ Together with a loan collection of Applied Arts*, Portland Art Association, Museum of Art, Portland, Oregon)

References of the period indicate that if there was a leading leather artisan in Portland it was Roma J. McKnight. She was the daughter of an early Oregon pioneer family who trained in New York City, specializing in design and jewelry making, but one with knowledge and sensitivity for the crafts in general. (Sunday *Oregonian*, May 24, 1908). Her Arts and Crafts Shop was mentioned as the one place in Portland where a person might get a glimpse of true art as the craftsman conceives it. The *Spectator* chronicles Miss McKnight's Arts and Crafts Shop activities from September through December, 1908. After that, the business was referred to as the School of Art and Handicrafts. In September, the article reported: "The business women who can spare Saturday afternoons are turning their attentions from matinees to the study of metal and leatherwork. Miss Roma McKnight, director of the School of Arts and Handicrafts, has quite a large class of business women each Saturday afternoon who are busy in the making of Christmas gifts both in the metal and tooled leather." (*Spectator*, vol.IV, no 3, September 26, 1908, p.15.)

After December, 1908, McKnight no longer advertised in the weekly *Spectator* and there were no further references to her shop. The Sunday *Oregonian* of May 9, 1909 announced that Roma McKnight was closing her shop in order to spend the summer in the Orient and that she would reopen in the fall. The Portland City Directories list her in an importers and craftworkers business with Mrs. R.R. Bartlett in 1910 and 1911; but no mention of her reopening her school. (*Arts and Crafts Movement in the Pacific Northwest*, p. 256.) She was not included in the catalog of the Third Annual Exhibition of the Arts and Crafts Society in 1910.

She may have curtailed her retail business side because of competition from the Arts and Crafts Society of Portland's new salesroom, the Shop of Fine Arts & Industries, which opened in November, 1908 and offered many of the same types of merchandise.

The *Spectator* reported:

The shop (located at Seventh and Salmon streets) will afford the people of Portland an opportunity to see and buy the best in art, handicraft work, reproductions, and bookmaking. Many notable artists have sent examples of their work and it will be at once an exhibition hall of what is really worthy in the fine and applied arts and a salesroom. The shop also serves as the headquarters of the Arts and Crafts Society, which is producing articles in silver, leatherwork, and jewelry. (Spectator 1V, no 4, Oct. 3, p 9, 1908.)

Throughout the next decade this location presented exhibits and items for sale by some of the best known Arts and Crafts workers and artists in America. Beginning with William Keith, a California artist, the shop also introduced the work of sculptor A. Phimster Proctor; color prints by Ruth Sypherd Clements, Helen Hyde, Ethel Mars and Maud Hunt Squire; metalwork by Mildred Watkins, George Gebelein, Dirk Van Erp and Arthur Stone; paintings and drawings by Josephine Rilkin of New York City; modeled leather articles from the Companeros Colony of Santa Rosa, California and the Ripley sisters of New York City; Indian photographs by Edward S. Curtis. (*Arts and Crafts Movement in the Pacific Northwest*, p. 73.)

The Third Annual Exhibition of the Arts and Crafts Society of Portland ran from April 14-28, 1910. There was a broad representation of modeled leather work by more than a dozen artisans. The largest offering—some 50 or more items—was by the Companeros Colony of Santa Rosa, California, with five handbags/purses, 13 table mats and a wide assortment of other personal and utility articles for the home. The Dolese sisters, Rose and Minnie, operators of the Wilro Shop of Chicago, entered bags, coin purses, card cases, and address books. Fanny V. Cross of Malden, Massachusetts, presented women's belts, traveling mirrors, desk pads, mats, pen wipers, blotters, and purses. Bertha and Ellen Kleinschmidt of Berkeley, California, supplied wallets, purses, an opera bag, table mats, card cases, bill holders, book and magazine covers, and a cigar case. A Miss Hemme of Berkeley, California, sent a writing portfolio, photograph case and a writing album; and Octavia Holden of San Francisco, California, provided three book covers. Nine Portland artisans' work was shown. Miss Lilly Fox, table mat, writing portfolio and a box; Mrs. F.G. Crocker, table mat, scissors and needle cases, portfolio and bolster cover; Mrs. T.T. Geer, book covers and a table mat; Anna E. Hoban, table mat, memorandum pad and fan bag; Mrs. H. N. Burpee, brown and red book covers; Miss Florence Knowlton, bag with metal top; Mrs. H.C. Holmes, shopping bag; Mae deWert, table mat; and Miss Cecelia O'Reilley, two book covers. (*Catalog, Third Annual Exhibition of the Arts and Crafts Society of Portland*, Portland Art Association, Museum of Art, Portland.)

The *Spectator* of April 23, 1910, reviewed the showing and commented:

This exhibit of the Arts and Crafts Society of Portland at the Museum of Art is considered the finest we have yet had, and compares favorably with those of larger cities. Famous firms of the East and local workers have given us their best. Beaten silver, in tea sets, spoons, cups and bowls in variety of designs, is the central attraction of the exhibit and has received much admiration. The leather is no less satisfactory than the silver. The beautiful tooled mats and other articles from the Companeros and the illuminated work of the Dolese in purses and bags leave nothing to be desired in this line of artistic work. Among them is a lovely box of soft green leather made by Miss Lilly Fox of Portland. Bertha and Ellen Kleinschmidt of Berkeley are exhibiting work of rare coloring, an example of which is a wallet decorated with green and purple thistle which exquisitely blends in tone with the leather. Awards of merit for distinguished work go to: Companeros, Rose and Minnie Dolese, Octavia Holden, Fanny V. Cross, Bertha and Ellen Kleinschmidt and Mrs. H.N. Burpee. (*Spectator*, Vol VII, 07: p. 9, 1910.)

Over the next decade the Society repeatedly issued calls for entries from local craftspeople, but few responded. The successes of the annual exhibitions were due, primarily, to the numerous professional consignments from the Midwest and East. The Society persevered and broadened its call for craft offerings from across the state. It even accepted student entries from the Oregon Agricultural College in Corvallis—now Oregon State University.

If it were not for Julia Hoffman's personal commitment and funds, and her recruitment of socially prominent Portlanders, the annual exhibitions would have expired long before the mid 1920s. However, as the nation's interest in the Arts and Crafts movement waned after World War I, Portland too was ready for a style change.

For a more thorough examination of Portland's role in the A&C movement, see a major work, *The Arts and Crafts Movement in the Pacific Northwest*, Lawrence Kreisman and Glenn Mason, Timber Press Inc., of Portland, OR, 2007.

In 1900 in Seattle and other Pacific Northwest cities, a few voices were embracing the principles presented by English Arts and Crafts English leaders Ruskin and Morris; and the American Elbert Hubbard.

However, the region's new artisans were at a disadvantage. Unlike Boston, Buffalo, New York City, and Chicago, there was no cadre of experienced metalsmiths, pottery artisans, or leather workers to lead hands-on training schools. The few enthusiasts who could afford it, went east for training. Others examined the new "how-to" articles in periodicals that covered their interest and became largely self-taught.

 ## The Women's Century Club

Seattle, Washington

In Seattle, the Arts and Crafts interest had coalesced in an organization called The Women's Century Club. Its members, inspired by the work and ideas of the Movement, planned the first call for handicraft entries for an exhibition in the summer of 1904. It met with strong public enthusiasm. The supporting reviews set the stage for a late May, 1905, showing of china painting, needlework, leatherwork, hand carving, and other handicrafts.

An item about the event in the *Seattle Mail and Herald* reported: "The result has far surpassed the wildest imaginations of the most optimistic member of the Women's Century Club, under whose auspices the exhibition was held, and the verdict of the public at large was that the artists of this part of the world need not fear to enter competition anywhere." (*Seattle Mail and Herald*, vol. VII, no. 31, June 17, 1905: 5.)

The significant public turnout and acceptance encouraged the club to prepare for yearly exhibits. Its 1906 effort brought even more and broader entries and in 1907 there was participation by Seattle artisans who earned their living by producing handmade items. These included hammered copper by Jessie Fisken and Mrs. John Ballard and photography by Adelaide Hanscom. (*Seattle Mail and Herald* X, no. 19, April 6, 1907: 9.)

As Lawrence Kreisman and Glenn Mason reported in a study of the club's activities: "The 1908 exhibition appears to have been the club's most ambitious undertaking, preparing the group for taking charge of the handicrafts exhibit at the coming Alaska-Yukon-Pacific Exposition the following year. An undated news clipping noted that the fifth annual exhibit of the Washington State Arts and Crafts Society was the best of its kind "ever held in size and quality." (Kreisman, Lawrence and Mason, Glenn, *The Arts and Crafts Movement in the Pacific Northwest*, Timber Press Inc., 2007, Portland, OR, p. 81.)

A newspaper account noted that "one of the most attractive features of the exhibition is the display of chinaware and needlework for which one room is reserved. In the same room is exhibited ornamental leather." (*Seattle Times*, 1908.)

The Washington State Arts & Crafts Society & The Alaska-Yukon-Pacific Exposition, 1909

Sited on what is now the University of Washington campus, the Alaska-Yukon-Pacific Exposition of 1909 began June 1 and closed October 16. The Washington State Arts and Crafts Society displayed handiwork from across the state in the rotunda of the Manufacturers Building known as the Women's Court.

A September 6, 1909, article in the *Seattle Post-Intelligencer* discussed a similar venue being displayed on the second floor of the Women's Building under the auspices of the State Federation of Women's Clubs. With more than 1,000 items, the story claimed this exhibit to be the largest of women's work of any exposition. Along with paintings and other fine art, the reporter also mentioned ceramics, hammered brass, tooled and burnt leather, carved and burnt wood and needlework of every description.

Not as well documented was the exhibition of applied arts by men. Even in the published newspaper lists of award and medal winners, the entries of regional male craftsmen were seldom mentioned. While the fine arts and exhibits warranted a catalog list for all the paintings and sculpture, there was no documentation of the applied and decorative arts in either the Women's Building or the Manufacturers Building. (*The Arts and Crafts Movement of the Pacific Northwest*, p.83.) Quite simply, there is no easy way to trace any leather work contributed by Washington artisans for there were no photos to identify the articles.

Of all the states with a dedicated building at the Alaska-Yukon-Pacific Exposition, California alone furnished a catalog of the fine and applied arts exhibited, including leatherwork. (*Catalog of Fine Arts Gallery and Exhibitors of Arts and Crafts*, California Building, Exposition Grounds, Seattle, 1909.) The Californian artisans included Elizabeth Eaton Burton, her father Charles F. Eaton, Charles F. Ingerson, the Companeros Colony, Lillian O'Hara and Grace Livermore, Ellen and Bertha Kleinschmidt, and Henry Busse. The quality and variety of their work was sure to have impressed the Seattle audience. Between them they took home numerous medals. *(See the California entries for more information)*

Other recognition was awarded to Mrs. A. H. Foote of Seattle, the grand prize for tooled leather, and Anne M. Holmes, a gold medal for tooled leather.

The Exposition drew four million visitors, 1.25 million more than the Lewis and Clark Expo of 1905 in Portland. The attendees were rewarded with the opportunity to examine the "now in fashion" manufactured items of the Arts and Crafts Era—Mission style furniture, ceramics, the newly produced electric lamps, and a wide variety of textiles.

Fine modeled leather articles were becoming available nationwide. The Roycrofters of East Aurora, New York, offered their first catalog devoted to modeled leather in 1909. Other companies such as Bosca, the Cordova Shops, and Meeker were just hitting their stride. An examination of the metal frames of most modeled leather handbags, will reveal manufacturing patent dates from 1915 through 1923.

Roycroft was also broadening its availability of modeled leather, hammered copper, fine books, and furniture. It formed alliances with local retailers in major cities and smaller communities. By 1915, many modeled leather objects could be purchased in the Oregon cities of Eugene, Corvallis, Independence, Lebanon, Marshfield, Pendleton, Portland, Roseburg and Salem. Roycroft's Washington affiliates were in Pullman, two in Seattle, including Frederick & Nelson, Spokane, Tacoma, Walla Walla, and Yakima.

Unfortunately, the Arts and Crafts movement in Seattle suffered an early demise. "No one organization or dedicated individual in Seattle, with the interest and determination to sustain the movement's ideals in people's minds, stepped forward to lead the effort. National and regional attention began to refocus elsewhere as World War I became an ever-increasing distraction... Seattle's interest in the Arts and Crafts movement waned dramatically." (*Arts and Crafts Movement in the Pacific Northwest*, p. 85)

LEATHER BOOK COVER
By Martha Sumbardo

*T*HE tooling of leather by hand is a very ancient and very delicate craft. Mrs. Martha K. Sumbardo, who has her interesting studio in West Seattle, is a most skilled exponent of leather tooling, this fine cover for a guest book being an example of her work. Mrs. Sumbardo was a student of the famous George Hulbe of Hamburg, Germany, who after years of research in the old monasteries of Germany, rediscovered and reapplied this enduring, practical and popular art. She is now passing on her knowledge of the craft to the students in her classes.

Selection of the right piece of leather (must be properly tanned, not too dry, nor too oily) is an important step in leather tooling. The general pattern is first traced on the leather, then it is carved, then to get the fine finished effect it is tooled from both front and back.

Visitors to Mrs. Sumbardo's studio are always impressed with her fine copies of the old masters' paintings, made during the twelve years she lived in Florence. The copies are of such immortals as Raphael, Del Sarto, Giorgione and Botticelli, etc.

〜 〜 〜

Seattle's leather artisan, Martha Sumbardo, maintained a studio and taught design and leather working into the 1950s. She cited her study of the craft with Georg Hulbe of Hamburg, in a story from the publication: *Craftsman's Guild of Washington*, Vol. 1, #1, May, 1940. *Courtesy Tom Wake.*

LESSER KNOWN LEATHER ARTISANS

While the highest quality, and most costly, modeled leather achieved acceptance, there was an enormous market for lower priced leather goods with some artistic merit. The superior artistic work served as models to be copied. These new mass-produced articles surfaced simultaneously—pre-World War I—and many thrived until fashions changed during the mid-1930s.

Following are some producers of this level of leather goods often offered on internet auctions. For a detailed view of these and others, examine the research prepared by Marion Spitzley, Publisher of Bagladyemporium.com and Bag Lady University.

Castle Leather Company
515 W. 156th Street, New York City, 1917

The Castle line of handbags thrived around 1920, likely due to its dual-sided embossed designs. The daisies on this handbag are identical on both sides. Some handwork is evident, besides the hand lacing. The frame is dated 1-25-21 and CASTLE is imprinted beneath a turreted fortress. 7-1/4"w x 6-1/2"h. *Courtesy of Faire Lees.*

Lyon Leather Goods
East Orange, New Jersey, July 3, 1916
Chicago. Illinois, 1929,
Merged with Enger-Kress of West Bend, Wisconsin, and the Guild Leather Company of Springfield, Ohio. The new corporate office operated from West Bend.

Simple yet attractive, this Lyon branded purse carries an embossed poppy design. Steel engraved and gold-washed frame dates to 10-5-15. Sewn handle on back allows easy grip. 6-1/2"w x 5"h. *Courtesy of Faire Lees.*

H.E. Rice
Muskegon, Michigan

Raised oval emblem of morning glory design on black and orange enameled Jemco frame. Fully laced body and handle. 7"w x 7"h. *Courtesy of Faire Lees.*

Small town Muskegon, Michigan, also had a show in the artistic leather handbag business. This offer appeared in *Trunks and Leather Goods* in September, 1928. *Courtesy Bag Lady Emporium.*

T&E Leather Goods
Milwaukee, Wisconsin

Restrained art nouveau daisy element on a fully-laced body and handle. Brass on steel frame bears the Jemco 1915 mark. Unique circle turnloc. 6-3/4"w x 7"h. *Courtesy of Faire Lees.*

E.J. Wilkins
Gloversville, New York,
as early as 1902

Wilkins of Gloversville, New York, large body purse with a Jemco frame that mimics a Mayan design. Turnloc tab is a stylized belt & buckle to resemble an art deco element. Strong repousse floral design has a moth or butterfly descending onto the foliage. 8-1/4"w x 8"h. *Courtesy of Faire Lees.*

Wilson Manufacturing Company
Boston, Massachusetts, 1912

The Wilson Company of Boston, Massachusetts, produced a very sturdy group of women's handbags. This 6-34"w x 7-1/4"h unit also has a repeat of its oak leaf design on the back. *Courtesy of Faire Lees.*

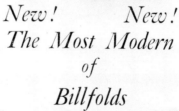
The Wilson Company of Boston looks like a player with this trade ad in *Trunks and Leather Goods*, June, 1929. *Courtesy Bag Lady Emporium.*

Unknown maker paperweight with Moth design, with felt on bottom, 3-1/2" dia. *Courtesy of Jessica Greenway.*

Perfect traveling personal accessories—leather containers for handkerchiefs, c. 1915. *Courtesy of Faire Lees.*

When men's shirts required detachable collars, a gent needed a new one daily. It would have been common to store them in such a case, even while at home. Likely pre-World War I, embossed and silk lined, 4-1/4"w x 10-3/4" l. *Courtesy of Faire Lees.*

No maker's mark, but a very respectable job of intricate modeling on the mirror back. This was once gilded and the foliage and flowers colored. 5-3/4"w x 10-1/4" l. *Courtesy of Faire Lees.*

Artistically styled carnations, inked and burned, combined with cutout design on suede leather. Embellished with small garnet colored stones and backed with orange silk lining. Unsigned, c. 1914. 6"w x 7"h. *Courtesy of Faire Lees.*

A checkbook cover style of wallet, with snap on the flap by Beach's of Coshocton, Ohio. Design on steerhide is stamped on all outside panels. 3-1/2"w x 4-1/2"h, 11" overall. *Courtesy of Faire Lees.*

Ships under sail were popular scenes for hand-modeled items, especially bookends by advanced amateurs. You'll find these produced in copper as well. Maker unknown on this 6"w x 5-1/2"h bookend. *Courtesy of Faire Lees.*

An exceptionally well-executed, hand-cut design on a women's belt likely before World War I, but unmarked. Its dimensions are 26" length x 2-5/16" width at back center. *Courtesy of Faire Lees.*

Brown & Bigelow of St. Paul, Minnesota, marketed a line of nearly hand-modeled work, but not totally. Under the brand of "Mission Leather" this checkbook style flap and snap wallet is described: "This is a genuine piece of hand-stained Mission Leather, from a hand-tooled design, conceived and executed by Brown & Bigelow of Saint Paul, U.S.A. 3-3/4"w x 4-1/2"h, 10-1/2" overall. *Courtesy of Faire Lees.*

Art nouveau stamped design on unknown maker's wallet designed for an inside coat pocket. 4-1/2"w x 7"h; opens to 8-1/2". *Courtesy of Faire Lees.*

Moore Leathercraft
Kansas City, Missouri

Another Missouri maker was Moore Leathercraft of Kansas City. Here's a two-toned nouveau styled lily with a few hand-tooled embellishments here and there, plus hand-lacing on all edges. The Jemco frame dates July 23, 1918. 7-3/4"w x 7-1/2"h. *Courtesy of Faire Lees.*

Souvenir purse from the 1904 St. Louis World's Fair. Braided 1/2" handle on a 7"w x 4-1/2"h body with kiss-lock closure. *Courtesy Faire Lees.*

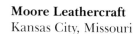

Octagonal 22" dia. Table mat. Dyed royal purple suede with four 8-1/2" wide white leather blossoms. Exceptional example of cut leather appliqué and careful sewing. Likely from World War I era. *Courtesy of Faire Lees.*

Rectangular 20"w x 17-1/2"h table mat. Dyed ox-blood suede with brown suede cut out hearts at corners. Dramatic 10"w x 5"h appliqué of green and brown suede pea pods is sewn within 1/32" of its edge. Outer curving border of maroon suede is also carefully sewn in place. Likely from WW1 era. *Courtesy of Faire Lees.*

ACKNOWLEDGMENTS

A Debt of Gratitude

This work was greatly enhanced through the contributions of those who share the passion for the Arts and Crafts movement. It includes data and images from scholars, antique dealers, and collectors, but most of all, offerings from the friends made as the data was being assembled. If I've somehow managed to not mention you, please accept my apology.

The extraordinary number of images of the leather artistry of the Roycrofters and Cordova Shops was only possible though the sharing of Boice Lydell. Together, in late June, 2007, we photographed dozens of these two company's leather articles at his Roycroft Arts Museum in East Aurora, New York.

This writer won't live long enough to be considered a Roycroft authority. That distinction already belongs to Boice, a passionate Roycroft collector, dealer and a preservationist of the ideals established by Elbert Hubbard and the devoted Roycrofters. Most leading Arts and Crafts scholars and collectors are in accord that there is no one better informed on all things Roycroft than he is. He is the keeper of the Roycroft flame and exhibits his collection in the Roycroft Arts Museum. It is housed in the original Alex Fournier residence known as the "bungle house" in the complex of buildings that makeup the Roycroft Campus in East Aurora, NY.

During research on this book we were in close contact for many hours. I listened as Boice's memory retold forgotten details about the artisan workers. Like a character storyteller in the Ray Bradbury novel, *"Fahrenheit 451"* Boice has become the Book of Roycroft. Mention a Roycrofter craftsman, even one with little notoriety, and Boice will recall their pedigree. If needed, he can consult his museum's monumental archives to refresh their contribution.

So the vignette on Roycroft modeled leather is a duet with Boice Lydell. The collaboration was also at work as we examine the Cordova Shops of Buffalo since Roycrofters Frederick C. Kranz and George L. ScheideMantel worked their craft there.

Other local information was provided by Mark and Joy Warren, Gordie Galloway, and Kitty Turgeon, the grand dame of preservation for the Roycroft campus. Don Meade, curator of the Elbert Hubbard Roycroft Museum, allowed access to the unique artistic leather styles of George ScheideMantel. The great granddaughter of Frederick C. Kranz, Marilyn Burch of Stuyvesant, New York, readily assisted with special information that could only come from a descendant.

The further enhancement of these, and many other never before seen digital images, was caringly produced by Marissa Natkin, photographer, of Seattle, Washington. The composed "still life" scenes of leather articles and Stickley furniture were made by her in the Kirkland, Washington, home of Jessica Greenway and Ken Nelson. They are collectors of all things Arts and Crafts, including leather articles.

Beyond this clutch of collectors I also thank, in no particular order, collectors who responded to my call for assistance. Jim Wear, a professional expert leather craftsman of Laramie, Wyoming, furnished the only known leather purses and a 1921 catalog from the Askew Saddlery Company of Kansas City, Missouri. He also contributed to the section on how to maintain and care for leather articles.

Sharon Darling of St. Charles, Illinois, provided the only known leather (a card case, circa 1904) attributed to Clara Barck, the founder of the Kalo Shop of Chicago. Paul Somerson (whose website is Chicagosilver.com) supplied items from the Forest Craft Guild and several artistically colored leather pieces from sisters Rose and Minnie Dolese. These, and many others, were produced around 1903 at their Wilro Shop studio in Chicago's Fine Arts Building. Other Wilro Shop of Chicago articles were supplied by Chicago writer/researcher Darcy L. Evon. An unusual set of hammered copper bookends with leather inserts was furnished by Steve and Mary Ann Voorhees of Voorhees Craftsman, Pasadena, California. The bookends are marked Gaw/Van Erp and were likely from 1910, the only year Ms. Gaw was working in the Van Erp studio in San Francisco. Before Erp, she maintained a Chicago design studio and was a graduate of the Art Institute of Chicago and a friend of Clara Barck.

The foremost authority on Forest Craft Guild, and the designs and teachings of Forest Mann, is Don Marek of Grand Rapids, Michigan. He shared the marvelous dark green suede leather purse with hammered, pierced brass that is adorned with a Venetian enamel cabochon. This and other visual treasures can be seen in his caring treatise on Mann and others in Grand Rapids Art Metalwork, his book of 1999. Still in Michigan, Marion Spitzley of Grosse Point leads the faculty at "Bag Lady University." She has long maintained vignettes of commercial leather producers, along with dozens of handbags and advertisements from leading U.S. makers. From her website, Bagladyemporium. com, she has contributed many of the handbag advertisements we show from the 1920s. Keepers of the flame of the Grand Rapids Arts & Crafts Society, Elizabeth Miele and David Lubbers, present an extraordinary display of period modeled leather at their site, Donatella.com.

Although there are many rare and unusual leather articles collected, perhaps the largest of these is an image of a 3-panel screen from the archives of Beth Cathers and Robert Kaplan. Its hand-colored, modeled, burned, and appliquéd leathers are of a Redwood forest scene and it was completed around 1900 by Elizabeth Eaton Burton of Montecito, California. She worked in leather before she became known for her hammered metal and sea-shell electroliers and other lamps.

The profile on Newcomb College of New Orleans, Louisiana, was enhanced by Jean Bragg, the Newcomb authority and long time antiques dealer of that city.

Across the nation, Arts and Crafts scholars and collectors contributed what knowledge they had about the hand-crafted artistic leather and the artisans who created the articles.

These include Barbara N. Fuldner, Peter A. Copeland, David Cathers, Paul Jackson, Jim Messineo and Mike Witt (JMW Gallery), Richard Blacher, Timothy Hansen, Allen and Vonda Breed, Paul Somerson, Stephen Gray, Bryan Meade, Isak Lindenauer, Bruce Smith, Lawrence Kreisman, Jerry Cook, Glenn and Judith Mason, Craig Levin, Bob Hulhizer, Andy Denes, George Sparacio, John Miller, Tom Maimone, Susan Kreigbaum-Hanks, Evelyn Haertig, Ken Nelson, Jessica Greenway, Lorrie Moore, Tom Wake, Anne Stewart O'Donnell, Stanley N. Hess, Pete Prunkl, Diane Dillon, Charles Sweigart, Patricia Shaw, Jane Clarke, Christine Larger, Patricia Green, Greg Frauenhoff, Sue Conrad, Lori Blaser, Mary Tanner, James Davis, Gus Bostrom, Pamela M. Gardner, Gail Gerretsen, Patricia M. Green, Madonna Swanson, Jean Oberkirsch, Pete Maloney, Robert C. Rust, Linda Schmetterlingtag, Ellen Warner Judi Wyant, Onda Dylewski, Evelyn McClure, Robert M. Storey Jr., Steve Schoneck, Gordon Hoppe, Nancy Rose, and the Reverend Dennis A. Andersen.

Museums and libraries are awash with information about Arts & Crafts furniture makers, potters and ceramicists, coppersmiths, metal workers, and weavers, but worthy data for leather artisans is woefully inadequate. One of the best providers of information is the New York City Public Library (through the NYPL Express). Its enormous collection of old periodicals reported on fashion and home decoration of the A&C Era—1900-1918. These often contain information about modeled leather and the producers.

The following institutions and their research people furnished important editorial contributions. These are: Art Institute of Chicago, Ryerson Library, Chicago, Illinois;

Chicago Historical Society, Chicago, Illinois, Colleen Beckett, research inquiries; Chicago Public Library, Newberry Library, Chicago, Illinois, Kathleen McMahon, reference department; Joliet Public Library, Joliet, Illinois, Roger Gambrel, information services; Bloomington Public Library, Bloomington, Illinois, Jane Chamberlain; Clark County Public Library, Springfield, Ohio, Cathy Hackett, reference librarian; Clark County Genealogy Society, Springfield, Ohio; Minnesota Historical Society, Minneapolis, Minnesota, Marcia G. Anderson, Senior Curator; The Minneapolis Institute of Arts, David Ryan; reference department, Washington County Historical Society, West Bend, Wisconsin, Janean Mollet-Van Beckum, Supervisor; research center; Grand Rapids History & Special Collection Center, Grand Rapids, Michigan, Rebecca Mayne, archivist; Grand Rapids Public Library, Grand Rapids, Michigan, Marcie Beck, librarian; Detroit Historical Society, Detroit, Michigan; Marianne Weldon, curator of collections; Wichita, Kansas, Public Library, Michelle Enke, reference librarian; Winterthur Museum, Garden & Library, as well as Bert Denker, librarian, Emily Guthrie, assistant librarian, Jeanne Solensky, Downs Collection of manuscripts and printed ephemera, librarian, Winterthur, Delaware; Hagley Museum & Library, Wilmington, Delaware, Marjorie G. McNinch, reference archivist; Schlesinger Library, Radcliffe University, Cambridge, Massachusetts, Jacalyn R. Blume, reference librarian-visual resources; The Society of Arts and Crafts, Boston, Massachusetts, Beth Ann Gerstein, director; Harvard University, Cambridge, Massachusetts,, OASIS, Online Archival Search Information System; Memorial Art Gallery, Rochester, New York, Lu Harper; Oakland Museum of California, Oakland, California, Amanda Jacobs, librarian; Santa Barbara Historical Society, Santa Barbara, California, Michael Redmon, director of research; Monterey Public Library, Monterey, California, Dennis Copeland; Sonoma Historical Society, Sonoma, California, Lee Torliatt; San Diego Historical Society, San Diego, California, Jane Kenealy; Joplin Museum, Joplin, Missouri, Brad Belke, executive director; Buffalo & Erie County Public Library, Buffalo, New York, "Ask Us" department; Portland Art Museum Crumpacker Family Library, Portland, Oregon, Debra Royer, library director; Seattle Public Library, Seattle, Washington, reference services; University of Washington Special Collections, Paul Allen Library, Seattle, Washington, Jane Chamberlain, archivist; King County Library System, Bellevue, Washington, Sharon Wilson, librarian; Louisiana State Museum, New Orleans, Louisiana, Suzanne Fischer, curator of material culture; Dallas Historical Society, Dallas, Texas, Rachel Roberts, historian; Nocona Public Library, Nocona, Texas, Alicia Walker, director; Museum fur Kunst und Gewebe, Department of Decorative Arts, Hamburg, Germany, Dr. Rudiger Joppien, director.

BIBLIOGRAPHY

This is the first and only work in print devoted to the artistic and modeled leather of the Arts & Crafts Era—1900-1929. Your internet search engine will produce thousands of citations to get up your hopes, but it rarely furnishes any that are worthy of examination. There aren't many print references because most of the books about the Arts and Crafts Era don't discuss artistic leather or the artisans. A major exception is *Head, Heart and Hand— Elbert Hubbard and The Roycrofters* by Marie Via and Marjorie R. Searl.

If your interest covers both American fine art and the decorative arts of the period, then investigate these publications in larger metro public libraries. *International Studio* covers the fine art of painting, sculpture and printmaking. *House Beautiful* and *Fine Art Journal* present items for personal or home use, jewelry-making, needlecraft and weaving, leather working, pottery, china-painting, metal work (copper, silver, brass of all types) and paintings. These also profiled individual artisans and featured their homes; and covered annual exhibitions of major Arts & Crafts Guilds or Societies.

A pioneering view into artistic leather, that became a fashion statement for women, is Evelyn Haertig's *More Beautiful Purses*, 1990, Gallery Graphics Press, Carmel, California. The huge work is well photographed and covers purses of all materials, shapes, and styles. Her tour d' force is beaded work. It offers an extensive look into commercial modeled and embossed leather handbags made at Roycroft, Cordova, Bosca, Meeker, Justin and other U.S. makers. An adaptation of the chapter was reprised in *American Bungalow*, (#32, May, 2002) "The Art of the Leather Purse" by Evelyn Haertig.

Perhaps the earliest thorough examination of one style of the art form is Arthur Inkersley's "The California Art of Stamping and Embossing Leather" presented in Gustav Stickley's *The Craftsman* magazine, Vol. VI #1, April, 1904. Don't despair if you can't acquire the original issue. Complete sets of *The Craftsman* issues are reissued in CD format and commonly available through internet searches.

Artistic leather features were expanded in succeeding issues. The father-daughter leather artisans, Frederick C. Eaton and Elizabeth Eaton Burton of Montecito, California, appeared a few months later. Look for "Nature and Art in California" written by Stickley, *The Craftsman*, Vol. VI #4, July, 1904. Reader interest must have resonated favorably for simultaneously the new magazine *House and Garden*, May, 1903 began featuring leather work and the artists. An extensive impression of Frederick Eaton's work and home appeared in *House Beautiful*, Vol. 16, February, 1905. There are citations directing you to the century-old reviews from these, *Vogue*, January, 1901 and other major magazines in the section end notes on Frederick Eaton and Elizabeth Eaton Burton and throughout this work. Another important publication, *Handicraft, the Journal of the Society of Arts and Crafts Boston*, suggested "The art form had merit when done by a skillful artisan, but condemned and decried what they saw as its popularity was producing some very bad leather work and it may seriously prejudice many people against all leather work." The comment is from a lengthy article, "Leather As A Medium For Artistic Expression" by Annah C. Ripley, appeared in its October, 1903 issue, Vol. II, No. VII.

Stickley also offered the home artisan full-scale design templates, plans, and materials to make their own items. These were augmented by articles about professional leather artisans among the regular Home Department magazine section. These include: "Re-bookbinding—a lesson in making over old books," Mertice Macrae Buck, Vol. XII, October, 1906, p. 137-146; "Albums, Portfolios and Guest Books," Mertice Macrae Buck, Vol. XIV, #5, August, 1908, p. 555-59; "Craftsman Leather Bags," Vol. XVIII, #2, May, 1910, p. 268-72; "Guest books in Tooled Leather—Craftsman Plans," Vol. XVIII, #3, June, 1910, p. 393-94; "Craftsman Leather Desk Set," Vol. XVIII, #4, July, 1910, p. 501-02; "A French Craftsman in Leather," Vol. XXI, #1, Oct., 1911.

There was rather widespread interest in leather working and craftspeople expected to see these designs of the artistic leaders. They are presented because they are so difficult to discover and because they represent the best detailed explanations of the craft in 1900. "The Art of Tooling Leather" by Katherine Girling, *The Craftsman*, Vol IV, #4, p. 298-302, July, 1903. "Gilded or Cordovan Leather," Mary Ware Dennett, *The Craftsman*, Vol IV, #4, p. 258-266, July, 1903.

In the first decade of the 20th century Arts & Crafts Guilds or Societies were loosely patterned after the Society of Arts & Crafts Boston and its success in the late 1890s. Leather working was most usually classified under "Allied Arts" or "Decorative Arts" to distinguish it from the "Fine Arts" of painting and sculpture. Along with jewelry-making/metal work, pottery, textiles and weaving, leather work design and modeling was offered as advanced course work at Pratt Institute, Newcomb College, the Art Institute of Chicago and others. Organizations typically held annual exhibitions of the year's accomplishments where the public could review and purchase the work. The Art Institute of Chicago held its first exhibition in the winter of 1902. The Handicraft Guild of Minneapolis followed suit in 1903. The exhibitions were significant and, besides student work, drew work from Tiffany, Grueby, Rookwood, Stickley, Teco, and other well-known manufacturers. These were often reported in depth in *House Beautiful* magazine. Look for their appearance in February or March issues following a pre-Christmas event. The Chicago and Minneapolis events offered more than 500 examples in the exhibit catalogs that can often be found in larger metro public libraries.

For a new Arts and Crafts Collector
If you are new to the individual and commercially made articles of this era, here is a "starter" group of diverse books that track the movement. Many are readily available at public libraries or for sale. Those that are out of print can often be located through nationwide internet searches.

Books and periodicals
Addams, Jane, *Twenty Years at Hull House*, Penguin, 1998.
Ayers, Diane, et al, *American Arts and Crafts Textiles*, New York: Abrams, 2002.
Batchelder, Ernest A., *Design in Theory and Practice*. New York: Macmillan, 1910.
Bragg, Jean Moore, and Dr. Susan Saward, *The Newcomb Style*, Jean Bragg Gallery, 2002.
Brandt, Beverly K., and Edward S. Cooke, Jr., essays, *Inspiring Reform—Boston's Arts and Crafts Movement*, The Davis Museum and Cultural Center, Wellesley College, Wellesley, MA, Abrams, 1997.
Cathers, David M., *Furniture of the American Arts and Crafts Movement*. New York. New American Library, 1981.
Clark, Robert Judson, ed., *The Arts & Crafts Movement in America 1876-1916*, Princeton, N.J.; Princeton University Press, 1972.
Conforti, Michael, ed., *Art and Life on the Upper Mississippi-1890-1915*; essay by Anderson, Marcia G., "Art for Life's Sake—The Handicraft Guild of Minneapolis;" Associated University Presses, Inc., 1994.
Congdon-Martin, Douglas, *Arts & Crafts: The California Home*, Schiffer Publishing, 2003.
The Craftsman on CD-Rom, New York: Interactive Bureau, 1998.
Darling, Sharon, *Chicago Metalsmiths*, Chicago Historical Society, Chicago, IL, 1977.
Denker, Burt R. ed., *The Substance of Style—Perspectives on the American Arts and Crafts Movement*, A Winterthur Museum Book, Winterthur, DE, 1996.
Green, Nancy E., and Jessie Poesch, *Arthur Wesley Dow and American Arts and Crafts*. New York: American Federation of Arts with Abrams, 1999.
Haertig, Evelyn, *More Beautiful Purses*, Gallery Graphics Press, Carmel, CA, 1990.
Hamilton, Charles, *Roycroft Collectibles*, SPS Publications, Tavares, FL 1992.
Kaplan, Wendy, *The Art That is Life—The Arts and Crafts Movement in America--1875-1920*, Boston Museum of Fine Arts and Little Brown Publishing, 1987.
Kreishman, Lawrence & Glenn W. Mason, *The Arts and Crafts Movement in the Pacific Northwest*,

Timber Press, Inc., Portland, OR, 2007.

Kriegbaum-Hanks, Susan, *Buffalo und sein Deutschtum (Buffalo and its German Community)* Translation by Kriegbaum-Hanks from German to English. It presents sketches of leaders, scholars and artisans of German descent in Buffalo, 1911-12. Website is archivaria. com/BusDHistory/, 2006.

Larson, Erik, *The Devil in the White City,* Random House, 2003. Here's a worthy view of the 1893 Columbia Exposition & World's Fair in Chicago, and the "new" architecture and culture blending in America's fastest growing city.

Ludwig, Coy, *The Arts and Crafts Movement in America—1890s-1920s,* Gallery Association of New York State, Gibbs M. Smith Publishing, 1983.

Marek, Don, *Grand Rapids Art Metalwork—1902-1918,* Heartwood Publishing, Grand Rapids, MI, 1999.

Rago, David, *American Art Pottery,* Knickerbocker Press, New York, 1997.

Shay, Felix, *Elbert Hubbard of East Aurora,* William H. Wise and Co., New York, 1926.

Smith, Bruce. *Arts and Crafts Ideals: Wisdom from the Arts and Crafts Movement in America,* Gibbs Smith, 1999.

Trapp, Kenneth R. *The Arts and Crafts Movement in California—Living the Good Life,* The Oakland Museum, Oakland, California and Abbeville Press, New York City, 1993.

Triggs, Oscar Lovell, *Chapters in the History of the Arts and Crafts Movement,* Chicago: Bohemia Guild of the Industrial League, 1902.

Via, Marie and Marjorie B. Searl, *Head, Heart and Hand—Elbert Hubbard and the Roycrofters,* University of Rochester Press, 1994.

Volpe, Tod M and Beth Cathers, *Treasures of the Arts and Crafts Movement—1890-1920,* Abrams, 1988.

Vonnegut, Kurt, *Palm Sunday (German culture in America),* Delacorte Press, New York, 1981.

Periodicals

American Bungalow (quarterly), 123 S. Baldwin Avenue, Sierra Madre, CA 91024
www.ambungalow.com

Style 1900 (quarterly), 333 North Main Street, Lambertville, NJ 08530 www.style@ragoarts.com

Leather Working Texts

Although there are many diverse offerings, we've chosen a selection that shows a wide variety of modeling, lacing and coloring techniques commonly used in leather production during the Arts and Crafts Era.

Bang, Eleonore E., *Leathercraft for Amateurs,* Beacon Handicraft Series, Boston, MA, 1927

Dean, John W., *Leathercraft Techniques and Designs,* Pratt Institute, Brooklyn, NY, McKnight & McKnight Publishing, Bloomington, IL, 1950.

Francis-Lewis, Cecile, *The Art & Craft of Leatherwork,* Seely, Service & Co. Ltd. London, GB, 1928.

George & Co., *Artistic Leatherwork,* Novello & Co. Printers Ltd., London, GB, 1924.

These rather rare examples are some of the finer modeled leather designed for a lady. On the left is a Cordova Shops of Buffalo teardrop handbag of a gold-filled design with hammered copper surrounds for its round braided handle. At center is the cameo figured repousse handbag work of George ScheideMantel of East Aurora, New York. On the right is a Roycroft glove case with repousse nasturtium design and signed with the Roycroft orb under the flap.

   They are shown courtesy of the Nelson/Greenway collection in Kirkland, Washington, and the collection of Faire Lees. They are discussed in greater detail in the Cordova Shops and Roycroft sections. Photograph by Marissa Natkin, Seattle, Washington.